GUMSHOE

Reflections in a Private Eye

Josiah Thompson

FAWCETT CREST • NEW YORK

A Fawcett Crest Book
Published by Ballantine Books
Copyright © 1988 by Josiah Thompson

All rights reserved under International and Pan-American Copyright Conventions. No part of this book may be reproduced in any form or by any electronic or mechanical means, including information storage and retrieval systems, without permission in writing from the publisher, except by a reviewer who may quote brief passages in a review. Published in the United States by Ballantine Books, a division of Random House, Inc., New York, and simultaneously in Canada by Random House of Canada Limited, Toronto.

Some of the names of people in this book (and some identifying details) have been changed for reasons of privacy.

Excerpts from *The Maltese Falcon* by Dashiell Hammett are reprinted by permission of Alfred A. Knopf, Inc. Copyright 1929, 1930 by Alfred A. Knopf, Inc. Copyright © renewed 1957 by Dashiell Hammett.

Excerpts from the Introduction to the Modern Library edition of *The Maltese Falcon* by Dashiell Hammett are reprinted by permission of Alfred A. Knopf, Inc. Copyright 1934 by Modern Library, Inc.

THIS BOOK IS FOR

Nancy, Lis, and Ev,
who lived it.

If you ask me why he is a private detective, I can't answer you. Obviously, there are times when he wishes he were not. . . .

But down these mean streets a man must go who is not himself mean. . . . The story is this man's adventure in search of a hidden truth.

—RAYMOND CHANDLER

CONTENTS

ACKNOWLEDGMENTS

My thanks go first to the numerous individuals who participated in these events, read the manuscript, and permitted the use of their real names in a story that is both theirs and mine. Their memories often corrected and deepened my own. The book could not have been written without their active assistance.

The events depicted happened eight to twelve years ago. In the intervening period, some participants have died and others have disappeared. Nonquitt Harbor is not a real place name, but its prototype exists and was the locale for the events described in Chapters 4, 5, and 10. In a few other instances changes have been made to protect the privacy of individuals.

I am grateful to William F. Nolan, who cited my August 16, 1977, report on Hammett in a footnote to his excellent biography, *Hammett: A Life at the Edge*. He graciously sent along my handwritten draft, scribbled out that August afternoon in the Carvells' sitting room.

Paul and Marguerite Harris gave much-appreciated advice at an early stage of the project. Jane Isay offered enthusiasm when I needed it. Michael Kohler gave advice and support, as did Aryeh Kosman, Sara Shumer, and Richard Bernstein. Gene Finley worked hard improving the Prologue and Chapter 1. Alan Silber helped me understand the end of *The Maltese Falcon*. David Kirp suggested valuable cuts and changes in the copyedited manuscript. John and Julia Poppy read the complete manuscript and offered essential advice and encouragement. Mary Ann Shaffer's criticism was the best and the bluntest.

Lis Thompson proofread the first draft of the manuscript and provided acute advice. Ev Thompson suggested important changes in Chapter 8. Nancy Thompson functioned as a sounding board throughout, suggesting invaluable changes while at the same time working to support all of us. The book, as well it should be, is dedicated to them.

Gerry McCauley labored through many years making the commercial arrangements for the book. Roger Donald believed in it from the beginning and gave me enough leash to write it.

Without the extraordinary assistance of my dear friend Cynthia Merman, this book would not exist. In line-editing it, she both taught me how to write and revealed what the book was about.

PROLOGUE

PARANOIA INVESTIGATORUS

FRIDAY, NOVEMBER 12, 1976

Until I saw the bullet hole, it was all playacting.

I moved into the shadow and tried the oversized aluminum doorknob. It didn't turn. Then I saw the bullet hole—flat and chest-high—just below the gold capitals of the cable-TV company's name. It was big—.30-caliber? .45? Seeing it made me lose my breath. The plate glass was an inch and a half thick, and the cracks spread outward from the hole like dividers on a dartboard. I didn't know what to do.

It was 5:45; they should be inside.

I tapped a quarter on the glass. Behind it was a staircase and an overhead light. If anyone was in there, the light should be on. It wasn't.

I tapped again. Two hundred feet down the street, a knot of strikers with printed picket signs huddled near the entrance to the parking lot. I couldn't stand in front of the door forever. The strikers were starting a fire in a rusted-out, fifty-five-gallon drum. I tapped a third time. Nothing. Up the street was a Denny's, probably with a phone booth.

It cost forty-five cents to call San Francisco. A gruff voice on the other end said, "Nine-one-three-seven."

"This is Thompson. I can't get in."

Hal's gravelly voice asked, "Where are you?"

Just my luck. He shouldn't be answering the phone. His staff does that.

"I'm at a pay phone in a Denny's down the street from the

1

plant. A bunch of strikers are out front, and the front door's locked. I tried to—"

"Didn't those assholes tell you to go in the back way?" Even over the phone I could hear him biting down on his cigar. "Jesus Christ!"

"No, Mr. Lipset," I stuttered. "They didn't tell me that."

Now it was "Mr. Lipset." Only days before, over dinner at Grison's, it had been "Hal."

"Where's your man?"

"He's on the picket line out front, sir."

"Well, for Christ's sake, get on him. I'm not paying you to stand around in phone booths talking to me."

"Yes, sir," I heard myself saying, "I'll do that right away, Mr. Lipset." There was a click, and the line buzzed.

I walked back. The day had been bright and clear, but now it was getting cold. This was the warehouse district of Oakland, and the water was only a block or two away. The streets were empty of parked cars; if left overnight, they'd be stripped by morning. A newspaper flipped over and blew across the street. Beyond were cinder-block walls, railroad tracks, patched asphalt, razor wire on cyclone fences, and tar roofs sprinkled with gravel. Things here were stripped bare, like the Tetons or the Sierras above the tree line. Nothing pretended to be other than it was. I zipped up my motorcycle jacket and was glad for the down vest underneath.

The bullet hole changed things. Until I saw it, I'd been able to tell myself this detective caper was all a lark. Underneath, I knew I'd gone to Lipset's office that afternoon not for amusement but for escape. But later, riding across the Bay Bridge, I'd also thought of the stories.

I'd be sitting in the faculty room having morning coffee, and Dean Potter would ask, "What'd you do on your sabbatical?" It would be comfortable there with the refectory table and the oil portraits on the wall. "There was the book, of course," I'd answer, "but I also worked a bit as a private investigator." "A real Sam Spade, eh?" Potter would ask, lighting his pipe. "Not really," I'd say, "but there *was* this one murder case. She had blond hair and legs that wouldn't . . . ."

That sort of thing.

But then I saw the bullet hole. It was like a sudden glitch, stopping the Walter Mitty film in mid-sprocket hole. Whoever put that bullet hole in the door, I told myself, isn't going to care you're some kind of college professor dicking around as a detective; he and his friends are only going to know you're working for the company, trying to put them in jail. The bullet that shattered the glass was real, and so were the Molotov cocktails that torched the trucks, and the rifle shots that blew up the transformers.

My man had on a denim jacket; there weren't any denim jackets in that little knot of people. He was blond with a reddish beard; only one white guy was there now, breaking up lumber scraps and feeding them into the fire. But he was short and dark.

I pulled on my helmet and pressed the starter of the BMW. I could cruise the area and see if he turns up. If he doesn't, I could try some of the addresses they'd given me. Goggles down, I pulled by the strikers and headed up the street. None of them seemed to notice.

At the end of the street, I saw him. He was getting on a Honda 450 in the Denny's parking lot. He must have come up a parallel street.

I cruised past and then slowed, watching the mirror. Soon there was a speck in its center that grew larger. I let him pass and followed a hundred yards back. His taillight went on as he braked for a light. I couldn't hang back in midblock; it'd look suspicious. I'd have to brazen it out. Earlier, he must have seen the Pennsylvania plate.

"I'm from out of town," I yelled over at him. "Trying to find my way to Haste Street in Berkeley."

"Follow me," he said, pulling away as the light changed.

I followed twenty feet back as he threaded through side streets and onto the Nimitz Freeway, melding into the right lane of the rush-hour traffic heading toward the Bay Bridge. There was a regular thump as the bike's wheels struck the asphalt joints in the pavement. He kept to a steady fifty in traffic, blond hair blowing in the slipstream. Then he motioned for me to come alongside. I blipped the throttle and slid in beside him.

"I get off here," he yelled, gloved hand to his mouth. "You keep going. Get off at Ashby. You got that, the Ashby Avenue exit?"

I nodded.

"Go up to Telegraph and turn left. You can't miss it."

"Thanks," I yelled as he hit his blinker and peeled off to the right.

SATURDAY, NOVEMBER 13

For a moment I thought I'd drifted off. The lighted window had been burning a pattern into my retinas for so long it felt as if I'd slipped into a trance. Finally there was just the image—the gold light cut horizontally by the covering venetian blind—and me.

Then, gradually, something changed.

It came first in places that were blackest—in parts of the parking lot outside the throw of the overhead lights, in the alley between the two apartment buildings. The black became gray, and shapes emerged in places where earlier there had been nothing. Garbage cans and a large cardboard box materialized in the alley. Things lost their contrast, and colors appeared in the flatness. The wall around the window—it was on the eighth floor—was red brick. Ericson's Toyota, sitting under the nearest eighty-foot light post, was yellow, not the tan it had seemed earlier.

The VW's vinyl seat crinkled as I moved. Sitting on my wallet all night had made me sore; I shifted and put the wallet into a jacket pocket.

Coffee and a doughnut would be nice, but that would mean leaving here for ten minutes. Ericson might get up early and be gone by the time I got back. Anyhow, I'd spent a nicer night in Russ and Tracy's car than I'd had any right to expect. When they sent me off to do an overnight surveillance on a motorcycle, what had they thought I'd do—curl up in a bush? Russ and Tracy had been amused when I'd burst in, asking to borrow their VW bug because I was "tailing" someone. Too bad the VW stalled at intersections. Still, it was a lot less conspicuous and more comfortable than the R90S.

It was light now. When Ericson got up, he'd probably raise the blind. I stretched. It was 7:45, and I was sore and hungry. The smokes were all gone, my face was stubbled, and I wanted to take a leak. The manila folder was on the floor. The map was lying open with a big ketchup stain in the top right corner of page 4. I wet my finger and tried to wipe it off but just made things worse. The ashtray was full. Russ and Tracy hated smoking, and I'd stunk up their car.

I was trying to get the ashtray out of the dashboard when something moved in the alley between the two buildings. Denim coat, sheepskin collar, dirty blond hair above: it was Ericson. He walked to the Toyota, dropped a package inside, locked the car, and came straight toward me. I ducked under the instrument panel and then realized I couldn't see anything. He could walk right up, open the door, and clobber me.

I edged an eye over the instrument panel, feeling silly. Ericson was right across the street, standing at the curb where the alley met Shattuck. He was reading a paper. Or was he just pretending to read a paper?

I kept my eye in line with the dashboard. There was a rush of noise, and a bus pulled in. It stopped for a few seconds and then gunned its engine, trailing diesel smoke. Ericson was gone. Had he used the cover of the bus to hide? No, dummy, he got *on* the fucking bus—that's a bus stop he was standing at.

I pulled out onto Shattuck.

The bus was a block ahead, but there wasn't much traffic this early in the morning. As we crossed into Berkeley, my adrenaline was pumping and I was feeling good. I'd stayed there all night and picked him up as soon as he came out. Maybe the bus trip was a complicated ruse to throw off a tail. If so, he hadn't fooled me. I was sticking to him—how did they put it in the movies?—"like glue." I hit a light, and the VW stalled. No matter, the bus was big as a house.

I accelerated when the light changed, but hung back about a block. Careful. Better figure out where we are, and where this bus is going. I looked down and flipped through the spiral map book until it showed where we were. Shattuck led into University, then there was a jag and Shattuck continued into north Berkeley. Would he get off at University or stay on through Cedar and beyond? I looked up. Two identical buses were now a block ahead, both cruising north on Shattuck!

I gunned the VW and caught up with them. One was number 87 and the other 134. But I hadn't noticed the number on the original bus. When it pulled away from the stop, its rear had been covered with oil. No luck: both were filthy in back. We were passing Durant now. Maybe I could get around in front and sneak a look at the passengers. Damn, another light.

I was closing on them for the second time when they peeled off, one turning right, the other turning left on University. I picked the one turning right.

Twenty minutes later, when it stopped in north Berkeley and the driver pulled out a thermos and a Danish, I knew I'd guessed wrong. Fifteen minutes after that, I was sipping coffee and waiting for breakfast at the House of Pancakes on University.

In the men's-room mirror, I looked haggard. I hoped I looked disreputable, but it was mostly haggard. The Belstaff jacket, with its black, goose-grease exterior, went perfectly with a day's stubble. "You sure as shit don't look like a college professor," I told the image in the mirror. On the other hand, the image didn't look much like a detective either. How about a shoe clerk competing in his first Baja 1000?

I was still chuckling over that when the seventy-five cents dropped in the pay phone. Nancy answered.

"Lis said you'd gotten the job, but that you'd had to run and just wanted us to know you wouldn't be home till after dinner tomorrow, which is—I guess—today."

There was a lilt to her voice. She was fixing breakfast with the sun slanting in over the Bolinas Ridge. The kids weren't up yet, and she seemed happy to be talking with me. So different from yesterday (was it only yesterday?), when we'd sat drinking coffee at the kitchen table, not willing to take up the argument again but not willing to put it away, either. Her voice was like I remembered it years ago, when we were in a different country, when neither of us wanted deception or felt tangled in it.

I gave her the thirty-second account of the last fifteen hours and asked if she'd save something for me to eat when I got home.

"You mean you've been up all night sitting in a car?"

"Yeah, but I feel pretty good. There's steak and eggs waiting for me at the table."

"Can you take time off from tailing people? I mean, can you quit for breakfast and lunch?"

"No," I laughed. "I was following this guy on a bus and looked down at the map. When I looked up, there were two identical buses going the same direction. So I lost him."

We were both laughing now.

"Two identical buses? Going the same direction?"

"Yeah."

"See you tonight. I'll keep something warm."

"I love you," I said. The line went dead.

Back at the table, I glanced at my watch: 8:45. The pink and cyan decor was the same in the House of Pancakes back at Haverford. We'd often gone there for breakfast on Saturday mornings. Come to think of it, the layout was the same too. Strange to be eating breakfast alone on a Saturday.

Three days earlier, at the end of the dinner at Grison's, Lipset had said I'd have to be interviewed by his junior partner, David

Fechheimer. And that's what I'd been expecting when I'd cruised in on the cycle. But there hadn't been any interview.

In the elegant Victorian on Pacific Avenue, the receptionist had been sitting at the phones on the left, electronic equipment—all dials and meters—filling the anteroom to the right. A bearded guy with rolled-up shirt sleeves had crossed in front of the door and turned. "You Thompson?" he'd asked, and then handed over a manila folder before continuing to the back of the house, where Lipset was talking on the phone. Wasn't it odd he'd been carrying *that* folder when I walked in?

The folder held a photo of blond Michael Ericson, with an address, phone number, and the license-plate of the Toyota Corolla. (Apparently they didn't know about the Honda 450; I'd better jot down the tag number if I got close to it again.) This information was laid out on a sheet with the Lipset Service letterhead. Typed near the bottom were other names, addresses, and license-plate numbers.

Hal Lipset had never come out of the back room. Fechheimer had passed by again a few minutes later. "The pay'll be eight-fifty a month. That OK?" Nodding toward the folder, he'd gone on, "You'll be on him starting at five-thirty tonight, and be relieved at seven-thirty tomorrow night. Come over here. I want you to meet Jack Palladino. He's running your operation."

Palladino had been sitting at a desk. He was wearing a tie, blue shirt with monogram above the cuff, and clear aviator glasses. Taller than Fechheimer and balding where Fechheimer was thick-haired, he appeared sleeker; in another life he could have been an intelligence agent or a casino pit boss. We'd shaken hands, and he'd quickly explained what the surveillance was about.

The strike against the cable TV outfit had been dragging on. The local was largely black, with white leadership, and the last several months had seen increasing violence against the company. Several trucks had been firebombed, and cable equipment shot up by rifles and shotguns. Not long before, a multimillion-dollar warehouse had been torched. Management had hired the Lipset Service to identify those responsible for the violence and gather evidence for their prosecution. Five tails would be out that night, each shadowing a particular union leader or striker who Palladino suspected might be involved in the violence. He'd brief us all at the plant at 5:15. The address of the plant and the phone numbers for contacting him ("Control") were on the assignment sheet.

On the surface, at least, Fechheimer seemed looser than Palladino, more informal, like a writer who'd just finished his novel and was doing this while he waited for the galleys to come through. Job interview or no, he had asked me no questions but simply handed over a Thomas Bros. map of Alameda County. "You'll need this," he'd said. "The next couple of months won't show whether you're a gumshoe, but they ought to show whether you're not one."

I didn't know what that meant, but I guessed I didn't have to. He'd been right, though, about the street map. Without it, the night before, I wouldn't have been able to find Ericson's apartment. He hadn't been there. Nor had he been at any of the other addresses on the sheet, where black teenagers had given me strange looks and catcalls near such beauty spots as Roundelay Lane off East 14th Street. Around eleven, I'd gotten frustrated enough to call Ericson's number. A white male answered, and I'd asked for Sharon, Sharon Kelly, the flight attendant who, I said, had given me her number on the Thursday-night Delta flight from Dallas. I figured it was Ericson. Ten minutes later, when I'd pulled in across the street, his Toyota had been in the parking lot and the lights had been on in his eighth-floor apartment.

After the steak and eggs, I had a second cup of coffee with a cigarette and took the freeway back to Oakland. The sheet said a morning strike rally was scheduled for 9:30 at the Labor Trades Building. Afterward, a caravan of strikers was to picket executives' homes in the Oakland hills.

The street in front of the Labor Trades Building ran four lanes wide in one direction. A drive-by turned up no Ericson; still, there was no better place to hunt for him. A side street half a block from the rally was virtually empty of cars, so I parked with just the nose and windshield of the VW peeking out from behind the corner of a bank building.

The "rally" consisted of forty or fifty people with signs gathered in a semicircle around the building's entrance. One of the leaders started to speak through a bullhorn from the steps. The wind caught phrases, sometimes complete sentences. After ten minutes Ericson appeared, smoking a cigarette.

Most of my car was hidden, and I was pretty sure he hadn't noticed it peel away from the curb on Shattuck earlier. What's more, the fact I wasn't around when he got off the bus would have cooled any suspicions he might have had. The goof translated into a bit of added safety, and that was welcome now. It had been fun and games for a while this morning, and nice to have had that laugh with Nancy. But somewhere between Berkeley and here things had changed, or I had changed, or something. Now the overcast skies, the signs, the voices on the wind, and the stone, especially the stone (the granite of the building nearby and the concrete of the sidewalk) made me think of the cracks around the bullet hole. They'd seemed so real, so impossible to argue with.

Not all the strikers joined the caravan into the hills. Two small groups of cars headed off in different directions, while the rest of the group dispersed. Ericson got into the passenger seat of a Vokswagen hatchback driven by a black woman; from the other side, two men squeezed into the rear seat. I followed a block and a half back, the morning's encounter with the bus fresh in mind. But a slow-moving convoy of four cars was such a challenge to incompetence that even I felt confident. At each stop in the upper-middle-class suburb, I jotted down street names and times. At least I could report to Control what addresses had been visited and when.

The routine was always the same: short speech, followed by walking up and down in front of the house with picket signs, followed by even shorter speech. Well-dressed neighbors sometimes stared from their decks or peered sidelong through draped windows. The well-kept gardens and sprinklered lawns, the asphalt driveways with late-model cars—were reassuring. These people were my class; surely nothing violent or ugly could happen in such surroundings. On the other hand, the strikers would have had to be deaf and blind not to notice the VW that kept such a respectful distance. Maybe they saw me. Maybe they didn't care.

The last vehicle—a rusted-out tan Datsun pickup—was now a quarter-mile ahead. It dropped out of sight beyond a small rise, so the road ahead was empty. The zone of the upper middle class, was left behind; eroded gullies with clusters of coyote bushes appeared on either side of the road. Near the ridge line, stands of eucalyptus moved in the wind. Lubricated by fall rains, clumps of earth had fallen away from their roots, leaving them exposed to the air. I'd seen no house or shack for the last mile or so. No matter. One of the executives must live farther out. He probably called his place a ranch and had a horse or two around. There would be a teenage daughter, and he'd drop her off at private school on his way to work.

I cleared the rise, and suddenly, three hundred yards ahead, the caravan was making a U-turn. The lead car was headed right for me. I whipped the wheel to the left and gunned the car through the mud and grass of the opposite shoulder. In second gear it pulled through, and I jerked the wheels back onto the asphalt.

The mirror showed they'd gained only about a hundred yards on me. The speedometer crept toward seventy. I took a left at the first fork and kept going. After several hard rights and lefts through roads and then streets, the mirror emptied. I pulled to the curb and turned off the engine.

The day was beginning to seem like a bizarre slapstick comedy. But it didn't feel like comedy. It felt frustrating and silly and, around the edges, scary. I was angry at myself, at the strikers, and at the Lipset Service for sending me out untrained. I was also trembling. I took a deep breath, turned the key, and drove to Russ and Tracy's.

They lived on North Street, a one-block street of squeezed-together frame houses just over the Berkeley-Oakland line in Oakland. If the California Left were ever to put together a register of historic places, North Street would be on it. On that August day in 1971, when Stephen Bingham left to visit George Jackson in San Quentin, he'd been living diagonally across the street from Russ and Tracy.

Tracy was out front, pulling up old tomato plants and sweet corn stalks in the ten-foot-square garden that separated the two-story house from the sidewalk. The landlord had painted the house dark brown, and the rough six-foot-high planks of the garden's fence clashed with the house's fresh paint.

"Come in and have some coffee," Tracy said. "You look like you could use some."

"Thanks. I can't. I'm supposed to be tailing this guy, and I've lost him twice already. Just now he spotted me; I was wondering if you had another car I could borrow."

"There's the van. I don't think Russ is using it."

She called, and Russ appeared on the porch.

"Mr. Spade himself."

"More like Inspector Clouseau. I just got seen in the VW. I

think the term is 'burned.' I was wondering if I might select another mount from your stable of vehicles.''

"The van's down the street, but it needs gas."

"I can fix that at the Shell station on the corner."

"You look awful. Been up all night?''

"Yeah. Staring at a window, for all the good it did."

"Wait a sec," said Tracy. "I've got an idea."

She came back with Russ's old leather jacket and black beret. We often kidded him about that beret. With his black hair and mustache, it made him look like Che Guevara. The jacket hung a bit loose on me. We were both five-eight, but Russ had a bigger frame.

We walked up the block to the Dodge van. It was white and of indeterminate age. I climbed in, put on the beret, and looked in the side-view mirror. It wasn't Che Guevara who stared back. Or even a shoe clerk just back from the Baja 1000.

"Berkeley's filled with old vans," Russ said as I turned the key in the ignition. "In the beret and jacket, no one'll recognize you." I smiled and started to drive off, but he gestured to stop. "On the other hand," he paused, grinning, "if they do, try not to get any blood on the jacket. It's a bitch to get out of leather."

A few drops of rain grazed the windshield as I pulled away. Neither Russ nor Tracy had asked about the job. Did they think it was bad manners to ask? Or had they figured out what it was and just wanted to avoid an argument about me working for management?

Two hours later, the rain had stopped and I was reading a properly left-wing paper while loitering near the entrance to the Berkeley Co-op on Telegraph. From inside came the smells of freshly ground coffee, spices, produce, and more granola varieties than Euell Gibbons ever dreamed of. I couldn't chance going inside and getting caught in a slower checkout line than Ericson and the woman he was with. I'd seen them come out of his building together—the long braid of her ponytail hanging down the back of her blue parka—and then I'd followed the Toyota as they'd driven up here. Here where Nancy and I'd shopped four summers back, where everyone we knew in Berkeley shopped. But now, instead of shopping, I was trying to look inconspicuous with the paper. Getting away from the van had seemed a good idea a few moments earlier, but now I felt stupid.

I dropped the *Bay Guardian* in a trash can near the Co-op

bulletin board and glanced left before crossing the parking lane. A yellow car was coming. Not just any car—Ericson's Toyota, passing now, Ericson at the wheel, talking to the woman. I ran to the van but fumbled putting the key in the lock. By the time I reached the exit, they were gone.

Mercifully, at seven-thirty I was relieved by a man of about fifty in gabardine slacks and a rumpled sports jacket. I was sitting in a vacant service-station lot near Ericson's building when he walked up.

"You Thompson?"

"Yeah."

"They want you back here at six-fifteen in the morning." His hooded gray eyes gave the impression he wasn't looking at you. Surveying the street, he went on, "Your location's better than mine. I'll back in when you pull out."

When I dropped off the van, Russ and Tracy offered a beer, but I set off right away on the motorcycle for Bolinas.

It seemed right that I'd spent the afternoon in Russ's too-large jacket. For that was how I felt—swimming in my job just as I was swimming in my clothes, for the last twenty-six hours losing Ericson every time he turned around. This surveillance was supposed to be about violence, but I'd seen no violence. I'd seen only a couple shopping at the Co-op, a man in a denim jacket getting on a bus, a rally, a ragtag cavalcade of cars.

But I'd also seen the bullet hole.

I was almost grateful for the sheets of rain that broke over me as the motorcycle topped the crest of Mount Tamalpais and sped downward through the redwoods to the sea. Riding a motorcycle in the rain was something I knew how to do.

SUNDAY, NOVEMBER 14

I had a direct view up the sidewalk under the colonnade of poles and overhanging wires. The nose of a midsixties green Chevy poked out of a driveway just this side of the house. Earlier I'd pulled into a parking spot diagonally across the street from it, but ten minutes at that location had been enough to start the hair rising on the back of my neck. It was too close. It felt as if a neon sign were blinking on top of the Volvo.

It was strange doing a surveillance so close to Russ and Tracy's. Their house was just around the corner from the intersection I could see in the mirror.

A couple of hours earlier, cresting Bolinas Ridge and starting the descent to Mill Valley, the stars had been clear and the smell of pine strong. The cold front had swept the rain before it, leaving behind a blustery, sun-swept Sunday morning.

At the filling station on Shattuck I'd found a young man in a windbreaker sitting in a dingy brown Pinto. The sun had been in my eyes as I'd bent over his window and taken the piece of notepaper with a name, address, and license-plate number on it. "The car's a tan Datsun," he'd said. "You can't miss it. It's got a big rusted crease across the driver's door."

A traffic accident had caused the change in assignments. The young man in the Pinto had originally been given this surveillance on Regent Street. Its "subject" (I was beginning to pick up the lingo) was another union activist, Miroslav Tabac, who lived in the house up the street. The night before, my relief—the fiftyish guy—had been broadsided by a truck as he'd pulled out of the filling station in pursuit of Ericson. He'd only been shaken up, but his Pontiac had been wrecked. Since Tabac seemed to be safely tucked in for the night, his tail had been switched to Ericson. Now I was picking up the surveillance of Tabac.

Could I take up the same position at the other end of the block? I took the binoculars from their case. Etched near the eyepiece was the white legend *"Carl Zeiss."* Inscribed on the bridge over the adjusting knob was *"J. D. Thompson—East Liverpool, Ohio."* My father's most prized possession, they'd come to me on his death the year before. They were "the best glasses in the world," he'd always said, prewar Zeiss, the product of three hundred years of refinements in the science of optics. I trained them on Tabac's house. The number plate over the door stood out crisply against the flaking white paint.

Someone had gone to a lot of trouble with that number plate, first chiseling the digits 3-5-4-9 and a daisy shape at each end, then painting the daisies yellow and the numbers between fire-engine red. Although officially in Oakland, the householders on this block tried to affect a Berkeley look by adding vegetation, shingles, or redwood siding. Only Tabac's house remained unabashedly Oakland, its flowered number plate signaling the values of a probably long-departed tenant.

I trained the glasses on the end of the block, where Regent

Street butted into Woolsey. They showed a black Ford sedan and a Peugeot station wagon. I'd have to stay here.

My father had taken his first set of Zeiss glasses off the body of a German officer during World War I. He'd lost them on the day before armistice, when he was hit by German shell fragments. Maybe that was why he'd gone to the expense of ordering these from New York, and why he'd always handled them with such care—as if they were some icon of visual potency.

I reached under the seat for the case and gently put the glasses back. Strange how the power of these glasses could come back to me sitting on an Oakland street thirty-five years later, how the feel of them could bring back Sunday hikes we'd taken together, could bring back the smell of the creek and the noise of twigs snapping under my feet.

I looked at the bag on the floor with the remaining doughnut. Better hold on to that. I lit a cigarette and looked over at a sandstone column. To its left was a telephone pole with a chartreuse poster attached to it, and then a mailbox. The building on the corner just beyond the pole was connected to Saint Augustine's, perhaps a Sunday-school or administration building. The parking spaces should start filling up soon, and I'd appear to be waiting for someone from early Mass. I took a drag on the cigarette and looked at my watch. It was already 7:45.

I was actually beginning to enjoy the game. There had been times the day before when I'd felt a strange rush. It had to do with watching and not being seen. I'd felt it following the bus, and then later, after the rally, when I'd fallen in behind the VW hatchback. There was even satisfaction in just sitting in the car, like now, watching.

Part of it was the novelty of the experience, the delight in doing something I'd never done before. But there was also something more fundamental, something "gritty" about it. I guessed that was what I liked best. You had to worry about elemental things—having food in the car or else going hungry, knowing where the pay phones were, which streets were one-way. And in this business, unlike teaching or writing, failure and success were obvious. The field of play was the world, in all its complexity and contingency. You had to stay alert and very quiet, paying attention to the slightest change.

Later I'd learn how to make of surveillance an arcane meditation. I'd learn how to adjust my antennae, and then throttle back remembering and anticipating, so that only perception was left, only the world disclosing itself second by second, minute by minute, hour by hour.

Unlike a story, a surveillance has no beginning, middle, or end. It goes on until something happens or until the shift is done. It's bound to the world of the mechanical, filled with moving from one place to another, switching one field of observation for another. So bound, it seldom offers an epiphany.

All of this I'd learn later, through months of practice. Now I was mostly bored, unaware of the changes boredom and tiredness were bringing about in my psyche, changes infinitely more important than anything happening on the surface.

The oversize container of coffee had raced through my kidneys, and I started to worry about where I could take a leak. I began thinking about what I'd been doing just two days before. It seemed like a century.

I'd been stewing. That's what I'd been doing. Stewing.

When Fechheimer called to set up the interview, I wasn't working on the Nietzsche book I was supposed to be writing; I was sitting at my desk, a blank page of journal open before me. I'd started the journal two months earlier, when Nancy left.

First there'd been the *Sturm und Drang*, the angry shouting after she found the letter I'd written to Philadelphia, breaking off the affair that had gone on too long. Then I'd taken her to the airport and she'd flown East to her parents', leaving Lis and Ev with me. She'd stayed away a month, returning only when I agreed to see a transactional analyst like the one she'd seen in St. Louis. That had lasted two weeks, long enough for me to manipulate the analyst into saying I was basically OK. But I hadn't been OK and Nancy hadn't been OK and our marriage, after eighteen years, certainly hadn't been OK either. In some subliminal and inchoate way, I'd conveyed to Nancy after her return the same message her own emotions were signaling—that she had to get even. Who knows what I had in mind? Probably some safe and pleasant form of getting even that I could control, as I'd controlled so many things. So when it came, when she came home that Monday night and said she'd had dinner with an architect at his home in Tiburon and taken a hot tub with him, I'd behaved outwardly like an approving modern husband while seething and scared within.

"What was his wife's name?" I'd asked, pleasantly enough.

"Nancy. She died in an auto wreck a couple of years ago. She was blond."

"Oh." I'd moved to the stove so she couldn't see my face. "Where did you meet him?"

Swiftly, then, had come her declaration of independence. "I won't tell you. Because then you could figure out who he is, and I don't want you to know that."

Days later, the wrangling had started, as my mask of approval slipped. Something of this was behind my asking Hal Lipset for a job, knowing only that my book was going nowhere and that I couldn't stay in Bolinas wondering, stewing.

When Fechheimer called, I was picking at the scab of my discontent, knowing that some change had to come, hoping that Lipset would hire me and, if he did, that working as a detective would be the distraction I needed. I was sitting in this car in Oakland, I supposed, not because of any great desire to be a detective or even much of a desire to *play* at being a detective for a week or two, but because I couldn't stand sitting around the house while Nancy carried on an affair with a nameless widower whose wife had also been blond and named Nancy.

If the night before was to be taken as a test, the anodyne was working. A chicken had been roasting in the oven when I walked in, and the four of us had had dinner at the kitchen table while I told of my first day on the job. Lis had been quiet, laughing only at my silliest misadventures. At twelve, she probably suspected there was more to my taking this new job than met the eye, while Ev, at ten, thought the whole idea of his father working as a detective was "far out." Nancy had seemed generally loose and happy and, when I'd mentioned how cold it had been in the car the night before, had retrieved a sleeping bag from the closet. It was as if a valve had been turned, relieving pressure. At least that was the way it felt at the time. Right now, sitting on this street, watching in my mirror as the early Mass was let out from Saint Augustine's, I didn't know what it meant for the future.

The rest of the morning passed uneventfully. Around noon I dealt with the coffee problem, urinating in the oversize styrofoam cup, opening the door, and pitching the cup and its contents under the car. In the early afternoon lace curtains stirred twice on a downstairs window across the street. The second time, an elderly woman's face peered sidelong at me. Not wanting to hang around to see what that meant, I moved the car to the far end of Regent. The black Ford had left, freeing a parking space closer to Tabac's tan Datsun.

By six o'clock my back hurt and I was thirsty and hungry. You should probably report in to Control, I thought, but with your luck, as soon as you break for a phone booth, Tabac will get in his Datsun and leave. Hold on until eight. On a Sunday evening, that should be late enough so he won't be going out, and the hamburger place on Telegraph—only a block away—has two pay phones.

I sat in the dark and waited.

The taillights and then the back-up lights of Tabac's car came on. At first I wasn't sure it was his car. I hadn't seen anyone and hadn't heard a door slam. When he pulled into the street heading away from me, I saw the rusted crease on the driver's door. I turned the key but waited until he reached the far end of the block before taking off.

Soon we were on the Nimitz Freeway. Passing the exit for the plant, I began wondering where he was going. Then it became clear: the Coliseum. The Warriors must be playing.

I hung one car back as the lane curled to the right into the arena's parking lot. Attendants were directing cars into long rows, and I was inserted, like a sardine into a can, two parking slots beyond Tabac. I had to move fast, gathering up the binocs and camera and stuffing them into the blue climbing pack.

Fifteen minutes later, inside the arena, it was easy to find Tabac with the glasses. Many people had binoculars, so my scanning of the crowd didn't stand out. Tabac and a woman were sitting in the upper third of a tier of seats halfway to the other end of the arena. They looked happy, talking and smiling in the interval before the game began. At the end of the first quarter, Tabac got up and returned with two soft drinks, stopping for half a minute at a pay phone on the way to the refreshment stand. I jotted down the time on a piece of paper.

The first half was sluggish, with the Warriors trailing by ten or twelve points throughout. At halftime I moved in Tabac's direction, looping the camera strap around my neck. The 105 lens wasn't really telephoto, but it ought to do fine from less than a hundred feet. Below them and off to the side, I started taking random photos of the crowd. Gradually I edged closer and cranked off three good shots, bracing the camera on a painted metal handrail.

Then I went to a pay phone and called Control.

I ran down what I'd seen that day and ended by saying I'd just gotten some photos of Tabac "and the woman he was with."

"What does she look like?"

"She's got on boots with two-inch heels and a leather mini-skirt. She's maybe five-three without the heels and has short dark hair."

"Terrific. That's his wife. She works for the phone company."

Five minutes later I was in the parking lot looking for my car. Control had told me to break off the Tabac surveillance and start tailing my old quarry Ericson. He hadn't told me why. I took it resources were being juggled, and Tabac's movements tonight made it unlikely he was up to anything. But where was the Volvo?

The guard shack was where it should be, at the end of the column of light posts. I counted the rows of light fixtures. This was the third row, so the Volvo ought to be right here. And where was Tabac's Toyota? It had been parked only two cars away. I looked at my watch: 9:20.

At ten o'clock I told a security guard I couldn't find my car. "Lots of people have that problem," he said, laughing. "The lots here are mirror images of each other. You must have come out the opposite side from where you went in."

I'd wasted forty minutes. If I hurried, I could still pick up a burger and coffee. This surveillance was going to run all night.

By midnight the car had gotten cold enough so I could see my breath, and fatigue was lowering my eyelids. Staying awake became an endurance contest. The sleeping bag in the trunk would make things warmer but also make it harder to fight off sleep. And I was being paid to watch, not sleep. If Ericson was planning to hit some transformers tonight, he'd wait until the small hours of the morning to make his move. When he did, I'd be across the street, watching.

Gradually, tiredness undermined resolve. Nothing is going to happen tonight, a voice told me. You're going to sit here watching this dumb window just as you did Friday night, and about eight A.M. Ericson is going to come down and get in his car and drive down to see how his pickets are doing. . . .

I jerked myself awake and looked around. The light was still on, and Ericson's car hadn't moved. I moved my watch so it caught the light from the street: 2:15. Hazy, fragments of a dream came back.

I'm sitting in a car, watching a door. Not just any door—the door at the plant. A car stops, and a man gets out. He raises his right hand, and then something happens to the door. The cracks spread from the hole, and shards of glass, in slow motion arc through the hallway. But it's silent. There's no gunshot, no crash of breaking glass, no noise at all. Then the man turns and sees me watching him. He points at me with his right hand, and I expect the windshield to explode. But nothing happens. He just points and laughs.

It seemed as though something else had happened, and I tried to bring it back. But I couldn't make it out.

I was fully awake now and knew I wouldn't have trouble fighting off sleep. There it was, the thing that had been troubling me all day, the thing that had struck me first with the bullet hole, and that I'd felt again on hearing of my relief's accident.

Sitting at the spot I'd chosen, he'd pulled out when Ericson left. The truck that hit him would have angled in unseen, from just beyond his peripheral vision. There would have been a split second when he knew it was going to happen and there was nothing he could do about it. He'd have grabbed the wheel and felt the crash and heard the scream of metal ripping. And then there would have been silence.

I'd been expecting it all day. I'd felt it there, just the far side of what I could see, unnoticed, like the cancerous lump before it announces itself. All I'd seen since Friday was the course of the world, ordinary people going about their ordinary business. That ordinariness had lulled me to sleep.

But now I was awake.

Was I overdramatizing? Was I fulfilling Hemingway's claim the old don't get wise, they just get careful? After all, I hadn't seen any violence. I was just a low-level operative tailing people in a labor dispute. Was I playing mind-games with myself?

Perhaps.

But then the bullet hole came back.

I looked at the window. Nothing had changed. The blind was still cutting the gold light into horizontal strips.

MONDAY, NOVEMBER 15

Paranoia is like that. It grows up around you before you know anything's wrong. It changes the world.

That's the way it had been with me. Only later—years later—when Fechheimer explained it to me, told me that what I'd gone through was what every detective goes through, only then did I recognize what it had really been about.

Sitting under Ericson's window, I may have dozed off a second time just before dawn. I was startled by how light it had become and by the condensation that had gathered overnight on the windshield. A bit before eight, Ericson came out and wiped off his windshield before driving to the plant. I followed half a block back and pulled into the Denny's up the street to call. Denny's was too close to the plant for a meeting, Control said, and gave me directions to a coffee shop a mile distant.

After our meeting, Control took my surveillance log and I headed for Bolinas. He said nothing about needing me later on.

At home, I fell right into bed. But less than an hour later, Control called and told me to pick up the surveillance of Tabac at his home as soon as I could get there. When I said I was wasted, he told me I could end the surveillance a half hour after Tabac's lights went out. But when I got to Regent Street, Tabac's car wasn't there. Sitting there trying to keep focused as the afternoon light faded, I began to suspect Control's motives. Why call me back from Bolinas to start a surveillance when Tabac wasn't even home?

I waited there several hours, looking at the tangle of overhead power lines, and after a while realized that although I'd been watching, I hadn't been seeing anything. I drove to the hamburger place and reported in. Then I sat in the car watching the traffic lights on Telegraph change from red to green and back to red. Back on Regent Street, I didn't bother to find a new parking spot.

An hour later, Russ's voice took me by surprise.

"What's this," he asked, at the same time pulling back on Sabra, their mixed-breed German shepherd, "the newest surveillance technique of the Lipset Service?"

"What?"

"Sabra and I were out for a walk, and I noticed you sitting here. You're pretty hard to miss with your headlights on."

I punched the lights off.

"You OK?" he asked. Sabra started to scratch.

"Yeah. I forgot about the lights. I was just thinking of something else."

"That's good. I thought it might be a new technique. Leave

your headlights on to throw 'em off the track. No one'll guess anyone sitting at the curb with his lights on could be a private dick.''

I got out, and we walked up the street together. His leather jacket fitted him better than it fitted me. Tabac's car was nowhere on the block.

A little after nine o'clock, it pulled into a parking spot on my side of the street. Tabac and his wife got out and went into their house. I sat there watching the lights come on inside. That was when the bad thoughts came.

They started with Fechheimer. When I'd walked into the office that first day, he'd been carrying the file on Ericson. Then, later that afternoon, Hal Lipset himself had answered the phone. That must have been part of it too. No one had told me to go in the back way; I was sure of that. They'd know I'd go to the front door and see that bullet hole. They'd known it would scare the shit out of "the Professor."

In my dream, the guy had pointed at me, but nothing had happened. The windshield hadn't exploded. I wasn't even sure he'd had a gun in his hand. What's more, he'd been laughing. That was the key to it. He'd been laughing at me just as they were laughing at me. Maybe they'd faked the bullet hole to scare me. Maybe there hadn't been any bullet hole. That would explain why Control told me so conspiratorially never to go to the plant. He'd said it was so my looks and car would remain secret, and I'd been flattered by that, made to feel important. But he'd simply been playing me, making sure I wouldn't see that front door again and notice the bullet hole had disappeared. It was all their little movie, and I was an extra in it.

Russ? He was probably playing along with them, checking on me to make sure I was actually there. Walking the dog—what a joke! Four years ago he'd never walked the dog this far from North Street. And how had he known I was working for the Lipset Service? I hadn't told him. Or had I? When I'd given Control the license-plate number of the VW, they must have run the plate and recruited Russ and Tracy behind my back.

There had been times yesterday when I'd thought Tabac and Ericson were in *my* movie. That was the high I'd gotten watching them, believing they weren't aware of me. But all that time I'd been a bit player in another movie—Lipset's movie, the one where Control moved me around like a piece on a chessboard.

I was exhausted and getting angry. They've been sitting back on Pacific Avenue laughing at me. Maybe they've been betting on how often I'd lose Ericson or Tabac. Ericson has something to do with the strike; he was there on the picket line. But Tabac? Maybe Tabac is someone they picked out of a hat, someone who "coincidentally" lives not far from Russ and Tracy. I'm sitting here watching the windows of someone who has nothing to do with anything. And I was doing this for six hours before he even got here.

The lights were unchanged. Just the fact they were unchanged made me angry.

I sat and stared and stewed.

"I've figured it out," I said aloud to all of them. "I won't be your pawn anymore. I quit."

It felt good. The car seemed to float down the street. On the right, I could see the hamburger place, closed but with the pay phones lit by the streetlight on the corner.

Nancy's voice sounded a world away. I ranted and raved, and she listened. Then, when I'd wound down, she said quietly. "Maybe they're testing you. Maybe they're seeing if you'll quit."

I don't remember what she said after that.

I sat in the car and watched the traffic lights for a while. Then I made one last circuit. Tabac's downstairs lights were off now. Only a TV flickered in the front bedroom. I pulled into my old parking spot and smoked a cigarette.

Half an hour after the flickers stopped, I drove to a motel on University Avenue and slept for the next twelve hours.

PART ONE

ONE

"IF HE'D BOUGHT IT,
HE WOULD'VE BOUGHT IT"

TUESDAY, JULY 26, 1977

Around me were shapes or presences, like coils of seaweed, indistinct yet somehow troubling. I was swimming through them, but in no particular direction. It wasn't unpleasant or frightening. It wasn't a nightmare. Just troubled sleep. Heavy and viscous. Flawed by some latch missing on unconsciousness.

The alarm hammered, and the coils retreated. I stumbled to the bureau and shut off the sound.

The toothpaste's bite took some of the cigarette taste out of my mouth. But it couldn't do anything for the lead in my muscles. What time had it been the night before when I'd turned up the driveway, scratching gravel, hoping the sound wouldn't wake anyone? Two-fifteen? Two-thirty? And what time was it now? Five-thirty. Forget shaving; I wouldn't be doing any interviews today. I picked up my pants from a pile on the floor. Nancy had rolled onto her left side, blond hair spilling across her head and shoulders. I looked at her. She hadn't stirred earlier when I'd moved close under the covers.

Quietly, I pulled on last night's clothes and buried my face in her hair. All the old scents of twenty years came back: Norfolk, St. Thomas, Oxford, Vienna, New Haven, Copenhagen, Haverford, and now California. I nuzzled her ear and she mumbled something I couldn't make out. At the bottom of the stairs I bumped Ev's skateboard and sent it skittering against the wall. The blue climbing pack was on the living-room couch. I picked it up and left the house.

25

Fifteen minutes later the Volvo labored up the second of four switchbacks above Stinson Beach. The road swung sharply to the right, and below were the lights of Stinson Beach and Bolinas, isolated pinpricks in the darkness. Soon they'd disappear and everything would meld into a wide-angle view of sea, sand, and marsh. Often, in the past, I'd felt a strange exhilaration in driving this road, a thrill that came not from the view but from the unreal clarity of the California light and shadow that dappled the road through overhanging oaks and greenish-gray lichen, so different from the flat, indifferent light of the East where I'd grown up. Now there was neither light nor exhilaration, just weariness as the Volvo's headlights tunneled upward through the darkness.

Soon the headlights picked up isolated stands of redwood, and the fog in my head began to clear. What was it about this case that was rubbing me the wrong way?

It wasn't having to get up at 5:15 to start a surveillance. In the past I'd done that, if not happily, at least with some curiosity about what the day might hold. But now I felt only a dull desire to be done with the case and with its dusty, bitter aftertaste.

It had all started with Bates, that simpering lawyer from Minneapolis. As he'd bent over David Fechheimer's desk to deliver the letter of authorization, I'd flashed on him as a kid in seventh grade, sitting close to the teacher, homework neatly arranged in front of him, looking up with arm raised, hoping she'd call on him. In Fechheimer's office, he'd sat on a green folding chair, fiddling superciliously with the gold chain that hung across his worsted vest, complaining of the "hot pants" Mrs. Cutler "seemed to suffer from." He'd given us Karin Cutler's address and phone number, the keys and registration to her Lincoln Continental Mark II, and a letter authorizing us to repossess her car and perform "whatever investigations are deemed appropriate to disclose whether or not she is committing adultery." He'd also turned over two photographs, one of her smiling vacantly with that pert blandness typical of Big Ten coeds' graduation photos, the other of her bikini-clad body stretched out on the afterdeck of a two-hundred-thousand-dollar cabin cruiser named *Pippin IV*. Why had the husband sent along a photo like that? Had he wanted to make sure we'd recognize her naked? "The rear end of the townhouse," Bates had said, "lies just a bit below Highway One-oh-one. And the drapes on the back bedroom are never drawn." Since we were the first detectives hired in the case, how did they know that?

There was a whiff of the prurient here. And, too, of the pathetic.

Consider the image of a distinguished white-haired man of sixty-six, member of the Board of Trustees of the Minneapolis Symphony, director of several Fortune 500 corporations, and chief executive officer of a family-held company that the year before had reported earnings in excess of twelve million dollars—consider the image of such a figure crouched in high grass and scrub oak just below Highway 101, peering through a chain-link fence in hopes of getting a glimpse of Karin Bohlin Cutler of the bikini and the Continental Mark II.

Bates, nervously fidgeting, had told us something of the Cutlers' story while I kept switching my eyes between the two photos of Karin. They'd married in January 1975, but things began to "deteriorate" shortly after Cutler was kept unavoidably in Spartanburg, South Carolina, by a court case. After a summer spent more or less together in the Sausalito townhouse, Karin hadn't returned to Minnesota with him. Now not only was she still in his townhouse and driving his car, she was also sharing house, car, and, more importantly, *herself* with a thirty-eight-year-old longshoreman and weight lifter who, Bates proclaimed, had "underworld connections."

How did Bates and Cutler know all this?

Well, it seemed Cutler had "visited out here with Karin" (such a strange rural archaism for Bates to use), and had met the longshoreman/weight lifter. A picture had begun to form in my mind, but Bates had moved on to something else. His client "particularly wanted to document the adultery through photographic means if at all possible."

The chubby lawyer's last remark had been enough to focus my thoughts, and I hadn't listened to the rest of the legal talk. It was another case about the failure of love, the slide from lover to voyeur. It was about Cutler getting his seasons mixed up and mistaking a few glorious days of fall for spring. His punishment was to climb through the scrub oak, gazing, expecting, hoping to see her. Terrified at the thought of losing her, helpless in any way to affect that loss, he sought to have her in another way: as object for his eye. Pathetic? Of course. But what followed was not pathetic. It was only mean.

Cutler also listened to the voice of the boardrooms. He was

being made a fool of by a woman, and by a woman less than
half his age. "Certainly, Clifford," I could almost hear his attorney, Bates' superior, saying, "there are steps we can and
should take. You have your rights, and they should be protected
with all the considerable resources at your command." And so
the resources had been deployed.

They'd purchased not only advisory counsel in San Francisco,
not only a free trip to San Francisco for Thomas Bates—where
he could cautiously, ambivalently take his affair with legal secretary Laura Bode out from behind the water cooler—but also a
private investigator who, at 5:50 A.M. in a roadside 7-Eleven,
had just purchased a chocolate-covered doughnut, a pint of orange juice, and coffee in a large Styrofoam cup. All this in the
service of Clifford P. Cutler's vengeance.

As the Volvo sped up the entry ramp onto the freeway, commuter traffic to San Francisco was already building. Each ramp
added a rivulet to the flow. In the next hour, as the eastern sky
turned from dull gray to orange, the flow would become a tor-
rent.

Perched on a hillside between freeway and residential street,
Cutler's townhouse was in the wrong place for a good surveillance. Since the house was sited above the street, with only one
door in back, you could sit in a car all night and (except for
seeing lights go on and off) have no idea what was going on
inside. I'd started the surveillance at seven the night before, after
checking that the black Lincoln with Minnesota plates was in
the carport by the kitchen. Later, a white Lincoln had pulled
into the complex—eight identical townhouses stretched along
the hill—at 8:13 P.M., but I hadn't connected it with Karin. It
wasn't until I'd walked up the stairs at the south end of the
complex and bushwhacked farther up the bank toward the freeway that I could see the white car parked next to Karin's in the
carport.

I flipped on the Sony BM-12 sitting beside me on the seat and
heard my voice from the night before:

This is Josiah Thompson in the case of *Cutler vs. Cutler*. The
date is July twenty-fifth, nineteen seventy-seven; the time is
seven-fourteen P.M. I'm commencing surveillance on Eighteen fifty-six Cordera Drive. Black Lincoln, Minnesota plate,
AGC nine-one-one, is in the carport.

Seven-forty: Late model Plymouth coupe, white male driving, just pulled into the driveway.

Eight-thirteen: A white Lincoln just pulled in. Couldn't see the driver.

Nine-twelve: I'm in place on the bank above Eighteen fifty-six. There's a cyclone fence just above me. [*I could hear my breathing, labored from the scramble up the bank.*] The white Lincoln is parked next to the black one. I'll get the plate later.

Ten-twenty: Karin just showed at the kitchen window, washing some dishes.

Ten twenty-two: White male, six-three, two hundred and forty pounds, no facial hair, is at the sink with Karin. He's naked from the waist up. This fucker's big! Huge shoulders!

Ten-fifty: Lights just went off in the kitchen. I can see some sort of flickering light in the left upstairs room. Probably a TV.

Eleven-thirty: Flickering light just went off.

Twelve-oh-seven: The white Lincoln—midseventies—has California plate one-five-oh MRP. I marked the right rear tire of both white and black Lincolns. Breaking off surveillance at this time.

Sitting there in the dark, waiting for the customary half hour to elapse after lights out, I'd decided to set up shop next day in the bushes. From the bank I could get some shots of the boyfriend leaving—not the photos Cutler wanted, but a nice touch for a court hearing and probably the best we'd get.

The Sausalito police had patrols all over this area. I'd called them before starting out the night before, giving my name, license-plate number, and a description of the Volvo. I'd told them we had a surveillance on for the 1800 block of Cordera Drive. That wouldn't help much now, because I'd have to leave the car at the Rio Vista exit, then hike a half mile down the freeway and bushwhack in from there. I might get spotted by a CHP car on the freeway, but after I started down the hill I'd be in high grass and Monterey pine. It'd be hot with the July sun beating down on the hill's eastern slope, but the boyfriend ought to be out of there by nine or ten, and it wouldn't have heated up much by then. I glided off under the freeway and parked on open gravel near the exit ramp.

The binoculars and camera were already in the climbing pack. I stuffed the recorder, doughnut, and orange juice in on top, locked the car, and started walking brisly down the freeway. I'd had only three hours' sleep, but the light weight tugging on the straps of the pack and the ground under my boots felt good.

I stepped over the metal guardrail and made my way down through sandy soil. Working off to the right, I climbed a six-foot cyclone fence and plunged deeper through grass and coyote bushes until I could see the "his and hers" Lincolns. The binoculars showed the two chalk marks on the right rear tires—right above where each tire touched the ground. Neither car had been moved.

But the angle was wrong. The cars obstructed the view of the back door. I slithered on knees and elbows to the left, pushed aside a coyote bush, and looked down. Perfect.

"Six-twelve A.M., August second," I spoke into the recorder, holding it inches from my mouth. "Beginning surveillance of Eighteen fifty-six Cordera Drive. AGC nine-one-one and one-five-oh MRP still in place. Tire marks still there." With the motor drive on the camera, I could shoot two frames a second. I'd zoom in on the boyfriend's face as he walked to the car; the last shot would be a close-up of his license plate as he backed out. Already there was enough light to shoot at 1/60 of a second.

I munched on the doughnut. It was quiet and pleasantly cool. The whole thing ought to be done by nine or ten; I could write it up, drop off the film, and take the rest of the day off.

I kept looking at a branch ten feet down the bank. With my luck, the boyfriend would come out the back, and the branch would block the camera's view of his face.

I sat there for two minutes, looking up and down the row of houses. No lights, no movement. It took only ten seconds to scramble down the open slope, break off the branch, and scramble back. No one could have seen me.

I finished the doughnut and took another sight through the viewfinder. As the day brightened, all sorts of details became clear. The light meter showed I could shoot at 1/125 of a second. There was nothing to do now but wait. The tiredness came back, and my mind began to wander.

Suddenly there was movement on my left. A Sausalito police car pulled in and stopped three doors down from 1856. Stretched prone on the grass, I could see the officer go up to the door and knock. No one could have seen me; it must be something else. He was talking now to a woman in a green bathrobe. He walked back to his car. Burrowing down in the grass, I heard him yell,

"All right, we know you're up there. Come on down." The seconds expanded as they ticked off. *Two* . . . Shit, I don't want to blow the whole case. *Three* . . . He's not going to want to come bushwhacking up that steep slope. It's too much work. *Four* . . . But there's that damn fence, and there's no way to do that invisibly. *Five* . . . He'll probably call for backup, and if he sees me go over the fence, he'll get CHP help from the freeway. *Six* . . . If they catch me after having to come in after me, they're gonna be pissed. *Seven* . . . . His voice broke the silence. "Now get the hell down here."

I raised my head and saw him going for his radio. It was decided. Grabbing the pack with one hand, camera around my neck, I stood up in clear view and scrambled down the embankment. I could feel their eyes on me. Not just the eyes of the cop and the green-bathrobed woman but the other eyes. Karin and her boyfriend's eyes. All the eyes I couldn't see. Wrapping me in contempt.

Spread-eagled against the side of the patrol car, I said, "For Christ's sake. I'm on a surveillance. I reported it last night. Didn't you hear about it?"

He was still frisking me.

"Can't we get this car out of here? Let's go out front, and I'll explain," I said.

He looked at me sidelong and motioned with his head to the car's back door. I got in. He spoke a few words to Green Bathrobe and then backed the car out.

When he stopped up the block, I was already rummaging through my wallet for one of David's cards. He switched off the ignition and, not turning his head, said, "All right, out of the car." He put my pack on the hood of the car. "Now open it." I pulled out the orange juice, the binoculars, and the recorder.

"You got some identification?"

I handed him David's card with my name in small print at the bottom.

"This doesn't tell me anything. You have a driver's license?"

I pulled out my Pennsylvania driver's license.

"It says you live at Five College Lane, Haverford, Pennsylvania. That true?"

"Well, not really. I've been living out here the last few months, working as a detective. That's why I gave you the card. I work for Fechheimer. Under his license. We called you last night to tell you we had a surveillance on."

He looked down at a clipboard and ruffled through some papers.

"It says here you're supposed to be driving a 'sixty-nine Volvo, license one-four-oh UNP. Where is it?"

"I left it up at the freeway exit and then came down the bank. I had to get some photos from the back," I said, risking a smile.

"How am I supposed to know that? You're supposed to be in the car, and you're not. Actually, you were trespassing." He paused for a moment. "What's this case about, anyway?"

"It's the usual thing," I said, thinking I couldn't go far down this road. "A domestic case."

"What house you working on?"

"I'm sorry," I said, hesitating. I couldn't go any further. I felt the gears shift, and my voice slipped into another tone and idiom. "I'd prefer not to say," I said.

"You'd fucking prefer not to say," he looked at me, color rising. "Here you're crawling around in the bushes with a camera at six-thirty in the morning. You show me some bullshit card that doesn't say anything, and you expect me to believe it. We've had a shitload of calls about a Peeping Tom out this way; maybe you're it. Get in the car. I'm taking you downtown."

As the car pulled away, I tried to talk my way out of it. After all, he had my name as the person doing the surveillance, and he'd seen my driver's license. He cut me off with a quick "Shut up!"

Fechheimer got me out of it.

I was working for him now. In early February he'd left the Lipset Service, set up shop in his apartment on Laguna Street, and invited me to join him as an apprentice operative. By that time I'd spent two months doing low-level work on the cable TV strike: continuing surveillance of Ericson, Tabac, and friends, running the video camera that peered down on the plant entrance, ferrying workers between the plant and a nearby motel where their cars were parked and guarded. New Year's Eve I'd spent tailing a black union member to a series of parties around Berkeley. Once I'd succeeded in photographing the passing of rifles from one car to another, but nothing had ever come of it. By late January Lipset was preparing to fold up the strike investigation, and I was suffering from what Kierkegaard called "the despair of finitude"—being bothered by too many little people about too many little things. When Fechheimer offered me the chance to join him, I jumped at it.

There had been times this morning, sitting on a hard wooden bench inside the fashionably shingled headquarters of the Sausalito police, when I'd wondered about that decision. When the desk sergeant called the number on Fechheimer's card, the answering service picked it up, and a new operator reported she hadn't the foggiest notion who I was. The sergeant asked her to let the call ring through, and finally a groggy Fechheimer answered. Two years earlier he'd worked on a jewel theft in Sausalito, and knew a couple of detectives in the burglary detail. It took only twenty minutes for him to get me released with a warning not to get out of my car again; if I did, I'd be busted for trespassing. One of the detectives told another patrolman to take me back to the Volvo.

It was 7:13 when I pulled through the townhouse parking area, confirming that the two Lincolns were still in place, chalk marks and all. I parked across the street, about 150 feet from the entrance, and settled in. I wouldn't get much warning when the boyfriend came out. I timed a blue Buick and found there was only about five seconds from the moment a car appeared until it was on the street driving away. This meant literally I couldn't blink.

This case seemed to be jinxed, and it was turning into an enormous pain in the ass. Bates had given us the wrong address, and three nights previous I'd sat on the wrong house for six hours before realizing something was wrong. A call to the tax assessor's office had given us the right address, but I might end up having to eat those six hours. And now this. I was sure Fechheimer would agree I'd been right to go in from the back to get a shot of the boyfriend leaving. Getting caught had not been due to carelessness, only to bad luck. But I'd made a mistake slipping back into the manner of the college professor: "I'd prefer not to say" instead of "Shit, man, I can't tell you that; I'd get canned if I told you that, and I need the money."

Discouragement rolled over me, mixing with the taste of the synthetic orange juice. Would I ever be able to shed the scales of that past life? Would I ever be able to move surely through the detective world—as, say, Fechheimer moved? Eight years younger, he was so much more accomplished than I. But he wasn't out here; I was. And for every dollar I was making tramping around in the underbrush, he was making three—in bed sleeping.

But my discouragement ran deeper. *Why* master the skills?

Why learn to move through a minefield with grace and confidence, when I could return to that Victorian house on the campus three thousand miles away? I didn't have to do this. I didn't have to get up at five in the morning after three hours' sleep and then crawl around in the bushes and get spread-eagled against a police car like a criminal. I didn't have to sit in a hot car, pissing into a plastic juice container, keeping watch as the hired minion of the likes of Clifford P. Cutler. And for what? For ten dollars an hour. What had I made as Professor of Philosophy? I'd figured it out once, and it came to something like seventy-five dollars an hour. Why was I doing this?

A flash of white caught my eye, and I raised the camera. False alarm. It was a white Ford driven by a little blue-haired lady. It was 7:28. Chances were Karin and her boyfriend had slept through the noise in the parking area. He should appear in the entrance in the next hour or so.

I called Fechheimer from a nearby pay phone at 1:15 that afternoon. By that time, rivers of sweat were pouring down my back and sides. I'd been eyeing a piece of shade across the street, but it was too close to the entrance; I couldn't use the camera there without running too great a risk of being seen. I'd also become angry—irrationally, implacably angry. Not at myself, or at the Sausalito police, or Green Bathrobe, or David. But at Karin and her boyfriend. Didn't he have a job? Some pressing reason to leave? I imagined them languidly awakening, making love, and then having a late, delicious brunch. I felt like Popeye in *The French Connection*, huddling in a doorway, nursing a tepid cup of coffee while the heroin dealer and his connection eat dinner in a luxurious French restaurant across the street. I called Fechheimer because I hoped he'd call the surveillance off. He told me to hold it until two o'clock and to break if off if the boyfriend hadn't shown by then. I checked the parking area again and resumed my position. Forty minutes more and I could take off.

At 1:37 the boyfriend showed. The camera whirred and clicked three times as he paused at the entrance. He turned left and sped past me up the street. The job was done.

But I wanted something more. I wanted to chase him, to get something that might embarrass him, to watch him without being seen, to feel some rush of power over this person who'd kept me sweltering in a hot car for six hours. Part of me knew it was stupid, but I persuaded myself I didn't have a good photo of his license plate and by tailing him I might pick up something. I turned the key, jammed the Volvo into first, and did a quick U-turn.

I caught up with him on Bridgeway but hung back almost a block, keeping several shield cars between us. As we expected, he turned onto the freeway toward San Francisco. Climbing the Waldo Grade, I got two clear shots of the car and its license plate. Then I decided to try something elegant. Speed was the key here. I pulled into the fast lane and began to overtake him. My passenger window was down, and he was two lanes over. I watched him out of the corner of my eye as I raised the camera with one hand, pressed the button, and listened to the motor drive whine and the shutter click twice. It was all over in a second; he didn't seem to have noticed. I pulled ahead for a short distance and then let the traffic overtake me.

With the Bay below and San Francisco shimmering in the distance, the toll plaza at the southern end of the Golden Gate Bridge was coming up. Should I follow him into the toll booth? We'd be stopped for ten seconds, and he might put together the image in his mirror with the car parked on the street near the townhouse. Or should I go for another lane and toll booth? I might get blocked and lose him. I saw an empty lane to the left and slid into it.

Coming out of the toll booth, we were almost even. I dropped back, and by the time we hit Lombard Street he was two cars ahead. A hole opened in the right lane, and for several blocks I tagged along in his blind spot, cruising ten feet behind his right rear fender. He made the turn onto Van Ness and then sidled over into the right lane. I slowed, watching him over the shield car between us. He took a sharp right onto Union Street, and I pulled into a red zone at the corner. Soon the tail of his Lincoln disappeared as he turned right again onto Franklin. By the time I reached the corner, he was making a third right onto Filbert. I gunned the engine, heart pounding, and pulled into a bus zone. "Breaking off surveillance at two-oh-four P.M.," I said into the recorder. "Boyfriend last seen going south on Van Ness at the corner of Filbert and Van Ness. Shit, I'm burned."

Hurrying up the stairs to Fechheimer's Victorian flat a few blocks away, I found David in the kitchen.

"You're early," he said, glancing at his watch.

"He showed at one thirty-seven," I said. "I tailed him to San Francisco and broke off when he went around the block on me at Filbert and Van Ness. I think he made me, David. We gotta get that car now, while he's gone, or we may never see it again."

I was thinking if he'd seen me, they might figure out Cutler had put a detective on Karin and hide the black Lincoln before we could repossess it.

"First," said David, "take a minute and tell me what you got."

I told him the results of the surveillance, beginning with the night before. He picked up a cigarette and said, "Go run the plate on the car. These turkeys gave us the wrong address to begin with; maybe this guy's her cousin. Let's find out who he is. Then come back; I want to talk."

I called Datasearch in Sacramento, a private outfit hooked into the DMV computer. For $3.75 they would run the plate and give us the name of the registered owner of the Lincoln. Anyone could get the same information from DMV, but by statute, DMV would report the request to the owner of the car. Private investigators, after some vehement lobbying in Sacramento, had been excluded from that part of the statute; we could get this and other information from Datasearch without the target ever being the wiser.

When I came back, David was smoking, staring out the window. I knew he wasn't pondering the Cutler case, in which he was only mildly interested. Was he thinking about his estranged wife, Renée, the bane and also love of his life? Or did that distant look mean he was plotting the angles in one of his other, private cases?

David was always oblique, even mysterious, a trait that seemed both natural and feigned. Natural because it was a good practice for a detective to work the corners, angling conversational shots off the cushion rather than firing directly into the pocket. Feigned because the enigmatic air had become part of his reputation, an alluring quality to the women who hung around him.

"How come you tailed him?"

"I screwed up, David. I shouldn't have. I was tired and pissed and thought I might pick up something."

"It's OK. From what you say, I don't think they'll spook much."

"If they hide the car, we'll have a bitch of a time finding it. Why not grab it now while he's gone? We've got the keys."

"No, it's too early. I'll call Minneapolis and tell them what we've got. All they want is evidence of adultery, and we seem to have that. We'll get the car later."

I started to walk back to the office.

"Wait a minute, Tink."

I turned and faced him.

"You're tired and frazzled. You haven't screwed up. Everything is gonna be OK. But you're straining. You're trying to push this case into your rhythm. The trick is to go in the other direction. Every case has its rhythm. You've gotta find it and fall in with it."

I looked at him steadily. There was no curl around the corners of his mouth. He was serious, and for only the second time since we'd been working together, he was actually giving me advice.

Once, months before, he'd talked to me about "paying attention," explaining that it was the only difference between a master detective and a bungler, and also the only insurance policy most of us would ever get. "Paying attention" meant things to him it didn't mean to me. For me it meant keeping my eyes open—really listening to what a witness was saying, always asking why if some expected piece of information didn't show up in a records check, staying alert to the changing mosaic of neighborhood sounds and movements on a surveillance. For David it meant other things. Like always checking his rearview mirror, even when he was out on a date. Or earlier, when the war between state and federal drug agents and a small group of San Francisco drug lawyers and investigators had reached its climax, checking under the hood of his car for extra wires from the coil.

For a while I'd taken these stories with a large grain of salt. After all, I told myself, state and federal narcs don't go around blowing up other people's cars. Then I read about some of the frame-ups that had embarrassed prominent drug attorneys, and more important, about Michael Murphy, David's last apprentice before me. Murphy was dead, killed in a freeway crash one April night in 1973. His autopsy had showed a stuporous level of blood alcohol, 0.30, and David had seen him cold sober two hours before the crash. They'd met in a café on Union Street and chatted about the case they were working on. Half an hour later, Murphy had called his wife and told her he'd gotten a call and had to "meet a guy." David was convinced Murphy had been led into a trap, injected with grain alcohol, and put into a car with a jammed accelerator. And David thought he knew who had done it.

What did I think? I'd never known Michael Murphy, and I certainly didn't know who had murdered him or even whether he *had* been murdered. But Michael Murphy's ghost lingered in my thoughts as a cautionary presence, underlining the importance of "Pay attention!" And now David was telling me something else. Not just how frazzled I looked and felt, but how to move out of it. "Find their rhythm and go with it." OK. So far today I'd made one error of instinct (with the cop), and one of judgment (following the boyfriend). The key was to stop straining. David looked back out the kitchen window.

"You remember Flitcraft, Tink?"

Flitcraft? Flitcraft? Who the fuck was Flitcraft? David was always doing this to me, asking me about some off-the-wall person or place. Now it was coming back. That motel near Fort Pierce, my first dope case with Fechheimer, lying back on the cheap bed reading *The Maltese Falcon* to pass the time, waiting for two days to hand over some newspaper clippings in a manila envelope to a pimply kid in the Tampa Airport. Yeah, I remembered who Flitcraft was.

I nodded.

"I've been thinking about Flitcraft just now. Maybe because half an hour ago Judith Krause called with a missing-persons case she's sending over. The client's a friend of hers and will be coming in at two o'clock on Monday. Her daughter disappeared from Wilmington, Delaware, three weeks ago after leaving a suicide note. I told Judith we'd talk to her and see if there's anything we can do. If you're free on Monday, you might sit in. Could be interesting."

He paused for a moment and took a drag on his Raleigh. Oddly, he collected the coupons that came in the cigarette packs.

"Hammett, you know, was right about Flitcraft. I've had a couple of skip-traces on middle-aged men, and you find them like Hammett said—through insurance companies. They always end up with a second family and pretty much the same insurance package. You ever think of running away, Tink, when you were back in that academic paradise?"

"No," I said, "the pension plan was too good."

As he turned from the window, I took his faint grin as an acknowledgment I'd learned something over the past six months. Once I would have answered his question with all the earnestness of a Labrador retriever returning a soggy branch to its master's hand. Between then and now I'd been thrown too many times in conversational jujitsu to risk such easy earnestness. I was learning the uses of ellipsis and indirectness. He stubbed out his cigarette in a Villa d'Este ashtray.

"Why don't you get some sleep? I'll call if Minneapolis wants another surveillance on tonight."

"Thanks, David."

"Thank *you*. We'll get the car. Don't worry about it."

Ten minutes later, I heard a *crunch* as the Volvo's right front tire collapsed a beer can near the curb.

This part of Grove Street lay only fifteen blocks from Fechheimer's middle-class neighborhood. A real-estate person would call it a marginal ghetto. On Grove Street, "gentrification" might mean something you did to your hair on Friday night; it wasn't anything you did to a building or a neighborhood. All that would come later. For now it was a hodgepodge of junk shops, two cheap restaurants, a grocery store, and, on my side of the street, wedged between a vacant storefront and a framing shop, a violin maker.

Up the street, the afternoon hookers were beginning to show while the secondhand dealers sat in front of their shops, talking or playing cards. The block looked safe, and during daylight hours it was. At night it changed. Only a block from the Opera House, it became a hunting ground for the muggers and car breakers who preyed on suburban operagoers taking advantage of the free parking on Grove.

I opened the heavy glass door to the building. The fake Spanish furniture was still chained to eyebolts in the brown tile floor of the lobby. The Areola Apartments, an eight-story brick building housing thirty-eight apartments of a style made popular in the early 1920s, was home to pensioners, addicts, young and poor gay couples, hookers, clerks. It was presided over by Cora and Herbert, an unlikely couple in their midfifties who in the mornings saw themselves as foot soldiers in the perennial battle against roaches and moral decay. Cora had told me only the week before, her slipping features trying to take on the lineaments of indignation, "You won't have any more trouble, Mr. Thompson, with that Mr. Duncan in three-oh-one. He's three weeks behind in his rent, and the parole officer picked him up this morning. The place was a pigsty. You wouldn't believe. And there were needles under the bed. I have a nice nightstand for you if you want it—five bucks."

Mr. Duncan had never bothered me, and I didn't want his nightstand. Now, since it was midafternoon, Cora's combat role was receding. Soon she and Herbert would be nursing their water glasses of straight tequila, clucking over the depredations of their tenants and the stolid indifference of the real-estate company as the light faded and the street noises changed.

I unlocked the double deadbolts of the door to my flat. The air was close; I hadn't been there for five days. When I opened a window, the odors from the Szechuan restaurant underneath drifted up past the lifeless plant some previous tenant had abandoned on the fire escape. The bed was unmade behind the double doors of the eight-by-ten-foot alcove that housed it. Months before, when Nancy and I'd first seen the apartment, what caught our eyes was the intelligence of the 1920s design—the ironing board that folded out of the wall in the kitchen, the sleeping alcove that turned a studio into a one-bedroom apartment. All for $150 a month.

The previous tenant had left a dirty patterned rug on the floor. It clashed with an orange vinyl chair I'd gotten from Cora and Herbert for five dollars. Nancy and I'd trooped next door to a secondhand store and come back with a lumpy double-bed mattress and box spring, plus a couple of motel lamps. When the bed was set up, she'd looked strangely at it. We'd spent a couple of nights there, but I knew she hadn't been comfortable. It was really my apartment, part of a life she'd learn about only through my words. And neither of us trusted the other's words much anymore.

There were six roach bodies lined up along the outside kitchen wall where the week before there'd been only two. Black Flag City Mixture was living up to its claims. I took a Coors from the fridge and looked over at the ashtray on the kitchen table. *Towne Motel*, it said, *Gordon, Nebraska.* Not quite the Villa d'Este.

I walked into the living room and sat down on the madras-covered daybed. It was cool in San Francisco, and my still-wet shirt gave off a chill. I pulled on a sweater and looked over at *The Maltese Falcon*, sitting in a jumble of books on a side stand. I riffled through it until the Flitcraft chapter came to hand. It began with the words *"In his bedroom that was a living-room now the wall-bed was up . . ."*

I looked over at the sleeping alcove with the unmade bed. Same era. And the Areola Apartments in the 1920s would have been just about Sam Spade's style. I could imagine Spade and Brigid O'Shaughnessy riding up in the elevator to the third floor, Spade opening the double deadbolts just as I'd done, taking Brigid's hat and coat, and asking her to sit down while he telephoned Joel Cairo. I could even imagine Spade telling her she'd gotten what she wanted, that Cairo had agreed to come over. In the book, Spade does all these things, and then suddenly, *"without any preliminary, without an introductory remark of any sort, [he begins] to tell the girl about a thing that had happened some years before in the Northwest."*

That "thing," of course, is the story of Flitcraft, a Realtor from Tacoma who went out for lunch one day and never came back. *"He went like that,"* Spade tells Brigid, *"like a fist when you open your hand."*

When I'd first read the book—lying on that motel bed months before in Florida—I hadn't been able to make much of the Flitcraft story. Nor, for that matter, of the whole book. I knew the movie. Who didn't know the movie? But the book was something else. It seemed dated, the "hard-boiled" style forced and contrived. Worse than that, it wasn't telling me anything about how to be a detective. I didn't run into clients like Miss Wonderly (a.k.a. Brigid O'Shaughnessy) or have strangers bearing mysterious packages expire on the floor in front of me. Back then, the book seemed just an exercise in hack writing; I'd liked the movie better.

During the past several months, though, I'd learned more about both the *Falcon* and its author from Fechheimer. This wasn't accidental; David probably knew more about Hammett than any of his biographers, people whose requests for information I often found lying on his desk. More to the point, back in the sixties the *Falcon* had had something to do with him becoming a detective. The story went like this.

In 1966 Fechheimer had been writing a master's thesis in American literature at San Francisco State. He'd stayed up all one night reading *The Maltese Falcon*. The next morning he'd called Pinkerton's, Hammett's employer fifty years earlier. "I suppose you don't hire people without experience," he'd said in his then tentative, graduate student voice, "especially people with beards?" The gruff voice on the other end of the line had surprised him: "You got a beard, buddy? We got a job for a guy with a beard, but only today. Come on down."

He'd begun by working undercover in a meat-packing plant (the beard), then ridden Muni buses, checking that the drivers were not pocketing fares. For two years he'd paid his dues, carrying out a variety of jobs for Pinkerton's. Then he'd quit, spending several months working in the public library before signing on with Hal Lipset. In case after case he'd proved himself, until finally, in the early 1970s, he became Lipset's junior partner in the best detective agency on the West Coast.

Through all these years, Hammett remained a presence in the back of Fechheimer's mind—both the impetus that brought him into detectivery and a shadowy ideal, the only modern detective writer who'd actually worked as a detective.

In his spare time Fechheimer pursued Hammett. Not as a literary critic, but as a detective. From a confidential source, he got Hammett's Veterans Administration file. By painstakingly following minute leads, he found Hammett's wife—long thought to be dead—and interviewed her and Hammett's daughter in Los Angeles. I'd end up helping in some of these researches, talking to several of Hammett's relatives in Maryland and checking musty archives in Los Angeles to get to the bottom of a phony rape charge filed against him in the 1930s. Through all this, Hammett became a kind of unspoken reference point—Saint Dashiell, mysterious patron saint of the shadowy craft we were each, in our own ways, practicing.

The fog was beginning to drift in. I shivered under my sweater.

Years after Flitcraft's disappearance, as Spade tells it, Flitcraft's wife heard that a man resembling her husband had been seen in Spokane. Spade was hired and quickly located Flitcraft, who now had a new wife (not unlike his old one), a new home (not unlike his old one), a new job (somewhat unlike his old one), and who continued *"to play golf after four in the afternoon during the season."* Sitting in Spade's hotel room in Spokane, Flitcraft tried to explain to Spade why he'd left. He'd never told his story before, says Spade, and it was somehow important to him to *"make its reasonableness explicit."*

One noon when he was on his way to lunch, with a game of golf scheduled for just after four that afternoon, it happened:

He passed an office-building that was being put up—just the skeleton. A beam or something fell eight to ten stories down and smacked the sidewalk alongside him. It brushed pretty close to him, but didn't touch him, though a piece of the sidewalk was chipped off and flew up and hit his cheek. . . . He was scared stiff of course, he said, but he was more shocked than really frightened. He felt like somebody had taken the lid off life and let him look at the works.

Before he'd gone twenty feet from the fallen beam, *"he knew that he would never know peace again until he had adjusted himself to this new glimpse of life."* Strangely enough, he wasn't bothered by the injustice of the accident that had almost struck him. *"He accepted that after the first shock,"* remarks Spade. *"What disturbed him was the discovery that in sensibly ordering his affairs he had got out of step, not into step, with life."* And so he acted: *"Life could be ended for him at random by a falling beam: he would change his life at random by simply going away."*

But why had he ended up living in Spokane, a duplicate of the life he'd given up in Tacoma? This is the part Spade likes best.

He wasn't sorry for what he had done. It seemed reasonable enough to him. I don't think he even knew he had settled back naturally into the same groove he had jumped out of in Tacoma. But that's the part of it I always liked. He adjusted himself to beams falling, and then no more of them fell, and he adjusted himself to them not falling.

Flitcraft adjusted. He *"had no feeling of guilt. . . . What he had done seemed perfectly reasonable."* The only thing bothering him was a doubt he could make that reasonableness clear to Spade.

The reading was making me sleepy. There was an idea here I was just starting to grasp. All the judgments in the story are the Flitcrafts': Mrs. Flitcraft thinks her husband is silly, while he thinks he is reasonable and, for a while, believes the falling beam has *"taken the lid off life and let him look at the works."* Spade doesn't get into the business of judging. He only relates what happened. And the same thing is true of the *Falcon* as a whole. It's a fable about the impossibility of judgment.

I couldn't hold the train of thought. I was falling asleep. I put the book down. Still, the thoughts ran on.

"Somebody had taken the lid off life and let him look at the works"—hadn't that been your vision of Fechheimer at the beginning? Someone for whom the lid had been taken off, someone who had *seen*? And hadn't that also been what you were looking for when you'd started working for him as an apprentice?

But has any of us *really* seen? The Flitcraft parable—what is it but a story, an invention, a piece of language that can be bent in one direction or another? Around the corners of my mind I could sense something growing, something I'd come to know all too well back in that "academic paradise" Fechheimer taunted me about. Hume called it philosophical despair. But that seemed too grand; it was simply a weariness with words. Words that spun words, words that led here and there but finally could not lead beyond themselves, could not *refer*. And opposed to words, silence and its uses. The silence in the background of Hammett's life. The silence that sometimes invaded my talks with Fechheimer, the silence implicit in his averted glance, his verbal gambits, his indirection. Silence . . . I was moving in the tidal surge. There were forms, but I couldn't make them out.

SATURDAY, JULY 30

Sean jammed the Dodge van into first, and we pulled away from the curb. He was laughing.

"You weren't there when that last call came in, were you, Tink?"

"No, why?"

"It was a pisser. Glenise took the call, talked to the guy for about five minutes, and handed it over to David. I couldn't figure out why she was laughing so hard. Then David told me this guy'd been an informer for the FBI in the Panthers. Then he got religion and broke with the FBI. All about eight years ago. Now he calls up sayin' the FBI is harassing him and he wants Fechheimer to investigate it."

"What's so funny?" I asked.

"Well, the reason he thinks the FBI is on his ass is that every time he goes out he gets a parking ticket. He claims the FBI has all these police departments in their pocket. Oakland, Albany, San Leandro, Alameda, Orinda, you name it. He thinks the FBI tails him wherever he goes. When he parks and leaves his car, they radio in and a traffic cop nails him. You know what David told him?"

"No."

"He told him this would be a difficult investigation to do because the FBI has so many resources. He said only an investigator with equal resources could handle the case. He told him to call Hal."

I laughed. "Maybe Hal could build him a helmet," I said.

"What?"

"Oh, I thought you were working for Hal when that happened. I heard about it later. Seems this guy walks in cold and starts talking about three or four people who have these transmitters. Maybe they're working for the CIA. I don't remember the story real well. Anyway these people have transmitters, and they're using them to control his thoughts. So you know what Hal asks him?"

"No."

"He asks him his hat size."

"His what?"

"His hat size. He gets the guy's hat size, takes a two-hundred-and-fifty-dollar retainer, and tells him to come back in two weeks. Then Hal gets together with Walt, and Walt designs a helmet. Apparently Walt went out and bought a motorcycle helmet and wired it up with a battery pack, transistors, diodes, and some other gizmos. The guy comes back, and Hal puts the helmet on him and shows him the switch. He turns it on, and you can hear this low hum. Hal tells him this is a special helmet that puts up 'a negative force field' to seal off his thoughts from the radio waves. The guy goes away happy as a clam, and the story is he calls Hal every six months to thank him."

"A lot cheaper than a shrink," said Sean, turning left. "How about telling me what we're doing? David said you'd brief me."

I gave Sean the five-minute version of Cutler, Karin, and the weight lifter and filled in on the events of the past week.

Sean didn't actually work for David but was called in for special projects. He was twenty-three and had the casual good looks and ease of manner you often see in young, native-born Californians. He was a motorcycle racer, a Porsche mechanic, and, according to David, a crackerjack driver with good nerves. Over a white, short-sleeved shirt, he had on a terrific jacket. Made of supple, dark-brown goatskin, it had the mandarin collar typical of motorcycle jackets.

"David called Minneapolis," I continued, "and they wanted more evidence of adultery. So I went back for two more nights. The weight lifter must live there, because he was there both times and even had the courtesy to leave at a respectable hour in the morning. Only one thing was odd. About eight Wednesday night they took off in both cars, and came back forty minutes later in his white Lincoln. Her car was gone on Thursday and Friday. It was sitting there at noon today when I cruised by on the cycle to check things out. I called David, and he called you."

"What do you make of it?"

"Probably nothing. I could've spooked 'em on Tuesday. It's Cutler's car, and they know he's got an extra set of keys. They could've changed the locks. Guess we'll find out."

Crossing the Golden Gate Bridge, we talked motorcycles. We'd taken a short run together the month before, but my BMW R90S had been no match for Sean's race-tuned Kawasaki Z-1. Nor had my reflexes been any match for his racing skills. I was thankful I'd had sense enough to roll off the throttle before wrapping the bike around a tree.

Soon we pulled into Cordera Drive and angled into a parking space two hundred feet short of the entrance to the complex.

"I'll see who's there and be back in five minutes," I told Sean.

Before reaching the crest of the entrance driveway, I saw we were in luck. Both cars were in their usual places behind the house, along with an old blue and white Plymouth with Minnesota plates. I'd seen the Plymouth there on Thursday; a call to Minneapolis had disclosed that it probably belonged to Karin's sister and brother-in-law, who Cutler heard might be visiting in August.

I walked down the row of townhouses. Through a window I could see Karin doing something at the kitchen sink. I kept my eyes and body pointed straight ahead, ambling down the asphalt, apparently unconcerned with anything going on in the townhouses. Then I went down the long set of steps and out to the sidewalk across the street.

I stopped and lit a cigarette before continuing back to the van.

"Hey," I heard from behind. "Wait."

It was Karin. She was leaping off the bottom step and moving in my direction. Above and behind her, the weight lifter was standing on the balcony.

"Give me a cigarette," she said, reaching out and patting the breast pocket of my sport coat. Weird! Even weirder was the full set of silver braces across her upper front teeth. Cutler paid for those too, I thought, reaching in for the pack of Kools.

"You've been following me," she said, as I fumbled with the cigarettes. "And I've had enough of it. You've been following me, and I want some identification or I'll put a citizen's arrest on you right now."

It flashed through my mind the boyfriend was only a few feet from a phone and the Sausalito police would not be pleased to be called here again because of me. I started to reach for my wallet, talking to Karin all the time.

"I don't know what you're talking about, Miss. I've heard California is pretty weird, but this is ridiculous. I'm a college professor from Pennsylvania, and I've only been out here a week. What makes you think I've been following you?" I said, opening my wallet.

"You just walked by my back window. I saw you," she said, her mouth tight and angry. She looked old for twenty-five, and her nose was running. Coke from the boyfriend?

"That's right," I said, moving onto the offensive. "I was visiting the Corbetts over in Eighteen seventy-eight. Just up there." I pointed to the other complex of townhouses, figuring she knew few, if any, neighbors. "I wanted to take a short walk before dinner. Is there any law against that out here?"

Now the clincher. I handed her my Haverford College ID card, my picture staring from the upper left corner. Slightly below my name it said *Tenured Faculty*.

A flicker of doubt ran behind her eyes as she examined the piece of plastic. There was a determined twist to her lips as she said, "There's no expiration date."

"At small Quaker colleges," I said wryly, "they don't put expiration dates on their tenured faculty. I guess they believe they'll be around for a while." The flicker of doubt grew into a first blush of embarrassment. I knew I had her.

"You seem upset," I said in an even, professorial tone. "Have you had these feelings about being followed for very long?"

She stared at me.

"Perhaps it might be a good idea to talk to someone about all this. It couldn't do any harm."

She turned on her heel and ran toward the steps. The boyfriend watched for a moment and then left the balcony. I strolled up the street, out of their range of vision, before doubling back to the van. The professor's tone had annoyed the cop, but it had worked perfectly on her. I climbed into the van through the rear doors.

"Man, I thought she had you," said Sean. He'd opened up two beach chairs so we could sit comfortably and look down the slight incline at the parking-area entrance.

"Old Mr. Chips strikes again," I said, and told Sean about how I'd conned her. "We're lucky," I said. "Both cars are there. But there's one sticky deal. I think her sister and brother-in-law are there too. At least, that old blue and white Plymouth with Minnesota plates is parked in back."

I looked at my watch. It was 7:35. I pulled out a legal-sized yellow pad, made a quick sketch of the area behind the town-houses, and marked the positions of the three cars.

"Probably all four of 'em will go out to dinner," I said. "They'll probably take one of the Lincolns. If they take the white one, we're in. But if they take the black one, we'll have to tail 'em and hope they don't go to some fancy place with valet parking. In any case, we ought to figure out how we're gonna snatch it from here."

"I think you'd better back the van down the row of town-houses," said Sean. "Stop when we get even with the black Lincoln. It shouldn't take more than fifteen seconds to snatch it. Get the van out of here right away, but hang around the entrance. If they come after me, you might be able to get in their way. If there's no fuss, we can drive back to San Francisco together."

"OK," I said, thinking I didn't like the idea of trying to take the car if the boyfriend was still inside. We settled down in our chairs and went back to talking motorcycles. I was telling Sean about seeing Reg Pridmore on a 90S blow the footpegs off a covey of Z-1's at Laguna Seca. Suddenly there was movement at the entrance to the parking area. The blue and white Plymouth appeared and, without stopping, turned right and sped away.

"How many? How many were in it?" I asked.

"I don't know," said Sean. "There was a guy driving, and I thought I saw some others. But the light was bad. Was that the boyfriend driving?"

"I don't think so," I answered. "There was more than one person in the car, but I couldn't tell who they were. Shit, they didn't even slow down."

"Yeah," said Sean.

"So now we don't know where we are," I said. "If all four of 'em left, it'd be a piece of cake to grab the car now. But we don't know that."

We chewed it over and agreed the sister and brother-in-law had most likely driven off alone. Had all four gone together, they probably would have taken one of the more luxurious Lincolns. That made sense, but was only a guess. Since it was not quite eight, the best thing was to sit tight and see what happened.

Our conversation became desultory, with frequent silences.

Eight-ten. Still nothing. There was a tightness around Sean's lips. If he was worried, I was even more so. I hadn't liked this case from the beginning. And over the week before there'd been too many foul-ups. I remembered David's advice: Find their rhythm and fall in with it. That's what we were doing. But what do we do half an hour from now? And why had the black Lincoln disappeared for two days? They could have changed the locks.

"Sean, let's go over the papers."

He opened the glove compartment and pulled out a manila envelope. Inside it were the Minnesota title in Cutler's name and a letter signed by Cutler authorizing us to repossess the car.

"Let me look at the keys."

He pulled out two keys on an aluminum ring.

"You know which one goes in the door?"

"The door key's the one with the diamond shape," Sean answered irritably. "I went to a Ford dealer this afternoon to make sure I knew how to start it. The ignition key will go in either way; you can't put it in upside down. Don't worry, I got my shit together."

"Yeah, OK," I said. We lapsed back into silence.

I didn't know where the tightness in Sean's voice was coming from, but I knew what was worrying me: the boyfriend. We'd found out enough about him to partially believe Bates's account. He was something of a heavy. Karin hadn't brushed my jacket pocket for nothing. She'd been feeling for a gun, probably because he'd told her to do it. Although he probably wouldn't run the risk of carrying one in the car, the house was a different matter. The black Continental was parked only about twelve feet from the kitchen door. Sean would have to open the door, start the car, and then back it into a cul de sac before pulling away. We had no idea what was going on in the boyfriend's life or how jumpy he was.

"Sean," I said. "I'm worried about the boyfriend having a piece in there."

"Yeah," said Sean. "I was thinking the same thing."

Again, silence.

As it got darker and we watched the entrance, my mouth grew drier. What's fear and what's a premonition? Fears you don't listen to; premonitions you do.

Five minutes later I'd decided to abort the snatch if we couldn't be sure the boyfriend was elsewhere.

At eight-thirty we took off to find a phone. We'd make a subterfuge call to her house, pretending it was a wrong number or—my specialty—chattering away in a fake Chinese dialect. At the very least we could find out if she was there, and if we got lucky he might answer the phone. I started scanning the streets for a phone booth.

Four blocks away, having traversed the side of the hill and then cut down to Bridgeway, we caught sight of a black shape and some Lincoln-style taillights. Soon we made out the Minnesota plate; he was driving.

"Piece of cake, Sean. They must have left as soon as we pulled out."

"Yeah. Maybe they made the van and were just waiting for us to leave. I'll hang back a bit."

We were in great shape. The riskiest part of a tail is the getaway from house or apartment. That's when the quarry is alert, checking to see whether anyone is following. Since we weren't even there when they left, they must believe everything was cool. The van was new on the job, and even if Karin hadn't bought my professor routine, there was nothing to connect "the professor" with the van. With a bit of luck we'd soon get the car, and the case could be closed.

They swung under the freeway and headed toward Mill Valley. Sean was driving a deft tail, holding three or four cars back and then tightening up when we hit some lights. They turned right off Miller Avenue just before reaching the center of town and pulled into the parking area of an auto-parts store.

We slid into a spot on the other side of the street and watched. Karin was wearing jeans and a beige sweater. The boyfriend had on jeans and an open-necked white silk shirt with a medallion. She took his arm when they reached the curb: your typical Mill Valley coke dealer and his lady out for a quiet Saturday night. Sean got out and followed on foot.

"Where'd they go?" I asked when he got back.

"Sequoia theater. I waited until they went in."

"When's the next feature?"

"Ten-forty."

"OK. We've got at least an hour and a half."

Sean was laughing. "You didn't ask me what film they're seeing."

"OK. What film are they seeing?"

"The Sting."

"That's great. The husband'll love that."

We pulled the van across Blithedale and turned it around so I could watch the street on the chance they might leave the film early. Sean walked to the car and unlocked the door. Twenty seconds went by, and no engine coughed to life. A Mill Valley patrol car passed without stopping. Sean got out of the car, relocked the door, and walked back to the van.

"The fucking key won't work. They must've changed the ignition lock. Now what?"

I thought for a moment.

"Let's tow it. We'll need a tow truck because of that steering-wheel lock."

"No, wait," said Sean. "David knows this guy who's got keys for just about everything."

"We've got an hour and a half," I said. "But that's not forever. I still think we ought to tow it. But OK, let's call."

Twenty minutes later I was wishing we hadn't bothered. We'd hit four pay phones, all out of order. Finally I got through to David, briefed him, and told him we had an hour and ten minutes left. He said to call back in three minutes. I knew why. He made it a rule always to take a minute or two to think over a decision; he once told me it had saved his ass a couple of times.

"I think you'd better tow it," David said laconically when I called him back. "You're running out of time."

Sean called a towing service and asked them to meet him at the Lincoln.

"You got enough money?" I asked Sean as we pulled into our earlier parking spot. He just smiled, got out, and walked to the Lincoln. I didn't know what Sean did, but I remembered that at the end of our motorcycle ride he'd paid for our coffee with a fifty-dollar bill.

I watched the corner in front of the theater as the minutes

ticked away. We had about forty minutes left when the tow truck showed up.

Sean talked to the driver for half a minute and then got out his wallet. The tow truck pulled in front of the Lincoln, and the driver crawled under the radiator to hook on the chains. I glanced at my watch—thirty-six minutes left.

After they pulled out, I followed for a few blocks, and then turned into a Shell station to call Fechheimer.

"They're towing it back to San Francisco," I told him.

"Swell," he said. "I'll call CHP and the Mill Valley Police. What was that license plate again?"

"Minnesota. AGC nine-one-one. That's Alfa-Golf-Charlie-nine-one-one," I told him, surprised that my memory of military phonetic equivalents had endured for eighteen years.

"Thank you, Lieutenant Thompson. See you guys in an hour."

As the van climbed the Waldo Grade, my adrenaline rush subsided. I felt relieved the case was finished but depressed by the whole thing. We'd gotten what Cutler and his lawyer wanted, and had billed about three thousand dollars. So what? I'd watched Karin and her boyfriend for a week, but had no idea who they were or what they were doing with their lives. Earlier she'd seemed content, hanging on his arm as they walked to the theater. Soon they'd come out, find her car missing, and call the police. They'd be told it had been repossessed, and would have to take a cab back to Sausalito. Karin would recognize that "the professor" really had been following her after all. "Have you had these feelings about being followed for very long?" That part I liked.

But the whole thing was tawdry. People fighting. Hurt, angry people. Was this the way Nancy and I would end? Hiring detectives and stealing cars? Would I—could I—ever come to hate her? And she me? I didn't feel that way. But where *were* we going? It was as if we were being led somewhere. Meanwhile, I was spending my Saturday nights stealing cars.

Sean took the car to a warehouse David owned on Potrero Hill. By the time I got there, the tow truck had left, and Sean was elated.

"You look in the trunk?" I asked as he slid into the passenger seat.

"No, why?"

"Just thought it'd be funny if a suitcase of coke was back there."

"Fat chance," he said.

"How much you give the driver?"

"Sixty bucks. Man, it went down like velvet. While I was standing there waiting for the truck, I was trying to figure out what to tell him. I mean, you know, it looked real odd. Here's some kid who wants a fourteen-thousand-dollar Lincoln Continental towed to San Francisco.

"I was lucky," he went on, loose and happy. "The driver was only about nineteen. I told him this bullshit story about the car being my old man's and I had to get it back to the city by eleven or my ass'd be in a sling. I told him I'd gotten an extra set of keys made and taken the car to Mill Valley, and now the damned ignition key wouldn't work. I showed him where the other key worked in the door lock. That may have helped, but I hit him with the cash fast, and I think that's what did it. Man, I don't know where that story came from. I just thought of it when I saw those tow truck lights comin' down the street."

We got to David's twenty minutes later.

Upstairs were two or three women I'd seen before and a couple of men I didn't know. David followed Sean and me into the office. Sean returned the keys and papers, and David handed him a check. In the other room, people were talking while *La Bohème* droned in the background. Sean left, and David asked me to drop off some legal papers with the Mill Valley Police on my way home. He'd called the lawyer in Minneapolis to tell him we'd gotten the car, and been surprised when Cutler himself came on the line. Cutler had been at his lawyer's office waiting for our report, and now he wanted the details. When David finished, Cutler had said only, "Hope the bitch had to walk home from the movies." Then he'd hung up.

I laughed and then said abruptly. "I was spooked there for a while tonight. Everything seemed wrong. We were gonna snatch the car from the house, but then I started thinking the kitchen door was only twelve feet away and the boyfriend might have a gun inside. I decided to call it off if we couldn't be sure he was gone."

David was looking down at his desk.

"I'm glad I did," I continued. "Sean would've gotten the door open but wouldn't have been able to start it. If they'd heard the car door open and come back to the kitchen . . ."

David looked at me straight on.

"Sean didn't have to go tonight," he said. "He took his chances, and got damn well paid for taking 'em. Better than you tonight, Tink. What'd you make? Sixty, maybe seventy bucks? That's why I sent him. You would have taken a chance on getting your head shot off for sixty dollars because you're too green to know any better. Sean isn't. He knew what it was about and what he'd get paid for it. If he'd bought it, he would've bought it."

I liked the play on words, but I wasn't sure I liked what was behind it.

Later, after dropping off the papers in Mill Valley, I thought about Cutler and his remark. The full moon cast deep shadows through the redwoods on the western slope of Mount Tam. I felt like some airman returned from a raid over Germany who'd chosen to take a moonlit drive through the English woods, not quite understanding what it was all about. The war between the Cutlers had moved into another stage. Who was right or wrong? What would happen next? I didn't know or care. There was no nobility tonight on Cordera Drive or in Minneapolis—only the tawdry afterskirmishes of a failed love. For a while I'd been a foot soldier in that domestic combat. How much had I made? Five hundred dollars? Six hundred? Not a bad week. I shifted into third as the car reached the bottom of the hill. "If he'd bought it, he would've bought it," I hummed to myself.

TWO

"THE EDGE OF EXPERIENCE"

Her name was Irene Kuznetzov—not eye-REEN but EE-ren—and she climbed the stairs briskly. Probably in her early fifties, she dressed like a Berkeley artist—long flowered skirt, white blouse over black leotard, macramé purse. She had never been a beautiful woman, and she knew it. Her features were long and somehow sorrowful, and on this Monday afternoon she seemed worried and ill at ease. All I knew about her was what David had told me the previous week and repeated twenty minutes before she came: her daughter disappeared a month ago from Wilmington, Delaware, leaving a note and some possessions for her mother and boyfriend. Judith Krause had referred Irene Kuznetzov to us and told David she'd be carrying a twenty-five hundred-dollar retainer. When the bell rang at 2:15, David was still in a towel. He asked me to let her in and begin interviewing her while he finished getting up.

I ushered her into the living room. Her eye darted around and fixed on a late-nineteenth-century landscape of a valley in New Zealand. I told her David bought the painting the month before in London, and we chatted briefly about it. While she was admiring the George III samovar on the parsons table, I noticed that as usual there was no place to sit down.

There was a desk chair in the office but no couch, no easy chairs, nothing to sit on except the three fold-up chairs that circled a small table in the kitchen. We always seemed to gravitate toward the kitchen, not just because it had the only chairs, but also because it had the most light. David's bedroom opened into the kitchen but had only one small window, as did the office between the bedroom and living room. The living room fronted on Laguna Street and would have been comfortable but for the fact it was virtually bare of furniture and the shutters were usually closed. The whole apartment was covered with mauve wall-to-wall carpeting.

Carrying the three kitchen chairs, I started back for the living room. The carpet seemed to muffle everything in this depressing flat. David would move from it as soon as his divorce from Renée became final; for now, the dark apartment with no chairs was all of a piece with the rest of his life. He was unsettled, in motion, even in conversation shifting from one foot to the other. Passing the bathroom, I heard the shower shut off; it would be ten minutes before he was ready.

"David suggested you might like to begin by explaining things to me," I said, setting up the chairs. "He'll be with us in a few minutes."

She turned from the bookcase, a volume of Jack Spicer's poetry in her hands.

"No," she said in a heavily accented, throaty voice. "I would prefer to wait and not have to tell the story twice."

She was right; it would be stupid for her to have to repeat it. I asked her if, in that case, she'd mind if I finished up some paperwork. I went into the room next door and wrapped up the billing on the Cutler case. Five minutes later I heard David introducing himself. I joined them in the living room, where we sat in an awkward triangle.

She told her story in a straightforward, logical way, sometimes referring to notes for details. There were no histrionics, but at times a tightness in her voice showed what she was feeling.

Her daughter was twenty-eight and had been working as a social worker in Wilmington. Her daughter's boyfriend, also twenty-eight and also a social worker, had gone to the daughter's place after being unable to reach her by phone for two days. He had used his key to let himself in and found a rambling suicide note, along with two boxes of possessions the note assigned to him and to her mother. Her car was missing. All this had happened three and a half weeks earlier.

As David asked her questions, I read a Xerox of the "suicide" note. It was disjointed and self-pitying but methodical when it came to practical arrangements. Its emotions were sharp. Irene Kuznetzov's daughter was desperate, pushing to break out of the box that was her life. She was also very much alive. The note—really a three-page letter addressed jointly to her mother and her boyfriend—must have given her pleasure. It was a gesture, a beginning rather than an ending. I agreed inwardly when David said, "First of all, Mrs. Kuznetzov, I don't believe your daughter's dead. She doesn't fit the profile of a suicide. She's trying to tell both you and her boyfriend something. Most likely she's taken off in her car and will show up in a few months. Did she have any oil-company credit cards?"

"Yes," the woman replied, referring to her notes. "She had a Sunoco card. Here's the number. But we haven't gotten a new bill yet. Oh, I almost forgot. She also closed out her savings account and took the twelve hundred dollars in cash."

"That's important," said David. "You don't clean out your savings account if you're going to kill yourself."

They talked a bit more about what had been done. The boyfriend had good contacts with the Wilmington police and had done all the obvious things. Irene Kuznetzov had talked several times with the missing-persons bureau. She complained of their lethargy, and David interrupted, getting up to walk around the room.

"You have to recognize, Mrs. Kuznetzov, that your daughter has committed no crime. She's twenty-eight and has a perfect right to disappear if she wants to. You can't expect much help from the missing-persons bureau. In any big-city police department they're last on the list for money and personnel."

I thought this might be the start of a pitch to illustrate the necessity of hiring private detectives. From our end, after all, the aim of this initial meeting was to get the case and the twenty-five hundred dollars. As David began explaining our rates and how we operated, I was thinking I'd probably get a trip back East. Then he shifted.

"Judith told me you were bringing along a retainer. I have to tell you that at this point in time we won't take the case. If you were independently wealthy, it'd be a different story. But as it is, I can't take your money. I'd be wasting it right now. It'll take about six months for her to get settled; then we might have a good chance of finding her. But right now she's still moving, and we'd have to be very lucky to find her. To try now would be to waste your money, and I'm not going to do that."

"But I can't wait six months," she said. "It's too hard. Won't you help me?"

"At this point there's only one useful thing to do. Information about her and the car she's driving should be entered in the NCIC computer. That way, if she's stopped for speeding or something and the officer runs a check on the car for her, it'll show up. You can have that done through the boyfriend in Wilmington or I can have it done from here, at no cost to you. But that's really the only useful thing to do now.

"Six months from now it'll be a different story," he continued, still pacing. "We'd be pleased to take the case then. But let me explain the conditions under which we'd take it. Your daughter has a perfect right to disappear; for that reason, I'd try to find her only on the condition we'd do nothing more than pass messages back and forth. In other words, even if I find her, I won't tell you where she is but will only function as an intermediary. With children it's different, but she's not a minor. That's the only way I take cases like this. After all," he said ruefully, a smile teasing his face, "I might want to disappear myself sometime."

Tears began to form in her eyes.

"But I brought the money. See?" She opened the macramé purse and showed a large wad of twenties and fifties. "I can't wait six months. I have to find her."

David sat down and looked steadily at her.

"I know it's rough. But you have to recognize your daughter has decided you're to suffer for a while. She's not dead, and she's probably not in any particular trouble. She has to break out, and for whatever reason, she also wants to make you suffer. I'm sorry, but sometimes you just have to take it. Maybe the most important thing is not finding her but figuring out what to do when she does turn up."

Irene Kuznetzov began to cry. Embarrassed, I got some toilet paper from the bathroom.

There was nothing more to say, and soon she was thanking us and making ready to leave.

I escorted her down the steps, and at the door turned toward her.

"Now may not be the right time to find her," I said. "She may need some time. The Greeks had a word for it: *kairos*, the right time. It may be a while yet before it's the right time."

"Perhaps," said Irene Kuznetzov, "I don't know."
We shook hands, and she left.

Forty minutes later, as the locksmith jockeyed his flowered
VW bug through traffic north of the airport, I was still thinking
of Irene Kuznetzov. I was proud of the way she'd been treated.
Any other detective would have taken her money and frittered
it away with a five-day trip to Philadelphia. Fechheimer didn't
subscribe to any code, yet hadn't he just demonstrated one? You
don't waste people's money; you treat them fairly; you tell them
the truth.

As the sun streamed down on the Bayshore Expressway and
the long-haired locksmith, Wally, gave me a hit of the joint he
was smoking, I felt extremely good about the fact I was a detective and working for Fechheimer. Today I'd been part of
something—even if it was a minor something—that seemed to
cancel out much of the tawdriness of the Cutler case. Perhaps
there was no code, no foundation underlying what Fechheimer
was doing, but Irene Kuznetzov had been treated well—
extraordinarily well.

As we pulled into the parking garage at San Francisco International Airport, Wally turned to me. "Which level is this
mother supposed to be on?" he asked. His T-shirt had *Maui
Wowie* emblazoned across the chest.

"It's supposed to be on Level Three. But who knows? We'll
just have to cruise around till we find it. It's a 'seventy-seven
Caddy Seville with Oregon plates."

This trip was a minor errand. After Irene Kuznetzov left,
David asked me to pick up a locksmith and go to the airport to
retrieve a car. He hadn't said much about it—only given the
description of the car, told me a locksmith would have to make
an ignition key, and enigmatically said not to look in the trunk.
After I got the car, I was to deliver it to a downtown garage.
The parking stub and Oregon registration should be in the glove
compartment.

We zipped around the garage, finally locating the Seville in a
roped-off temporary construction zone. I told a construction
worker what we were doing and asked if we could lift the rope
and park next to the Seville. He shrugged and walked away.

According to the parking stub in the glove compartment, the
Seville had been there eleven days. It would cost sixty to seventy

dollars to get the car out, but I had $150 in cash. The locksmith checked the chassis number and referred to a small handbook.

"Shit," he said. "I can't figure this out. I'll have to call the office."

I sat in the driver's seat of the Seville, musing. A button inside the glove compartment would release the trunk lid, but I wasn't tempted.

I was thinking of Karin Cutler. Just before I left for the airport, she'd called David to bitch about some things of hers that were still in the trunk of the Lincoln. David had humored her, telling her he'd have anything she wanted delivered to her if she sent him a written list. I hoped I wouldn't end up being the delivery boy. On the other hand, that might be pretty funny.

The locksmith came back. The code he was using didn't apply to new Sevilles, so he'd have to take the steering column apart and install a new ignition lock. As time passed, I was impressed both by the complexity of General Motors' antitheft devices and by Wally's manual dexterity after smoking the joint. Reduced to holding the nuts and screws he extracted from the steering column, I let my mind wander back to Karin Cutler. Those braces!

"Freeze!" I heard from behind me, on my left.

I turned and looked directly into the barrel of a large, ugly revolver. Eight feet away, behind the gun, stood a San Mateo County deputy sheriff. He was holding the gun in classic firing position, both arms straight-elbowed in front of him, left hand cupped. Behind him stood another deputy sheriff, holding another gun in the same way.

"Don't move," said the first deputy, "or I'll blow your head off."

I didn't breathe. In slow motion, with perfect clarity, the thought ran through my mind: These turkeys are dangerous. They had already made a bad mistake by both approaching the car from the same side, even though they could see two men in it.

"Now put both your hands on top of the steering wheel."

I did.

The door opened and I felt a hand grab me roughly by the shirt collar.

"Now both of you get out. Slowly."

As I eased out of the door, a screwdriver fell from the locksmith's pocket. There was a metallic *ping*, and the deputy's hand tightened on the revolver. He threw me roughly against the side of the car, cuffed my hands, and started to frisk me. The second deputy did the same to Wally, who looked bewildered. After the frisk, the deputy bent me over the trunk and pressed the side of my face to the cold metal.

"You guys weren't paying attention, were you?" he said.

"I don't know what you mean, officer," I replied, trying to be deferential. "I'm a private detective, and he's a locksmith. We were sent to pick up a client's car whose keys were lost."

"We'll see about that," he said. "Just keep kissing that metal."

I hadn't been handcuffed since the old antiwar days. As usual, the cuffs were too tight. The second deputy was going through Wally's billfold. Just beyond him, a middle-aged businessman and his family—two dark-haired kids and a wife with glasses and a red nose—were looking on in horror. I thought how they'd tell the story that night—the guns, the two criminals handcuffed and bent over cars. I could have been him, with Nancy, Lis, and Ev along.

"Shit, Luke," said the second deputy, holding up a card, "he really *is* a locksmith!"

The deputies holstered their guns and allowed us to straighten up. I noticed how big they were—six-three or -four, both in their late twenties, with paunches stretching the gabardine over their gun belts.

"Now, who are you?" asked the first deputy. I tried to get my wallet from my back pocket, but couldn't reach it.

"If you'll get my wallet out of my back pocket, Officer," I said, thinking of the unopened trunk, trying to be as inoffensive as possible, "I can show you."

He fished out the wallet.

"There's a card on top there."

He took out one of David's blue and white business cards as the other deputy rummaged around in the front seat of the Seville.

"It says here 'David B. Fechheimer.' That you?"

"No. My name's Thompson. It's in smaller type in the bottom corner. I work for Fechheimer."

"You said you're a detective. Your license in there?"

"No. I work under Fechheimer's license. If you call him at the number on the card he'll explain everything. He's there now."

I heard a click, and the Seville's trunk lid flipped open.

The second deputy must have found the release button in the glove compartment. The first one was still examining the business card as his partner went to the trunk. Everything was running in slow motion. I could only keep quiet and wait.

The first deputy spoke into his walkie-talkie. His partner looked around the trunk. The first deputy repeated Fechheimer's name and number; then his partner's right hand reached up and slammed the trunk lid shut.

Wally was talking rapidly now, pointing out that all he'd done was come out here to make a key for the Cadillac. I wasn't saying anything, waiting to see how things developed.

After a few minutes, they uncuffed Wally. He rubbed his wrists vigorously and stood talking to the deputies. I was obviously the heavy. They were going to leave my cuffs on until they got clearance from higher authority. We still weren't out of this.

The radio crackled. I could hear only part of the transmission: "You can let those dudes go. We called [static] Lieutenant Davidson says he knows Fechheimer and he's legit. You won't need to file [static] after you get to Level Two [static]. Over."

The first deputy took off my cuffs.

"Hope we didn't scare you guys too bad," he said. "We get a lot of car rip-offs in the garage. Especially Porsches and Caddys. Next time, check with our office first."

I said the expected lines, and the deputies moved off. Wally went back to work, and I punched the trunk-release button. Inside were two large suitcases and a cosmetics case. I didn't try to open them, but instead went around and got in front with Wally.

Twenty-five minutes later we were on our way back to San Francisco, Wally in his VW bug following me in the Caddy.

What the deputy had said was both true and false: "You guys weren't paying attention, were you?" Even if I'd seen them coming, there would have been a hassle and we would have ended up getting handcuffed. I shivered, remembering the gun pointed at my face, realizing only now that the hammer had been pulled back.

How dangerous had it been? Who knows? Probably not very. Then a thought struck me: This is the way it will happen if it happens. Not when you're doing something glamorous or important, but when you least expect it. Not for any good reason, but due to some stupid foul-up, being at the wrong place at the wrong time, or being taken for the wrong person.

I used to argue the same point in teaching Merleau-Ponty. Death seldom comes like a railroad locomotive, getting closer and closer until it's finally here. It comes like a rifle shot from the rear: Nellie Connally saying to John Kennedy, as the limousine turns onto Elm Street, "Mr. President, you can't say Dallas doesn't love you." Kennedy agreeing with her, waving to the crowd at the corner. Death catching us unawares, blindsiding us. That's the way it would have come had it come today—a jumpy deputy, a screwdriver drops, his hand tightens on the trigger . . . Surely no one's fault, just a regrettable accident. Was Camus surprised just before Gallimard's car hit the tree?

There was much hilarity back at the office. "The Professor" had done it again. Picked up by the police twice in one week! Several people were standing around in the kitchen, and the story did seem funny—especially when I stressed how bewildered the half-stoned locksmith had been.

Then David led me into his office.

He was amused but serious. He agreed it would've been unwise to check with the sheriff's office first—too many questions—and was pleased to learn neither deputy had jotted down the license-plate number of the Seville.

"You'll be going East later on in the week," he said. "Why don't you spend tomorrow and the next day wrapping up odds and ends? I want you to meet with someone here at four on Thursday. OK?"

SATURDAY, AUGUST 6

The seat-belt sign had winked off long ago. Lunch was served and glasses refilled. The plane settled into its long lumbering passage over the American heartland: Salt Lake City, Grand Junction, Denver, Kansas City . . . The warmth of the double bourbon spread from my stomach. My mind wandered, and I began to think.

Not about the case. That would come later, much later, when I would have to take seriously what I was supposed to be doing on this little expedition. It all had started with that Thursday meeting two days before in David's office. There was the can to find and the paper bag containing thirty thousand dollars, hidden under the floorboards of the attic. But that was for later. Apart from the fear mixing with the bourbon in the pit of my stomach, none of the details seemed real or would become real before the plane's wheels touched down in Boston. Then I'd have to make some decisions. Now I could settle back and enjoy the luxury of passivity, encapsulated in the dead space and time of a transcontinental air journey.

I looked at my watch. One o'clock San Francisco time. Three and a half hours from now I'd be back in the East, back in that part of the country where I'd spent nearly all my life.

I remembered the day we'd left. Had it been only thirteen months since we'd set out for California, luggage carrier and trunk stuffed to overflowing, heading west on the Pennsylvania Turnpike?

It had been hot and muggy that July morning, the air redolent of new-cut grass as the college's tractor and gang of mowers circled Merion Field. Lis and Ev had squatted cross-legged on the ground, subdued, talking in quiet voices to their friends from next door, planning a reunion the next summer in California, hesitantly beginning to experience the leaving that was only minutes away. Where had Nancy been? Oh, yes. She'd gone to have a last cup of coffee two doors away with Ann Davidon.

I'd locked up the old Victorian house and walked down to the duck pond. The ducks had been circling the pond in the dead calm of morning. I'd watched them cruise, stopping now and then to dive for food, and had a sharp premonition it would be the last time I'd stand at that spot.

All through that last year at Haverford things had felt like that—strange. Walking back from teaching my last class, it had struck me I wouldn't be teaching any more classes. Ever.

It had made no sense. After all, I was just going off for a year's sabbatical to write a book on Nietzsche. In a year I'd be back; Haverford would be the same and also not the same; a book would have been written or not written; I'd start teaching again. It had always been that way. Yet this would not be like the other times. Something was going to happen. Turning back to the car, I'd looked back at the pond and the circling ducks and wondered what it would be.

Now, the American Airlines 707 was filled with rows of businessmen, some reading papers, others tabulating their expense accounts, still others sleeping. The cabin was cozy and reassuring, the red, white, and blue decor familiar. Reassuring too was the regular drone of the engines. Pushing the fear away once again, I looked at the somnolent businessmen. Had I been like them? Had I been like a drowsy, well-fed air passenger lolling back in his seat, fully at ease in the comfortable and the familiar?

Maybe. But there'd also been that inability to rid myself of the notion something was missing, that the edge of experience lay elsewhere.

I rolled that phrase—"the edge of experience"—in my mouth. It seemed orotund. Was I really such a figure? A man at ease in the comfortable and the familiar who always wanted something more? Or was I a broken-down college professor living out a spasm of middlescence on the golden coast of California?

Twenty years before, at Yale, it wasn't the edge of experience but its center that had intrigued us. Sitting in George & Harry's, we'd talked about life as a kind of stream, bemoaning the fact we were still in the shallows. Yale in the fifties had been a good place for such conversations—for dreaming, if you will. There'd been no pressing social problems, no messages from the outside world to threaten our vision of ourselves as an elite that would naturally and necessarily govern. That we would succeed was taken for granted. What was not taken for granted was that in succeeding we would live deeply or well. And so, endlessly, we'd talked about it, throwing in whatever came our way through courses or reading. We'd read Sartre, Camus, Hemingway, Faulkner, and Fitzgerald, writers who, we believed, knew about living, whose characters we could emulate.

Hemingway became for me a kind of reference point. I wanted a life like Frederick Henry's, or Robert Jordan's, or even (except for his injury) Jake Barnes's. I wanted a woman to love me as Catherine Barkley loved Frederick Henry. I wanted to shred my hands for her as Frederick shredded his hands for Catherine, rowing through the night across Lake Como. I exulted in Hemingway's critique of the big words, "obscene beside the concrete names of villages, the number of roads, the names of rivers, the numbers of regiments and the dates."

In some way, I suppose, we saw ourselves as existentialists, opposed to the pomposity and slipperiness of the big words yet captivated by the literary ideal of a life lived cleanly and well. Few of us knew tragedy in our own lives, yet we packed Richard Sewalls's lectures on tragedy because they were—how to put it?—"edifying." We had not known war or poverty or personal disaster, or even in any significant way enjoyed happiness or the love of a woman. But we'd climbed mountains and hitchhiked from coast to coast and wrestled in the back seats of '55 Chevys. And so we'd transformed dormitory parties into Pamplona revels, and picnics in the Connecticut countryside into fishing trips along the Rio de la Fabrica. We were playing, insulated by Yale's wealth and power, secure in our sense of being the elite of a truly worthwhile society. On Monday afternoons, we put on ROTC uniforms and drilled on the playing fields where ten or fifteen years earlier another generation had wheeled and turned to the same cadences before going off to fight a just war in the hedgerows of Europe or the atolls of the Pacific. We were playing, yet the play always seemed to have the same direction and purpose: to turn life into literature, experience into story.

For me, this meant something special. It wasn't just that I wanted to be the author of my life; in a sense that was inescapable. I wanted something more. I wanted to be both author and central character in the novel that was my life.

So what? I asked myself now. All that is true, but how does it explain your flying across the continent in the service of a dope dealer's lawyer? Or, to push it further back, how does it explain your successful failure as husband, father, and college professor?

My mind drifted back to the duck pond and to the time I'd spent at Haverford. It seemed shorter than eleven years as I thought back on it, shifting in my seat so I could peer down on what must be the Missouri River making its final turn before meeting the Mississippi at Alton.

In many ways Haverford had seemed like a miniature utopia. There'd been the small amenities—the luxury of being able to walk to work, for example. I'd loved those morning walks up College Lane to my first class, watching the sun form shadow-patterns through the branches of the oaks lining the lane, aware of leaves falling in autumn and new buds appearing in spring. My first class had always been an introductory course, the fall term spent on Plato, Hume, and Kant, the spring term on nineteenth- and twentieth-century philosophy. Usually a knot of students had hung around after class asking questions. We'd talk for a while, often ambling along the path to the dining hall. After lunch had come the advanced class, with everything usually over by four o'clock, leaving time before dinner for a brief spin in the countryside on the motorcycle.

I missed those late-afternoon runs; now I got to ride only on weekends. They'd offered a strange meditation as I cruised the familiar roads, my mind lulled into reverie by the regular beat of the engine.

All that leisure to read and think and talk was now in the past.

That was what had been so fine about Haverford, the opportunity for reflection and friendship. It was a self-contained community of leisure—two hundred acres of carefully kept lawns, rolling hills and woods, an institution with a long and proud history, gifted students, a distinguished faculty. It was a good place, a safe place. Why had it become for me, finally, such an unhappy place?

The setting had been part of it. Not the physical setting but the human setting—the sense we were all parodying ourselves. Often it had seemed as if Haverford were a stage set for a comic novel or movie about life in a small college.

I could even remember the exact moment when that singular thought first struck me. It had come at the end of my first faculty meeting.

Lis had been only a year old that September, and we'd been living in a tiny ninety-dollar-a-month apartment on Railroad Avenue. As I'd straightened my tie in the hall mirror, Nancy had kidded me about it being my first faculty meeting. The day had been overcast and cool for late summer. I'd hefted my briefcase and set off across Merion Field, pausing in front of the duck pond before making my way up the lawns beyond to Founder's Hall.

The faculty was assembled in its own oak-paneled meeting room. Looking at the intense, tanned faces of my colleagues, I'd been impressed. Haverford was a prestigious institution, and its faculty looked the part. Tweedy in dress, bright-eyed and intelligent in expression, they seemed to have come right out of central casting.

The room helped.

Staring down from the walls were oil paintings of legendary faculty giants. Serious, even dour, they appeared to be passing judgment on the present occupants of their chairs. Carved with great care and highlighted in gold on the oak panel above the fireplace was an inscription ascribed to Isaac Sharpless, president of the college in the late nineteenth century. *"I suggest that you preach truth,"* the inscription read, *"and do righteousness as you have been taught, whereinsoever that teaching may commend itself to your consciences and your judgments."* It ended with the imperative not to *"sacrifice one iota of the moral freedom of your consciences or the intellectual freedom of your judgments."*

The meeting was brought to order by the president, a kindly

man named Hugh Borton, who asked department chairmen to rise and introduce new faculty. I was introduced and made my little bow. Reports from faculty committees were read and discussed; announcements were made. Finally the floor was opened for new business.

A balding, rather severe-looking chemistry professor rose and began discussing a "problem" that had recently been brought to his attention. He wore a bow tie and used the word *concern* a lot, as is the Quaker custom. For some minutes I couldn't grasp what was bothering him. Then, face flushed, he launched into a jeremiad about the sexual promiscuity that had become rampant at Haverford. Apparently a Haverford student had impregnated the seventeen-year-old daughter of some friends of his. Now, according to him, no female in the surrounding community between the ages of twelve and sixty was safe from the lascivious attentions of Haverford students. Speaking quickly and vehemently, with only a trace of irony, he ended with a practical suggestion: a condom machine should be set up in the basement of Founder's Hall.

I looked around. No one was laughing or even smiling; only rank on rank of thoughtful, serious faces.

The discussion began: "This is a community problem." . . . "I wish to thank Henry for his courage in bringing his concern to all of us." . . . "We must think long and hard about this." . . . "A matter of conscience" . . . "The disastrous consequences of the new sexual morality" . . . "I'm glad I have only sons." . . . "We have to think of our reputation." . . .

Finally discussion focused on the suggestion. Should the condom machine be in Founder's or another building? Perhaps several might be installed; they could be put next to the washer/ dryers in each dormitory. Should the idea of a machine be given up, and condoms dispensed free of charge by the college nurse? Would gratis condoms imply faculty approval of sexual activity? What about Haverford's relations (the word drew a titter) with nearby Bryn Mawr?

There was a break in the discussion, and Professor Wallace MacCaffrey rose to his feet. The reigning chairman of the History Department, MacCaffrey, who would shortly move on to Harvard, enjoyed universal respect. He said slowly and simply, "I do not believe this matter is of any concern to the faculty of this college." He sat down. A brief silence followed, and the president adjourned the meeting.

Taking a last look at the faces peering down from the walls, I'd made my way to the door. Not only had central casting assembled a remarkable cast, but the director had just brought off a brilliant comic scene. The whole meeting, the detailed set with the portraits and the inscription over the fireplace, the cast, the lines spoken, the abrupt ending—all of it had been part of a movie. Bravo.

Had that been it? The growing awareness no one could take himself seriously in this stage set, that the affairs of this mini-utopia were an endlessly repeated comedy of manners—had that been the cause of the accelerating unhappiness I'd felt in the early seventies? It had been part of it, but not the whole story.

The core of it, I thought to myself as the stewardess refilled my glass, was the fact that by 1970, at the ripe age of thirty-five, I'd come to think of myself as superfluous. Sartre would have liked that, I thought: *de trop* at thirty-five. Yet it had seemed true.

I was a father, but—so I'd told myself—a superfluous one, content to look on as my children flourished like young plants in rich soil, watered regularly by Nancy's attentions. They hadn't needed me.

As husband?

Well, that was more complicated, I had to admit. But there too I'd functioned in the conventional way, providing money and a stable life, again superfluous, a presence along the horizon of Nancy's life.

As professor?

My job was safe, that had been clear: early tenure, three books in philosophy, a Guggenheim, and a nomination for a national teaching award. I could be fired only for some cardinal academic sin: "moral turpitude" or "academic incompetence."

As teacher?

There too I was superfluous. The students were talented; they came from liberal, advantaged homes and would get educated no matter what I or my colleagues did or didn't do. As teacher, I was only honing the already liberal outlooks and competent minds of the sons and daughters of the upper middle class.

Perhaps that was putting it too coldly. It was difficult to remember how I'd actually felt in those years. *Unhappiness* was too strong a word, for I hadn't been unhappy, or even bored. There had just been a vague restlessness gathering in the background of my life. Month was following month, year following year, but I wasn't changing: time was simply accumulating. I'd felt frozen, I suppose, like Kierkegaard's chess piece in that line from his journal: *"At the present time I feel like a piece in chess of which the opponent says: that piece cannot be moved—as an idle onlooker, for my time is not yet come."* That was it. I'd become an idle onlooker, gradually turning older, wearier, deader. And looking ahead, all I'd seen was more of the same.

Superfluous and restless in my public life, I'd constructed a secret life out of politics and sex.

In the sixties, "the news," especially TV news, had mesmerized us. Every night at seven we'd switch on the set to see what new atrocity had punctuated the last twenty-four hours. It was a time of bulletins and breaking stories, of Walter Cronkite's friendly and dependable face chronicling the latest turn of the downward spiral. For a while, the microcosm of the small college seemed to have been absorbed into a wider world. And of course, it had been possible not only to watch this wider drama but to participate in it. There'd been the antiwar movement.

At the outset everything had gone on in an atmosphere of earnest respectability. Nancy and I had come early to the antiwar movement, organizing marches and vigils in 1965 and 1966. I'd been arrested in the usual well-mannered ways in Philadelphia and Washington. Consistently polite to the authorities, we'd even permitted members of the Philadelphia police civil-disobedience squad to attend our premarch meetings. There'd been little violence; it had all been a battle of words.

When had things changed?

It was probably 1970. We'd spent that academic year in Denmark, where I'd read the Danish papers for news of Cambodia and Kent State. We'd returned to Haverford in the late summer, and you didn't have to be an Eric Sevareid to recognize that the balance had shifted. Resistance had replaced dissent; criminal conspiracy had taken the place of political organizing. On the one hand, there were draft-board raids and sabotage missions: in March 1971 the files of the Media FBI office were elegantly stolen and selectively released to the press. On the other hand, there was the ever-present danger of government phone taps and penetration by informers. For a brief moment, respectable middle-class citizens could function as criminals, backed not only by moral purpose but by the vocal enthusiasm of the intellectual community.

The wheeling columns of uniform-clad young men performing their maneuvers "for God, for Country, and for Yale" had receded into the past. The society was no longer integral or obviously worthwhile. Our attention turned to the "good Germans," the Circle of the Rose, or, alternatively, to Camus and Sartre and their compatriots in the French resistance. My Navy training in commando and demolition raids could be used to advantage. It was a time of secret meetings and secret plans, of coded phone messages and watching one's rearview mirror. When Haverford's president announced he might honor the FBI's request to examine the college's Xerox machines, I helped shift the offending roll to the president's personal machine. When Hoover's short-haired under-cover operatives appeared in Powelton Village, a neighborhood warning system of hand-held sirens alerted the troops. It was David against Goliath. We were the best of our generation, we told ourselves, ready to take risks and do things others only thought about.

Had I been happy? Yes. It was an engrossing "story."

At the same time, I became an unfaithful husband. That, of course, was another "story."

Some stories leave their engrams not only in the experiencing and then remembering mind but also in the world, a small rearrangement of physical reality, a precipitate of the event. I wondered whether the smudged handprint was still on the door between the kitchen and dining room of the Haverford house. It had been there the previous year. I remembered glancing at it that last morning before we left.

I'd always liked that door, so reminiscent was it of similar doors in the house I'd known as a boy—a heavy swinging door anchored in metal plates at floor and lintel. The college had painted it white. But the paint had been applied too thick, or the house had settled, or something. In any case, the door had stuck. That had seemed a significant flaw to me. The door was so well designed, it deserved to swing freely.

And so that October evening, the evening of the day on which another door had opened, I planed and rehung the door. So enamored of free movement was I, so desirous that the door swing silently and effortlessly, that I'd taken motorcycle grease and lubricated its moving parts. When I was finished, with only a slight push, it swung neatly to and fro. Above, along its top edge, I'd inadvertently left a handprint.

The leaving of the print had been inadvertent, but not its preservation. I'd noticed it that night, and in some inchoate way decided not to erase it, wanting it left (so to speak) as "evidence," an empirical trace of an event that remained secret to all but Carla and me. Over the next six years I'd often glanced at that print. It would be easy to say it functioned as a kind of silent reproach, but it didn't. Rather, it reminded me of my surprise in discovering, that evening, that I didn't feel guilty.

I'd expected guilt. I'd believed guilt was part of the bargain I was striking in crossing that threshold. One didn't become unfaithful after twelve years without paying a price—or so I'd thought. I'd been wrong. Or for a while, at least, it *seemed* I'd been wrong.

It had started—but of course really *hadn't* started—that morning. I'd awakened slowly and luxuriously, pushing back the web of sleep, and rolled over to my left. (Yes, it was to the left, I thought as the engines droned and the plane steadily bore eastward over Indiana. I always slept to Nancy's right. How is it, I wondered, that these small details of intimacy become fixed?) I'd rolled over and stretched my hand easily to Nancy's stomach, before moving it up to feel the rise of breast. She hadn't responded. There'd been no turning toward me, no subtle or unsubtle sign of wanting me, or it, or anything. Nothing.

Minutes later, staring at my stubbled face in the mirror, I'd been angry, and had known that, as always, the anger would be with me all day. "Enough," I'd said to myself, not fully aware of the cliché I was enacting. "If she doesn't want me, I'll take care of myself."

How much suppressed anger lay behind her unwillingness to open not just her legs but her heart, I hadn't then perceived. But I'd known my anger, and my weariness with that anger, and that had been enough.

Later that morning I'd taught the usual classes. We were reading the *Phaedrus* in the introductory class, and its quiet indolence, its evocation of spirits so at home in a scene so clearly *beyond* the city's walls, had stayed with me through the day.

In the early afternoon I'd walked the half mile to Carla's apartment. Carla! What could one say? To describe her as courageous and smart is not to do her justice. Carla was a friend. We'd done things together. We liked each other. Before this day, there'd been no thought of even a hesitant flirtation. Carla was too direct for that, so clear-eyed that flirtation would have seemed silly, even insulting.

We'd met in the antiwar movement a few years earlier. She

taught at a downtown Philadelphia university but lived on the Main Line. We all knew one another. Nancy and I had often had dinner at Carla's, or she'd come to our house, and less frequently we'd hiked together at Valley Forge.

Carla and I had smoked a joint that October afternoon, then lain around languidly talking and listening to music. I'd taken her hand and drawn her down beside me on the carpet. She'd been trembling, wanting yet not wanting to continue. Soon we'd moved to the bedroom, and there made love without embarrassment or awkwardness, again and again and again, as the breeze rippled the curtains and the Indian summer sun fell in longer and longer shafts through the trees. We'd come together, and I'd felt released from anger and brought into some kind of mystery. It had seemed like a time-warp, a standing-out from the day-to-day, only partially fueled by the languor of the afternoon and the tetrahydrocannabinol. Afterward, we'd rediscovered the room and the other time that had continued to tick away on the mechanical Big Ben on her bureau.

Walking home among the leaves and ginkgo berries that lined the walkway over Railroad Avenue, I'd braced myself for guilt. But it hadn't come: I'd felt hungry and very much alive. At dinner there'd been much animated talk. Then, carrying the dishes into the kitchen, I'd encountered the sticking door.

My decision to fix it then and there was no simple response to accumulated annoyance. It obviated the risk of conversation, something I feared that night because it brought with it the chance of discovery. This was new and unknown territory, but I didn't want to turn back. I wanted to see where it led.

And so the story unfolded.

At first Carla seemed uncomfortable, perhaps guilty, about betraying Nancy. She knew and liked Nancy, and could empathize with her pain should she find out. I told her Nancy and I seemed freer and happier together. This was true, and it seemed to help. But more important was the fact Carla herself was becoming more vibrant and animated. The fear or guilt was cerebral; emotionally she was happy and getting happier. Our sexual connection grew. Within a month or two it became obvious we'd started on some course the ending of which wasn't clear and needn't be clear. Something was happening. I didn't want to control it. I wanted only to experience it, to follow the hidden story developing around us, through us. Whatever we were doing and wherever it led, it had vitality, I told myself; it expressed the truth of the senses.

And for a long time it did.

For two years it flourished: meetings at the Jersey shore and in California, afternoon and evening trysts at Haverford, walks, meals, films.

And then gradually it began to sink under its own weight. Why? In such matters do we ever know? Was it the onus of familiarity? The lack of momentum, of any future we could live toward? Was it simply Carla's independence, her unwillingness to pull any of the manipulative levers that would have thrown us into a common life? Or was it my fear of the unknown, my reluctance to cash in a known and basically happy life for something indeterminate? Was it all of the above, or none of the above? I only knew the story was ending.

We'd always argued. Argument had been a form of play. But toward the end, the arguments were followed by an uneasy silence. She came to resent the urgency of my desire for her. It made her, she said, feel used. Why couldn't I be satisfied more often with just talking, or walking, or shopping, or doing any of the things most people did? I answered that we were not "most people." We were lovers trying to carry on something clandestine with never enough time. But the arguments never got anywhere; they only marked the place where we'd arrived. Slowly but irrevocably we drifted apart.

After Carla—in fact even during Carla—there were others. So many women—one-night stands, one-week stands, six-month stands. I hadn't intended to become a "womanizer." But womanizing became habitual, a series of new experiences, perhaps new mirrors for the self. Occasionally I felt sad when the affairs were over, but never for very long and never very intensely. There were always complications, of course, and sometimes there was callousness. The complications often ran both ways, for it's always painful for two people to admit that although they've experienced each other, enjoyed each other, been naked in many senses before each other, even learned from each other, it's now time to move on. Often, after the sex was over and the alcohol or marijuana had faded, I wanted to escape. Usually I stayed on, keeping up appearances, listening to the harsh words bounce off the walls of yet another anonymous motel room, waiting for the storm to subside and the clock to release me.

Each affair was a kind of story, created and sustained by the ambiguous wishes of both parties. Each moved in its ambience of secrecy. Each drew to it the taste of the illicit. In each was a scent of danger, a probing of the limits.

Oddly, during this time, Nancy and I were never indifferent to each other. Through each affair, I remained sexually obsessed by her, my fantasies stoked by memories of the curve of her breast, the touch of her hand, the sound of her voice. A primitive connection endured. And because of that connection, all the affairs were attacked from underneath, shadowed by fear of discovery and by the knowledge that what I was doing was unfair, indefensible.

She never asked troubling questions, and was satisfied with partial answers. We lived those years at arm's length, careful not to disturb the established balance. Although the term sticks in my throat, I suppose we'd made an "arrangement."

Watching the ducks turn in circles on the pond that humid morning a year before, I'd known a pattern was slipping out of focus. My dual life could not be sustained indefinitely, nor did I want it to be. Underground political activities were already a thing of the past, overtaken by Watergate and the fall of Saigon. And my womanizing had become threadbare, a series of endlessly repeating cycles, each less satisfying than the last. Standing there, I'd felt grateful for a significant break, a change in geography that might knit together the public and private skeins of my life. Underneath everything, I'd become weary of deception. I wanted to be done with it. But I hadn't then dealt with my predilection for the dramatic, nor had I acknowledged the price of candor.

Now, stewardesses passed up and down the aisle collecting cups. The seat-belt sign winked on, and my ears told me we were settling into our final descent to Logan Airport. I hadn't been to Boston in fifteen years. Now it would be different; not because of a new skyline or a few new freeways, but because Boston was where the case would begin. My stomach tightened—the case!

THREE

"A LITTLE MORAL INSTRUCTION"

SUNDAY, AUGUST 7, 1977

The first problem was getting into the house. At least that was the way it looked to me as I dipped the spoon into the bowl of clam chowder and looked around at the tables of tourists. It was eleven-thirty on a Sunday morning and already The Captain's Table was filling up. At each butcher-block table, a large white paper napkin held knife, spoon, and fork of heavy-gauge stainless steel.

That was when I decided to do it.

Holding the spoon in my right hand, I slid my left hand over the pile of cutlery, palming the knife and slipping it up the sleeve of my tweed jacket. It was easy then to drop my hand into my jacket's side pocket, where the knife fit easily.

Outside, I opened the trunk of the Mercury Cougar and dropped the knife into the wheel well holding the spare tire. There was a small Hertz sticker on the rear bumper. I got a fingernail under it and slowly lifted it off; I'd already pried off the one inside the windshield that morning, waiting at a light just north of Logan Airport. A small precaution learned earlier from Fechheimer—why advertise you're driving a rental car?

The knife was my own idea.

I'd thought of it a bit after stopping at the light, after the Cougar, like a homing pigeon, had slipped off I-95 and headed up Massachusetts 28. Reading disappeared in the mirror and Route 28 became a wide avenue, bisecting the Andover campus. Off to the right stood the white chapel where on other Sundays

76

we'd trooped in coats and ties to hear the sermons of the Reverend Baldwin and Headmaster Kemper, and where, on a plaque near the entrance, was a quotation from Henry L. Stimson. Driving down that wide avenue, watching the chapel get closer, it had struck me all the hardware stores would be closed, and I'd nothing to force the lock with. It was there I'd thought of the knife.

What would they all have thought?

In the 1930s Stimson had declined to establish a code-breaking unit in the State Department, explaining, "Gentlemen do not open each other's mail." What would he have thought of one of Andover's sons passing by on a mission to recover a can of evidence and thirty thousand dollars in a paper bag, all in the service of a Stanford-educated dope dealer? Would he have been standing by the road, eyes alert for the Cougar? Would he have waved and asked me to pull over: "See here, my good man, I think you could do with a little moral instruction. Why don't you step over here into the chapel"? or would he have smiled benignly, letting me pass, knowing he had more pressing moral concerns closer to home on the Andover campus?

Silly or not, that knife in the trunk made me fell better as I nosed the Cougar into the stream of traffic heading south on 495 toward New Bedford. I hadn't slept much the night before at the Airport Hilton. Fechheimer had gotten back to me with final clearance a little after one, and I'd been awakened at seven by a breakfast I hadn't ordered. But now things were beginning to click. It was a beautiful day in New England, and the traffic was only spotty on the two-lane Route 140.

The can was hidden outside a house in Nonquitt Harbor, the same house where thirty thousand dollars might lie in a bag under the attic floorboards. I'd been sent East to retrieve both.

Why?

Well, that part got complicated. It had to do with the fact that a dope dealer named Jamie Reynolds was sitting in jail. I was also carrying ten thousand dollars of Jamie's money to deliver to his brother. The whole situation was surreal; perhaps that was why I'd almost expected Henry Stimson to be standing by the roadside in Andover. The bizarre had become commonplace so often over the last nine months that now nothing seemed bizarre. Like, for example, that night the spring before in Dixon.

From I-80 twenty-five miles west of Sacramento, all you can see of Dixon is a giant orange ball on a two-hundred-foot-high

steel pillar. If you turn off there and pass by the hamburger shack
at the base of the pillar, you end up on a two-lane road angling
southeast. Down that road is an abandoned Army Signal Corps
base, renamed DQ University. I'd driven down that road the
previous March to see an American Indian Movement leader
who had (or had access to) the murder weapon in the Skyhorse-
Mohawk case. At least that was what we'd been told. So I'd
driven down that road under the giant orange ball, turned into
the parking lot at DQ, and followed him around for a day and a
half until finally, after midnight on the second night, I'd found
myself standing naked in the stubble of a winter wheat field,
looking at the lights of split-level tract homes a quarter mile
distant. Behind me, hot stones were being shoveled into the
center of the sweat lodge. Then the five of us—the leader, myself, and three of his aides—had crawled inside.

The language of the ceremony was Lakota, and its origin lay
hidden in prehistory, passed on by generations of Sioux warriors
for hundreds if not thousands of years. On that June evening
one hundred and one years before when the 7th Cavalry confi-
dently made its way up Rosebud Creek, this ceremony was being performed in sweat lodges along the Little Bighorn. And
now it was being performed again, almost within earshot of the
split-levels where Johnny Carson was about to sign off.

It mattered not that later that night I'd sit in the leader's trailer
with a kerosene lantern swinging over the table as we ate the
meal prepared by his women and he told me what he knew of
Marvin Redshirt and the knife used to murder William Whaley.
The job, the success or failure of the task at hand, could not
normalize the situation. Some distinction between the real and
the surreal had been dissolved. After that night, or after several
nights like that, I no longer came to expect things to be "regular" or "normal"or "usual." It hadn't seemed "strange," then,
to be doing what I was doing.

The night before, at the Airport Hilton, it had seemed more
than strange. It had seemed downright scary. But now that the
night was over and I was actually doing it, it seemed less so. A
storm had passed through a day or so before, leaving the atmosphere bright and clear. The black ribbon of asphalt unwound
in the sunlight, and soon I made my turn off Route 140 and
headed seaward. Abandoned farms dotted the landscape, their
weathered wood and creeping vegetation like an Andrew Wyeth
painting. Then the flow of cars picked up, the road widened,

and a shopping center burst into view. I pulled into the lot to check map and notes.

This was it.

The shopping center was the first landmark. A left turn at the intersection beyond would take me around a point of land and over a bridge, and then, two hundred yards farther along, a road would angle in from the right. That was the lane.

I opened the trunk and took the padded mailer from my suitcase. Merleau-Ponty's *The Phenomenology of Perception* and *Humanism and Terror* easily slipped out. The sealed envelope with ten thousand dollars in cash remained inside. I folded the mailer in half and wedged it into the wheel well with the spare tire and the knife.

Twenty minutes later, I didn't recognize the house.

Reynolds's girlfriend, Sheila, had described it to us last Thursday, but her memory of the house and the rather solid post-Victorian structure partway down the lane didn't match. The lane dipped to the left to pass the boatbuilder's house, garage, and dock, all on the left. The house stood just to the right of the lane where it made its dip. Back in San Francisco, Sheila had described a house that was vaguely Colonial. This couldn't be it. But it must be, for beyond it was the vacant lot and then the dark-brown, shingled guesthouse with the green shutters.

The Cougar ground to a stop in the gravel before the guesthouse. Professor Thompson from Haverford had just arrived for a brief vacation in New England.

"We can put you up as long as you might want to stay," said a dark-haired woman in a Shetland sweater behind the desk. Her accent was not New England. As she led me down the corridor, I asked where she was from. "Los Angeles," she said, and briefly explained how the marriage of her daughter to a contractor in New Bedford had brought her East.

Fifteen rooms were still being rented in what earlier had been a small hotel of thirty rooms. A large veranda looked down over the water and a dock the hotel shared with the boatbuilder. There were heavy chairs on the veranda, caned with bark an inch wide and painted dark green. My room was on the first floor, just to the left of the entryway. It had a single bed with heavy blanket, reading lamp and chair, closet, and sink. The bathroom was down the hall.

I put the two volumes of Merleau-Ponty and a copy of *The Maltese Falcon* on the bedside table. For the last time, I took out the envelope on which I'd scribbled Sheila's directions and description of the house. The location was accurate. The house was actually at a fork where the main lane dipped to the left and a smaller lane turned up the hill to the right. The bush with the can under it was the first one beyond the house along the upper lane. Sheila hadn't known where the money was, only that it was in a paper bag stuffed under the floorboards in the attic. I walked to the end of the hall and flushed the ripped-up pieces of envelope down the toilet.

I dived off the end of the pier and swam straight out. The water was cold and clear. A hundred yards out was a float, and beyond it some flat rocks. I swam to the float and then back to the dock.

The sun felt good on my back as I sat against a piling, looking at the house. The Sunday *New York Times* lay beside me on the dock.

They'd come to the house in late July and rented it for a month. Reynolds's family had often summered here in years past, and he had a special affection for the area. He also had a special affection for not being busted, and increased surveillance by the Coast Guard and the DEA had made smuggling marijuana into Florida and the Gulf states increasingly risky. This was to be his first attempt to land a large load (over twenty tons) on the New England coast.

Something had gone wrong—there had probably been an informer—and arrests had been made on the night of the dress rehearsal for the landing. Reynolds, Sheila, and another couple with them in the house had been taken into custody. Sheila and the other couple were quickly released for lack of evidence, but Reynolds was still in jail on federal charges. He'd been arrested in a rented Peugeot near one of the landing sites. No dope had been found, and the mother ship hadn't yet been located by the Coast Guard. The only problem was the Peugeot's glove compartment; the authorities said it contained fourteen ersatz Colombian Quaaludes and something less than a gram of coke. That plus the DEA's continuing interest in him accounted for the $1,250,000 bail Reynolds was being held under in Boston. The Seville in the San Francisco Airport parking garage was his.

When Reynolds was arrested, the crucial question was evidence. Planted or not, there wasn't much to be done about the contents of the glove compartment. But had the government proof of actual smuggling?

Sheila had hidden the can under a bush. It held a navigation chart with plots of the mother ship's expected positions and radio frequencies. It also contained Sheila's diary, which might or might not prove incriminating, and possibly some drugs. If found, the can's contents would be the first evidence of actual smuggling in the whole case. The same applied to the thirty thousand dollars. Reynolds could care less about the money or what was in the can. What was important was whether the government had found either.

From the dock I could see the front of the house but not the bush where Sheila had hidden the can. That would be the easiest part. If the house was unoccupied, I could take care of that later that night. Sheila had warned me they'd rented the house from the boatbuilder and that he kept up the grounds. He wouldn't be keeping up the grounds at night.

But how to get into the attic to look for the thirty thousand in cash?

A Pontiac sedan pulled into the circular driveway by the house. I got only a quick look as they went into the house: two dark-haired, fat kids, a woman in a flowered dress, and a heavyset man smoking a cigar.

Twenty minutes later the man with the cigar ambled down to the dock. His belly pushed over the white belt of his trousers. He was wearing a white T-shirt, and his right bicep carried a heart-shaped tattoo with the word *Mom* in its center. On his left wrist was a huge leather watchband that dwarfed the diver's watch it held. I buried myself in the *Times*. He looked out over the water for a few minutes and then headed back to the house.

Thirty-five minutes later I was back in the shopping center at a pay phone.

"David, I think the bad guys are in residence," I said.

"OK, call me back in ten minutes."

That meant I was to call him back in ten minutes at pay phone number one. Had he said twenty minutes, it would have meant pay phone number two in twenty minutes. I got change at a Long John Silver. At the operator's signal I dropped in quarters.

"He smelled cop all over, David. He really did. I didn't see any other men around. But remember, all this happened only forty-five minutes ago. I haven't had a chance to reconnoiter things."

"That's OK. I think your instincts are right. It'd make sense for them to sit on the house and see if anyone shows up. You say the plate on the Pontiac was New York?''

''Yeah.''

''Could be some DEA agent getting a cushy week's vacation with his family at government expense.''

''Could be.''

''Look. Take a vacation for a couple of days while I sort this out. Don't do anything. Just read your philosophy books, swim, and eat lobster. Call Wednesday noon. I should have more information by then. And give me a contact number.''

I read him the number from the guesthouse matchbook. We said goodbye, and I was alone again.

That night the fog came in with the darkness.

I'd been sitting above the house where the lane became gravel and curved up the hill between fir trees. A granite outcropping with soft grass in its shelves overlooked the curve of road, and the early-evening sun slanted through the tops of the firs and threw speckled shadows on the buildings. I'd been sitting there on the grass, my father's binoculars braced against my knees, watching.

The combination of eastern woods and my father's glasses brought back memories of other Sundays when we'd hiked together along the Beaver Creek near Fredericktown. I remembered how he'd pause at creekside, raise the glasses, and scan the shallows for evidence of a beaver dam. Then he'd pass them to me, and I'd turn the knurled knob on their bridge to bring branches, leaves, and running water into focus. Often there'd be a small animal in the viewfield, and once I'd seen the snout of what my father said was a beaver poking out from a pile of branches. The glasses seemed as mysterious to me now as they had seemed long ago on those Sunday hikes, as if they had the power to change my position in the world, to insert me into the smaller frame of the beaver or the squirrel poised on the branch, or now—a world away—into the spider web that hung above the door of Cigar's house.

I was thinking of that, watching the light fade on the clapboard siding of the house, when the fog came in. It wasn't like San Francisco fog, with its picturesque ''fingers'' spreading through the Golden Gate and curling around Telegraph Hill. It rolled in from the sea, heavy and dense. One moment everything was clear, and then the fog was there. First the house disappeared, then the lane, then the trees on my side of the lane. My watch said 7:45, but it seemed later than that. Shivering a bit, I stuck the binoculars into the side pocket of my sport jacket and moved down the hill.

The fog could be a real break. Along the upper lane, the nearest bush to the house was only about fifteen feet from a line of kitchen windows, and the light from those windows fell on it. Sticky. The fog, though, changed all that. David had told me to sit tight. But why do nothing when this might be the best night I'd get? It was obvious only Cigar and his family were inside. I waited.

An hour later the kitchen light snapped off. Other lights came on and went off, but the fog made it impossible to tell in which rooms. I waited ten minutes and then worked my way over to the bushes just below the lane. On hands and knees, I felt around the trunk of the first bush. Sheila had said the can was square and that she'd left it unburied alongside the trunk of the first bush. Nothing. Had she been mistaken? Had they found it? Anyone who looked could have found it easily. But had anyone looked? That, I reminded myself, was why I was here. The second bush also held nothing. And the third. And the fourth, fifth, and sixth. "They must've found it," I told myself. "Sheila couldn't be this far off."

But she had been. Under the eighth bush, well down into the middle of the yard, my hand brushed something metallic. My fingers traced the edges of a metal box maybe four inches by four inches, and eight inches high.

Two thoughts raced through my head. First: this is a trap and you just fell into it. Second: you won't be able to explain that damn ten thousand in cash in your trunk. They're going to get a warrant and crowbar and break into your trunk and then they're going to make you eat that ten thousand dollars and the envelope it came in, the one with your nice fingerprints all over it.

Dummy.

I took my hands off the can and held absolutely still. Nothing. No noise of running feet. No searchlights. No commands to "Freeze, motherfucker!" Just the fog and the sound of my breathing. I waited. Still nothing. I felt in the dirt around the can for wires. Again, nothing. But if they'd put an alarm on it, they would have used a transmitter and a motion detector. I'd brushed the can, but hadn't disturbed it. Maybe the alarm hadn't gone off. There was one sure way to find out.

I grabbed the can and ran, plunging through the fog and the

fir trees toward the upper lane, breath blowing out in front of
me, branches catching and pulling my jacket. The open space
of the lane appeared and then disappeared. There was a tree
trunk and some rocks on the bank beyond. I grabbed the trunk
and scrambled toward a fir tree. Under its boughs, the needle-
strewn ground was soft. I slithered to a stop.

My breathing was labored, but beyond the envelope of the
tree there was only silence. Nothing.

You've done it, I thought, you've actually done it!

Then: That's right only if there's something in the can, only
if some savvy deputy sheriff hadn't found it first, ripped off the
drugs and whatever, and left the empty can behind. And there
might be a beeper on the can; they might have wanted you to
find it.

Fine, I told myself, you can figure all that out back in the
room.

Walking down the lane, I checked myself out. The binoculars
were safely in my pocket. I didn't seem to have any scratches
on my face or rips in the tweed of my jacket. My knees were
wet and dirty from crawling around, but the dark flannel pants
wouldn't show much. I should pass muster if anyone was in the
hallway when I got back. What time was it? Ten-fifty.

Back in the room, I locked the door and sat down on the bed.
Not bad, I smiled to myself, not bad for the first day.

Now, what was in the can?

The lamp on the bedside table was the only bright light in the
room. I pulled over the chair, removed Merleau-Ponty and
Hammett from the table, and set the can down in the circle of
light. It had a handsome green label on a light beige background
that showed it once contained five hundred grams of Fortnum
& Mason Royal Blend Tea. Sheila seemed to have an eye for
design; she probably picked it especially to use for their drug
stash.

It wasn't empty.

The navigation chart had been folded and rolled into a cylinder six inches long. On it were navigation plots with dates
alongside. Across the bottom were numbers that looked like
radio frequencies. Stuffed in the cylinder was a foil package.
When the foil was stripped back, I could see the dope wrapped
in fish netting around a central spike. It looked like half a shish-
kebab and smelled old and moldy, more like hash than sensi-
milla. I figured it was a Thai stick.

Upright along one side of the can was a four-by-six-inch book with a paisley cover. You'd take it for an address book if it weren't for the ruled pages and writing inside. I flipped through it. Interspersed between what looked like accounts of erotic dreams were descriptions of meetings and meals. The people only had first names, but the entries were dated and the place names were given. I didn't know enough to interpret it.

I put everything back in the can after wiping down the surfaces, inside and out, with a washcloth. Holding the can in a towel and its lid in a washcloth, I forced the lid back on, put the whole thing in my suitcase, and lay down on the bed.

I'd succeeded. Half the job had been accomplished on the first day. There was no beeper. Clearly the authorities had never found the can. But the early success created a problem: what to do with the can? The safest place was the locked trunk of the Cougar. But how do you like the idea, Professor, of driving around with ten thousand dollars in cash plus the diary, chart, and half a Thai stick in your trunk? Not much.

You could bury it. But where? And how?

Or you could let it stay right where it is—under a shirt in your suitcase.

That would be really stupid, I thought. After cleverly cleaning the can of any prints, you leave it in your suitcase. If you're found out later on, the first thing they'll do is search your room.

So what do you do?

The real problem isn't the can, but the thirty thousand dollars that may or may not be in the house. With Cigar and his family living there, how are you going to get in to see?

A break-in would be risky. You don't even have someone to play lookout.

You might be able to rent it. But how would a professor from Pennsylvania happen on that particular house as a late-summer rental?

If it were for sale, it'd be easier. And, come to think of it, it might well be for sale. The boatbuilder probably wasn't tickled with the police raid on his house. He may be fed up with the hassles of summer rentals. But there isn't any For Sale sign on the house. If it was for sale, you'd think there'd be a sign. You could check some Realtors' windows tomorrow morning.

What about reporting in?

You've succeeded only in the easiest part of the job. And you did go against David's direct order. You can call from town tomorrow midday. And the ten thousand dollars? You better get rid of that tomorrow too.

MONDAY, AUGUST 8

I noticed the bag as I was getting my jacket out of the closet. Just an ordinary supermarket paper bag. Inside were a couple of used Kleenex and the cardboard cylinder from a tampon. I got a towel and wiped the top of the bag where I'd touched it. Then I took a washcloth, picked up the can from my suitcase, and placed it inside. Not leaving any prints, I rolled the top down neatly and placed the bag in the back corner of the closet. Then I put my suitcase in front of it. If the maid had missed the bag earlier, she couldn't even see it now. If I got arrested later on and the room was searched, there was nothing to tie me to the can.

Whoever belonged to those Kleenex and the tampon cylinder might be linked to it, but not me.

Not bad, I congratulated myself. Elegant!

By ten-thirty that morning I'd located the house in the second Realtor's window I'd looked in. Four bedrooms, two and one-half baths, kitchen, dining room, living room, porch, cellar, and attic—all for $67,500.

The Realtor was in his late fifties, a strange-looking character in cowboy boots. Right off, I gave him my Haverford card. I told him I was looking for a house I could use both for summer vacations and as my family's home during the sabbatical year I was just starting. Merleau-Ponty's *Phenomenology of Perception* was in my hand as I ran through this. The house was fourth in a group of five houses I picked to look at with him the next day. I didn't want to move too quickly while still holding the ten thousand dollars. We shook hands and agreed to meet at his office the following morning. The rest of the morning I spent in the library, reading up on the Reynolds drug bust.

The arrests had been made two weeks earlier. As I'd expected, the news reports gave no indication as to what led to the raid, but they did point out that Reynolds and friends had been "under State Police surveillance" for the week prior. The use of the plural *houses* implied that another house besides the boat-builder's had been under observation.

When I called the office at one-thirty I got the "call me in twenty minutes" instruction. I waited, called pay phone number two, and explained to Fechheimer I had the can and would be viewing the house the next day. He was delighted and gave me no grief about disobeying his order. We chatted for a minute longer, and then he asked for the number I was calling from. He said he'd call me there exactly fifteen minutes later.

When I picked up the phone, it was clear he was back in the office. We talked about innocuous things for a while, and then he said, "That can you picked up, Tink. Be sure to safeguard it and bring it with you. It's evidence." I answered "OK" in a bewildered tone, and he hung up.

What the hell had he meant by "evidence"? Evidence for the prosecution, sure—evidence that could fry our client? It didn't make any sense for me to bring it back as evidence. And why mention the can over the office phone? Why bother to call me back at all? Weird.

At seven-thirty that evening I wheeled the Cougar into the driveway of the house where Briar Reynolds was staying. I'd called him that afternoon, and he'd suggested I come by between seven and nine. He was visiting friends, and they'd be out for dinner then. In his early forties and divorced, he was six years older than Jamie. He'd spent a number of years at Paine Webber in New York, but for the last fourteen months had been functioning as the captain of a forty-five foot yawl owned by Jamie. I didn't think either he or the yawl had been part of the smuggling operation. He must have known what was going on—it was paying his bills—but probably had been separated from any direct contact with it. All he knew about me was that I was one of Fechheimer's people and was delivering ten thousand dollars of his brother's money.

After we exchanged formalities and I accepted a cup of coffee in the kitchen, I handed him the envelope.

"I'd appreciate it if you counted it," I said.

He laid the bills out in piles of ten. There were only nine bills in the last pile: $9,900 in all.

"Please count it again," I asked.

He came up with $9,900 again and looked at me questioningly.

"There must have been a miscount in San Francisco," I said. "I'll report back that you got only nine thousand, nine hundred. Do you want me to initial anything to that effect?"

"No," he said, eyeing me strangely.

I could read his mind. This guy obviously ripped off the hundred bucks, but why did he ask me to count it in front of him and then ask if I wanted a receipt for the lower figure? He must know you don't give receipts in this business.

Irritated by the whole thing and unable to show it, I left.

I'd counted the ten thousand myself, sitting on Fechheimer's floor. Counted it twice, as a matter of fact. Then I'd put it in the envelope and sealed it. The same envelope that had just been unsealed before my eyes. How? Must have been a miscount.

I drove on, leaving my lights on bright and pushing hard on the accelerator. Everything goes well and then some dumb thing happens. I'm making my usual out-of-town hundred a day. If I have to come up with that missing hundred, I've just lost a day's pay. A hundred a day for the chances I'm taking? Shit. And what sort of game was Fechheimer playing earlier?

Then, suddenly, I saw it.

Fechheimer was protecting me. "Evidence"? That made no sense at all. He was creating a defense for me in advance. If I later ended up getting popped, I'd turn out to be the inexperienced dummy who'd just been following his boss's orders. That was why he'd made the call from his office. If a tap was on the line, it would save my ass. The call would also appear on David's bill as a toll call, and undoubtedly he'd had his own recorder running. The tape would go into his desk drawer for use if necessary.

Would I have to eat the hundred? Not if I came up with the thirty thousand.

TUESDAY, AUGUST 9

"I can't make an offer until I've lived in the house," I was telling Arnold "Slim" Whitridge as I looked out the window at the tourists and the harbor beyond. "I've got no trouble with the price. Well, a little trouble. Let me rent the house for a week or two just as soon as it opens up. Whatever it's been renting for, that's fine. After that, I'll let you know. And if I buy it, I want the rent taken off the purchase price. I don't know how you write that up, but that's what I want to do."

"Well, I tell you, Professor," said Whitridge, leaning back in his chair so his cowboy boots showed underneath his tweed pants, "the house just came on the market last week, so I don't really know what the Carvells have in mind. We haven't had other offers yet. It's been renting for two-fifty a week. That OK?"

"Uh-huh. Let me rent it for a week at that price. If after a week I decide to buy it, my offer will be sixty-five thousand minus two-fifty, or sixty-four thousand, seven hundred and fifty. But I want to get into it right away and resolve things. I gotta have a place to live next year. How're the schools up here? Nancy will want to know."

"I imagine you'll find them a lot better than you're used to in Philadelphia. Let me give the Carvells a ring and see if we can't put something together."

Everything about Whitridge was elongated—his legs, his arms, his thin tie under the green cardigan, even the '68 Eldorado he'd been driving me around in all day. I couldn't figure him out. There was a Saint Christopher's medal embedded in the car's dashboard. Did that mean he was a Catholic in a Protestant town, or had the car come equipped with the medal? I'd been sliding left and right on the slick maroon leather seats all day as he'd snaked his way around the roads near Nonquitt Harbor, showing me houses ranging in price from $47,500 to $75,000. In between houses, he'd told me almost all of Mike Dodge's "Bert and I" stories, passing them off as authentic Down East folklore. I'd used the stories to point up the difference between urban and rural culture, finally steering the talk around to the "drug problem in the cities." Whitridge had taken the bait and told me everything he knew about the recent bust. He knew only what had been in the papers, but I could use what he'd told me to open the topic with the Carvells. I could hear him talking to them on the phone, explaining who I was.

The Carvells' house had been fourth on the list. When we got there, Cigar was sitting on the porch, reading the *Boston Globe*. The woman and kids were down swimming, and Cigar didn't bother to get up from his paper as we moved through the house. It was a lot of house for $65,000—sturdy, well insulated, and spacious. I took special pains looking at the basement and the attic. Somebody had been at those floorboards. The nails in several had been removed and replaced.

"You're basically saying you and your wife need to stay in the house a week to make up your minds. That right, Professor?" Whitridge was holding the phone in one hand, the Carvells still on the line.

"Yes. That's right. At the earliest opportunity."

I was thinking that Nancy had unknowingly just won the August vacation prize—a trip East.

Whitridge continued to talk over figures and dates with the Carvells. I wandered over to the door and looked at the harbor. It was genuinely picturesque. Flat granite rocks awash near a pine-covered island, seagulls turning near the boat dock, overcast now and cool. Whitridge put down the phone.

"The Carvells wondered if you might be willing to drop by for a chat. You see, it's the old family home—they live right across the street—and they don't want to make any deals over the telephone. I hope you understand."

"No problem. The guesthouse I'm staying at is right near there. What time did they have in mind?"

"Ben said Ellen would be back in about twenty minutes. Why don't you make it five-thirty or so? They're nice folks, I'm sure you'll like each other. Why don't you figure on dropping back here around ten tomorrow and we can write up a rental contract? The family in there now will be out on Sunday."

"Terrific. I appreciate your help in all this, Mr. Whitridge."

"That's how I make my living, bub," he said, switching into a Down East accent. "Sure you can find your way?"

"East Vasselboro?" I asked, trying my own imitation of the accent and referring to one of Mike Dodge's stories he'd told me earlier. "You can't get there from here."

With the Carvells, I suppose I expected some rough edges. Ben Carvell was a boatbuilder. To me that meant someone who worked with his hands—a craftsman, to be sure, but also a manual worker, someone who trusted wood and steel, not words. And Ellen Carvell? I imagined she'd be homespun and simple, a dependable and self-effacing companion for her grizzled husband.

I expected canvas. What I got was far smoother.

Ben Carvell met me at the door. He was short—a trifle shorter than my five-eight—and in his midfifties. He had on a sport coat over a crewneck sweater and buttoned-down shirt. His hair was gray and receding in front. His complexion was ruddy but not noticeably weathered, and he had very clear blue eyes.

Ellen was sitting on a flowered couch in the living room. There were Oriental rugs scattered around, and *The New Yorker* was sitting on the coffee table along with a bottle of Beefeater's and the fixings for martinis. Ellen put down a martini glass as she extended her hand. There was a brisk, windswept quality to her. She'd probably be more comfortable in a parka and turtleneck than in the Ann Taylor dress and cableknit sweater she had on.

"What do we call you, Professor?" asked Ben Carvell. "At Dartmouth almost everyone was a 'Doctor,' so we just used 'Mister.' "

"That suits me fine," I said. "I got used to the same thing at Yale and at Haverford, where I teach now."

"We looked at Haverford a couple of years ago when Adam over there"—he stretched and pointed to a photo of a lacrosse player on the piano—"when Adam was looking around at colleges. Terrific place."

"Thanks. Where did Adam end up?"

"He's a junior now at Amherst," said Ellen Carvell. "But this summer he's off in Alaska climbing some mountain in the Brooks Range. Did you ever call the Hollisters in Darien, Ben, to see if they've heard anything from Bruce?"

Ben said he hadn't, and the conversation moved on to mountain climbing and why young men did it. As the martinis were poured and we became more comfortable with each other, they asked about my family, and I gave the usual answers.

Then, oddly, I heard myself saying, "A lot of couples split up on their sabbaticals. That's why I wanted to make sure the house is comfortable. I'm sure—or at least I hope—Nancy will love it."

It just popped out. It wasn't that I hadn't meant to drop a few hints of trouble; a bit of irrationality might prove useful later on, when I'd need a reason for not going through with the deal. But I hadn't planned it. The words were there in the room before I knew it. Their looks told me the seam had registered.

In nooks and crannies along one wall of books were hull-design models. It was Ben's specialty, and he liked explaining the qualities a successful hull must have. An idea of his had been used in *Courageous*, the current defender of the America's Cup. He turned to replace the model on the bookshelf, and I made my move.

"Slim Whitridge told me you had a little excitement here earlier this summer," I said.

"I hope Arnold got it right," said Carvell. "What did he tell you?"

I gave him Whitridge's account.

"Well, that's basically it. But nobody knows about the funny part, I guess."

"What's that?"

"It was that damned antenna," said Carvell, a grin beginning to spread across his face. "I guess that fellow Reynolds thought no one'd notice it."

"What do you mean?"

"These dope dealers," said Carvell. "They think they're so damn smart. I guess in the cities no one pays any attention to anything anymore. He must have thought no one would even see it. Actually, I didn't notice it for a day or two."

He paused while Ellen Carvell refilled our glasses. I was already feeling a glow.

"Arnold rented the place. I didn't know they'd paid with a cashier's check until I asked Arnold about it. I didn't think anything about it. There were these two couples, and they didn't have any children. Ellen, you thought that was strange, didn't you?"

Ellen nodded. Her eyes began to glaze over. She knew she'd have to hear it all over again.

"Anyway, a couple of days later I saw that antenna up on the roof. I thought about it for a day, and then I called Gus. He's been a colonel in the State Police for eight years; we went to high school together. I told him what I'd seen, and we joked about it. Then at the end of the call he got serious and said that since enforcement had gotten heavy in the southern states the smugglers had moved north, and he'd check this guy out.

"That's when I asked Arnold how the rent had been paid. To make a long story short," Carvell said, eyeing Ellen, "Gus asked permission a couple of days later to put a surveillance team in our garage. He said that antenna was for single sideband transmissions, and the DEA had a lot of raw intelligence on this guy but no arrests. He must have thought he was being so clever coming up here where no one knew anything about dopers and dope smuggling. Well, he was just a mite too clever. We weren't as dumb as he thought we were, and now they tell me he's sitting in jail up in Boston."

"Maybe so," said Ellen, "but didn't you tell me they never did find any drugs? If he was such a big dope dealer, how come he didn't have any dope?"

"That isn't the point. This fellow was setting up to bring in tons of dope. He wouldn't use it himself. He probably thinks dope is for high school kids."

I thought of the Thai stick in the can.

"You can say what you want, Ben," Ellen said. "But it just may turn out your crony Gus Hummel isn't the supercop you think he is. And if he gets sued for false arrest, we just might get sued for putting him up to it. Some dope dealer he snags— no dope, no guns, no money."

"What d'you mean, 'no money'?" asked Ben. "You were with me when we went over there and Gus showed us the twenty-eight hundred dollars from the bedroom nightstand."

"In the detective novels I read," said Ellen, "people make dope deals with suitcases of money, not twenty-eight hundred dollars. But surely this must be boring Mr. Thompson?"

"Not at all," I replied. "It's a lot more excitement than we get down at Haverford during the summer."

We never did get to the nitty-gritty of the deal. Whether it was WASP unease in talking about money or an unspoken under-standing that Whitridge was to handle such matters, I never found out. I left at about seven-thirty.

There was no fog. The sky was clear. Beyond the dock, a pair of mallards skittered to a landing on the water, just short of the flat rocks.

WEDNESDAY, AUGUST 10

By the time I reached the Pennsylvania Turnpike it was early evening. The traffic was sparse, but I kept the speedometer at fifty-five. The can, still in the paper bag, was wedged in a crev-ice behind the spare tire.

I felt uneasy, but I didn't know why.

Everything had gone incredibly well. What the Carvells had told me was more important than the can in the trunk or the cash still to be retrieved from the attic. Reynolds didn't have to worry about the testimony of an informant somewhere down the line. Basically, the government's case was known to us, and it was thin. Since the Carvells hadn't mentioned it, I knew the cash was probably still in the attic, and as soon as Cigar moved out on Sunday, I'd move in and pick it up. Cigar, Fechheimer had told me when I'd called the night before, was really a DEA agent out of Boston. The New York plate on his car had come back "no record to be released," and a couple of phone calls to Boston had produced a name to match the description I'd passed on. David was amused that narcs on the East Coast were still registering their cars out of state on the presumption they'd be harder to trace. He was pleased with the latest news and said the case would pick up the "full tab"for Nancy's trip East, including the cost of a baby-sitter.

The meeting with Whitridge had taken eight minutes. I'd signed a rental contract for a week and given him two traveler's checks and a fifty-dollar bill.

So why didn't I feel terrific?

Maybe it was driving five hours on interstate highways. Maybe it was the light.

On a nice day in northern California, the sky was a deep, clear blue. Here, in the haze of the great Northeastern Corridor, it was white. The sun glared, breaking down colors and shades. It left nothing deep, clear, or new. Gone was the high desert clarity of California light with its perpetual promise. In the brightness of that light, you could think of new beginnings and believe in their completion. Northeastern light was the opposite. It brought to mind the raw bone of the actual. Maybe it was the light that made the East seem so dirty.

I was off the Turnpike now, following the meanderings of Old Gulph Road as it made its way from King of Prussia to Haverford. In twenty minutes I'd be there.

Dirty was both the right and the wrong word for the East. Right because it expressed its drab, shopworn quality—the mottled surface of the Henry Hudson Parkway, the newspapers and light garbage clinging to the vertical cement railings of the bridge over the Schuylkill River. Wrong because dirt was on the surface, something you could wipe off. What I was picking up, what was making me anxious, went deeper than dirt.

Take that cliff with the small overhang above the road I'd just passed. There'd been a controversy about it ten years before, when the state Department of Transportation had proposed widening the road and removing the overhang. Apparently Old Gulph Road had been around for several hundred years. Washington had moved his troops over it leaving Valley Forge, and the overhang was mentioned in several Colonial diaries. The Department of Transportation lost the debate; it was left untouched, and several years later I'd nearly demolished the roof of a rental truck on it. Still, it was nice to drive down a road that had accommodated Washington's men.

The maintenance of the past in the present, the coming together of different historical strata in the same building, stretch of road, or curve of river—that too was the East. It wasn't dirt, because it wasn't on the surface. But it showed on the surface as a kind of patina, a mixture of styles and stories. For me, visiting the East was a lot like the visits Julia and Smith make to old London in Orwell's *1984*. Old London is threadbare and decrepit, but its tawdriness exhibits a reality modernity cannot achieve. The East was like that—drab and old. It spoke of limits and restrictions, of culture and tradition, of an actuality that was rooted and immovable. That was why returning to it was making me anxious. By juxtaposition, it raised the one question a California dreamer couldn't answer: Are you dreaming?

I swung right, into the campus, and stopped at the guard shack. The guard didn't know me, but that was no problem. Like many things at Haverford, the security system was too well mannered to work properly. I passed by and pulled up in front of the house we'd left a year before.

"Anybody home?" I yelled through the screen door.

A student came to the door, eating a slice of pizza. "May I help you?" he asked.

"I'm Professor Thompson," I said. "This is my house. You must be one of the subtenants who're staying here this summer."

He told me he was, and that none of the students I'd rented the house to was in town. We had a beer in the kitchen, and he talked about his summer research job at the Center for Non-Violent Conflict Resolution. It seemed that his project, mediation between two Philadelphia youth gangs, had come to a stand-still with the untimely demise of the mediator, a thirty-eight-year-old expert on youth gangs. He gave me a solemn account of how the "expert" had been shot and killed by a police stakeout team while trying to hold up a liquor store on Frankford Avenue. Before he could explain how the Center was shifting its study to focus on police violence, I left him in the kitchen and carried the paper bag upstairs.

The house was in better shape than I'd expected. In the study, a chain and padlock bound the file cabinet where my Kennedy assassination materials were stored. The combination 5–3–6–6

opened the lock, and the chains fell away. I stuffed the paper
bag into the top drawer and relocked the cabinet.

Downstairs, we said the usual things. I told him my wife and
I might be dropping by later on in the week. To his question of
what I was doing in the East, I replied only, "Business."

Walking to the car, I thought of ambling over to the duck
pond. But by the time I'd reached the curb, I wanted to leave.
The lights were coming on up and down College Lane. I turned
the key and headed out of the campus.

SUNDAY, AUGUST 14

Nancy stayed in the car while I went in to get what I wanted
from the hardware store. It was the one with the Glidden paint
sign in the window, two hundred feet from the ferry slip. Ten
minutes later I was back. I hesitated and then opened the trunk,
unzipped Nancy's suitcase, and placed the paper bag from the
hardware store inside it.

"What'd you do with the stuff you bought?" Nancy asked.

"I put it in your suitcase."

"Why couldn't you just leave it in the trunk? It'll mess up my
clothes."

"If I left the bag in the trunk, there's a chance Ben and Ellen
Carvell might come over to the house and see it when I open
the trunk to take our bags in. They might wonder how come
we're arriving for a week's vacation with a light, an extension
cord, and a crowbar."

"That's silly," said Nancy. "You could work things out so
we'd leave our things in the car if they came over to the house
with us."

I pulled away from the curb without saying anything. Why
did she have to argue about everything? I was just being careful.
She let a couple of blocks go by in silence. Then: "I don't like
any part of this. I didn't want to come, and now I wish I hadn't.
The big David Fechheimer treasure hunt. Did he really say 'No
problem, Tink, I'll send you a wife Saturday,' or did you make
that up?"

"That's what the man said. No big deal. Lizzie or Janet
would've come for the plane fare just to get East again."

"I'll bet they would. And you all could've had a marvelous
time with that Thai stick you tucked away in your toilet kit."

She looked at me and then away, out the window. I watched her out of the corner of my eye. Back in those forties movies, Veronica Lake's hair used to fall over one side of her face; Nancy's hair sometimes fell like that, but it was shorter and never fell so directly in front. Nor did her face have Veronica Lake's softness. It was more classically direct, like Julie Christie's in *Doctor Zhivago*, with high cheekbones and a fine nose, blue eyes and a fresh complexion. Seeing her for the first time, you might take her for Scandinavian or North German. She had on a heavy black sweater and a tight green skirt. She looked gorgeous.

We passed around the point of land, where weeds and bushes crowded in from either side. I looked past her at the giant green stalks and oversize leaves creeping onto the roadway. They grew in such riotous profusion here in new England, as if they meant to defy the march of the seasons. Strange, I thought—winter buried in the heart of summer.

We crossed the bridge, and I turned up the lane. Quickly, the gray-blue mass of the house loomed in front of us. There were no cars in the circular driveway, so I parked where Cigar had left his Ford Fairlane the week before.

"Let's go meet the Carvells," I said.

Nancy took my hand as we walked down the asphalt to the Carvell's Cape Cod-style house near the dock.

"I'm sorry," she said as we walked. "I'm just jumpy about this whole thing. And I miss the kids. But I'll be OK. I promise."

As I rang the bell, I could hear Ellen Carvell talking on the phone. Apparently Ben wasn't there. Ellen came to the door and gave us the key. She shook hands with Nancy, and I could see a question shift behind her eyes.

"Ben and I are going over to Shore Acres as soon as he gets back from town," she said, "but the house is all cleaned up. The other tenants left early; he had to get back for something or other. Perhaps you'd like to come by for cocktails tomorrow at five?"

We accepted the invitation and ambled up to the house.

"It's a real bitch, Nancy," I said. "You're too good-looking to be a Haverford faculty wife. Ellen Carvell was wondering about that. I should have had Fechheimer send me a real dog for the week."

"Flattery will get you everywhere. But you've still got all that junk in my suitcase, all that junk you were afraid the Carvells would see."

Later, breathing hard from lugging the suitcases up the stairs to the big bedroom in back, I said, "Come on, let's take a look."

A window on the north side of the attic gave just enough light. The attic was bare, the roof sloping to the floor everywhere except where the dormer window cut in. Near the center, the cracks in the floorboards seemed a trifle larger. Earlier, with Arnold Whitridge, I'd thought I could make out something different about the nail holes in this area, but now I couldn't be sure.

"What do you think, Nancy?"

"This one area looks strange. But the light's so bad I can't tell. When are we going to start prying up boards?"

"Ellen said they'd be leaving as soon as Ben got back from town. Why don't we look around the rest of the house and keep our ears open for their leaving?"

Forty minutes later we'd finished our tour and were sitting in the kitchen when Ben's car drove in next door. Ten minutes after that, it left and we were plugging the light into a wall plug in the attic.

Near the center of the floor a number of boards had been disturbed. When we looked closely we could see pry-marks around the nails and the places where new nails had been used. Nancy held the light as I worked the pry bar. The boards came out with no great difficulty. In the next half hour we pulled out half the boards that had been disturbed. There was insulation underneath, and here and there we could see the indentation of a hand.

"Somebody's already been here," I said. "Shit. They must have found it."

"I hope they did," said Nancy. "Then we can forget all this hugger-mugger stuff. We'll spend a couple of days here to make it look right, and I can get back to California early."

I looked at her but didn't say what had crossed my mind. I started working on another board.

By the time it started to get dark and the light in the attic became visible from outside, we'd lifted every floorboard that showed signs of tampering. I was dripping with sweat. Nancy unplugged the light and rolled up the extension cord, and we clambered down the attic steps.

The call to Fechheimer went much like the initial call the week before. I reported our failure, and he told me to stay put until he spoke directly with the person who'd hidden the thirty thousand. Nancy became impatient as we walked aimlessly around the shopping center, waiting for the pay-phone maneuver to be accomplished. I got annoyed at her impatience. We ate in silence at a crowded restaurant on the waterfront.

MONDAY, AUGUST 15

We were sitting on the bed talking. It was after midnight, and we'd been working on the Thai stick since around eleven. A gas heater was hissing in the corner.

"I had a funny time down in Maryland," I said. "This Catholic priest hung up on me as soon as I got the name Dashiell Hammett out of my mouth. Great start. But then I actually found a relative of Hammett who went to his funeral. She ran a beauty shop and was a real gas. Her mother, Effie, was probably the model for Effie Perine in the *Falcon*."

"Do you like the way this girl has her hair cut?" Nancy was reading *Playboy*, pointing to a blonde with a kind of pageboy cut. "What do you think?"

"I like her," I said.

"Would you like me better like that?"

"Probably not."

"Do you think that would go for most men?"

"Probably."

"OK. I won't have it cut, then." She put the magazine down, and her voice turned serious.

"I never leveled with you about something."

"What's that?"

"Remember that call you made to me from LA after you'd been home to Ohio?" She lay back on the Victorian bed and flicked ashes into an ashtray.

"Yeah."

"I've never had a Thai stick before. Have you?"

"Nope," I answered. "I guess we're both virgins."

"The call was about a jealousy dream you'd had. Do you remember?"

"Sure. It was a couple of months ago."

"You told me you woke up at two-thirty in the morning with

this dream about me walking hand in hand with some faceless guy in the backyard of your parents' home. I think you told me it was out by the swing, back where you used to put up a tent and camp out as a kid.

"Anyway, you had this dream and you called me a couple of nights later. I think you'd gotten back to the West Coast by then. You were in LA or somewhere down south. You called me up and laid out your dream and I pooh-poohed the whole thing, said it was all your imagination. Remember?"

"Yeah."

"But you were right. You knew that, didn't you? Your jealousy sniffer was right on. Even the time was right. I know because I looked at my watch when I left. Two-thirty Eastern time was eleven-thirty Pacific time, and that was when I left his house. You woke up from your dream at the moment I left his house."

"You sure?"

"Of course I'm sure. That's what upset me. I mean, how accurate you were from three thousand miles away."

"Tell me more."

"I don't know. . . . You really want me to? I wouldn't even think of it if I weren't so stoned. OK, why not? Holding out on you has bothered me, and I knew you knew in spite of anything I said. Can you really handle it?"

"Try me."

We were both getting high on the Thai stick. Nancy sat up and tucked her legs underneath her. She was wearing a black bra and half-slip, her blond hair cascading to her shoulders. It seemed longer than I remembered.

"It was a Sunday night, as we both remember. The kids were occupied doing something or other. You'd been in the Midwest for the last ten days. And I was bored. There was a movie on at the film series downtown, so I went. He sat down beside me and started to talk. We hadn't seen each other for a month or two, so when he sat down I was surprised. Then the movie started, and afterward it was the most natural thing in the world to have a drink at the Gibson House and then go to his house for a nightcap or an evening cap or whatever. I remember I got my things together and left at exactly eleven-thirty. And three thousand miles away, in a small town in Ohio, you woke up."

"And him? Is 'he' him?"

"The very one."

She put her hand on the back of my neck.

"Is that why you want to get back?" I asked.

"No. Right now I don't want to go anywhere. Do you?"

I quit pulling back. We kissed and touched and played and danced the old dance. At first I kept expecting it to run as it always had. But then the rhythm changed. Some knot loosened, and I started to lose track of who we were. It didn't seem to matter.

Still, I couldn't let it go.

"So what will happen when you get back? Will it be more of the same?" I asked.

"Not unless you want it that way and can't accept what I'm trying to give you. I'm tired of playing games and pretending to be something I'm not. We've hurt each other enough. I want the war to be over."

Gradually the net of irritation and recrimination that had bound us for so long fell away. It had been so long since we'd made love without anger, the whole experience seemed new. The August breeze riffled the curtains on the window and flowed over us. We moved in the stream and then lay still.

Afterward, we went downstairs and fixed ourselves a snack. We sat at the wooden table in the middle of the kitchen and let the Thai stick clear our bloodstreams. I raised a glass of milk and winked at Nancy.

"Success to crime!"

"I was just thinking of that," she said. "What happens if we really do find the thirty thousand? I noticed you weren't above ripping off the client's very excellent Thai stick. What about the thirty thousand? A sixty-five-thousand-dollar house with thirty thousand in cash in the floorboards is a bargain. We ought to buy it."

"That," I said quickly, "would be really stupid. Buying it, I mean. But the thirty thousand, that's something else. On top of half pay from Haverford and the money I've made as a detective, thirty thousand dollars would make this year a real zinger."

"I guess I was thinking something like that too, but if we took the money, wouldn't both Fechheimer and this guy Reynolds be after us?"

"Not likely. Given what I've already told David about the handprints in the insulation, everybody in San Francisco must be thinking the money's gone. That's exactly what *I'm* thinking. Even if it never showed up as evidence in the case, they'd just figure one of the cops ripped it off. If, due to some colossal good luck, we ended up finding the cash, we could probably rip it off.''

"But like our ex-President said, 'We could do that, but it would be wrong!' "

"True. But this treasure hunt isn't going anywhere. Everything we saw yesterday says the cops—or *a* cop—already picked up the money. All we have is a can with some dumb documents and the Thai stick. You really think it was dishonest of me to rip it off?''

"Sure.''

"That's what I thought you'd say. What if I told Fechheimer I took it? Would it still be dishonest?''

"No. Then I suppose it'd be some kind of 'tip.' He'd think it was funny the professor managed a tip for himself. And he might begin wondering if you also arranged a slightly larger tip.''

"Actually it was only half a Thai stick.''

"So?''

I put the milk down and began spreading peanut butter on a piece of whole wheat bread. The munchies. Nancy was still looking at me.

"Don't you like this better than being the wife of a college professor?'' I asked.

"I don't know. When people ask me what my husband does, I don't tell them he's a private detective. I guess I'm just not used to it. I tell them you're a professor on sabbatical. The other's just a bit too—I don't know—sleazy.''

"You mean private detectives are the kind of people who are sent after money and who, if they get a chance, take the money and run? While college professors teach courses in ethics and talk a lot about 'principles' and are never sent after money in dope cases?''

"Maybe.''

"And if they *were* sent after money in a dope case?''

"They'd probably sit around the kitchen with their wife having a dumb discussion about nonexistent money. They'd talk the issue to death but would never find the money. And if by some thundering good luck they did find the money, they'd dutifully turn it over because they were too scared to do anything else. That about right?''

"Yeah.''

"I thought so. It fits that weird prejudice you have about

college professors being sissies. So I guess you've got a choice: either be a sleazeball or a sissy.''

She got up, put her glass and plate in the sink, and pulled her robe around her.

"You think the kids are OK?'' she asked. "It's only ten-fifteen California time. We could go to the shopping center and call them.''

"Let's go to bed,'' I said, putting my arm round her waist as she passed my chair. "It's late.''

FOUR

"I MIGHT'VE MADE
THE WHOLE THING UP"

TUESDAY, AUGUST 16, 1977

I watched from the sitting-room window as Nancy pulled out of the driveway. The Pennsylvania plate on the back of the Chevy wagon got smaller as she turned left onto the lane. That Pennsylvania plate had been one reason for starting from Philadelphia. Last Friday at the Philadelphia airport, the Hertz clerk had said a station wagon was available. I would have settled for a large sedan, but a station wagon was better. The usual fingernail under a couple of Hertz stickers, and we had the perfect vehicle for Professor Thompson's nuclear family. Nancy had arrived in early evening; we'd spent that night at a downtown Philadelphia Howard Johnson's, neither of us wanting to drive out to Haverford.

That was four days ago.

This morning we'd gotten up luxuriously late. Sunlight filled the kitchen as we drank coffee and juice and ate blueberry muffins Ellen Carvell had given us the day before. The muffins hadn't caused the fight, but they'd been part of it.

"I just don't feel right about it," Nancy had said. "They're being so nice to us. I really like them, especially Ellen. I think they like us. And we're manipulating them. How can you sit there and eat those muffins and not feel anything?"

"Look, it's a business deal," I'd said. "Nothing more or less. I pay them two hundred and fifty dollars of Reynolds's money, and they rent us the house for a week."

"You know there's more to it than that. You've told them you

104

might buy their house. They're really expecting it. They're not pursuing other offers. We may be costing them a lot of money. The summer's almost over."

"Costing 'em money? How about the money they cost Reynolds? By the time this quiet little disaster is zipped up it will have cost him millions, not to mention the time he's spent in jail and will spend in jail. All because Ben fucking Carvell got a little curious and let his high-school chum put a surveillance team in his garage. What are the ethics of that? You rent your house to someone and then call the cops on him?"

"The ethics of that are reporting suspicious circumstances to the authorities. When did you get so solicitous for the financial wellbeing of dope dealers? I'll tell you when. About the time you started working for 'em! Something's happened to you, Tink. I don't know what it is, but something's happened to you. You're getting hard in ways I don't understand and don't really like. Sometimes I don't recognize you, I don't recognize that sweet, sort of literary fellow I married almost twenty years ago—"

"Jesus fucking Christ! Literary—"

"That's another thing. You use *fuck* a lot more than you used to. It's vulgar."

I drove to the store and bought a paper. Then we agreed that Nancy would drive into town and take a sightseeing boat around the harbor. I needed a couple of hours to write a report on the two days I'd spent the previous week doing research on Dashiell Hammett.

After watching Nancy leave, I gathered a yellow pad of notes, *The Maltese Falcon*, and a book on Maryland history and spread them out on a table in the sitting room.

The history book was called *Yesterday in Old St. Mary's County*. I'd purchased it at the Historical Society early that first day, when it had seemed I wouldn't have much to report to David. When it became clear I'd be sitting on the East Coast for several days with nothing to do, he'd suggested I do some research on Hammett's origins. I was being paid a hundred dollars a day whether I did anything or not, so whatever David wanted was fine with me. I'd looked forward to being a scholar again, if only for a day or two.

I started leafing through the book. The author had been born in Saint Mary's County on the night in 1910 when "Halley's comet passed over." I checked the index for *Hammett* and found only one reference, to a Dr. Charles Hammett, apparently a

Washington, D.C., eye specialist. The book might give some general background on Saint Mary's County, but it wouldn't provide much on the Hammetts in particular. No matter; I'd gathered a lot of Hammett material on my own.

I laid out my notes.

How to organize them? Memorandum? Letter?

Why not use the standard of the detective trade, the "Report of Investigation"? After all, I'd been paid to do the work as David's operative. I might have thought of myself as a literary type while I was doing it, but I was really only an operative doing legwork—the same thing Hammett used to do. I'd be just one "op" writing up the background of another.

I started to write on the legal-size pad:

August 16, 1977

David B. Fechheimer
1803 Laguna Street
San Francisco, California 94115

Re: Samuel Dashiell Hammett
File # [Not Assigned]

REPORT OF INVESTIGATION

Saint Mary's County, Maryland, was visited on August 11-12, 1977. It is located approximately sixty miles southeast of Washington, D.C. In many respects, the countryside resembles tidewater Virginia—gently rolling hills with rich, dark earth growing corn, tobacco, and vegetables, many small towns, and here and there a plantation dating back to the seventeenth century. Leonardtown is the county seat, but Lexington Park—adjoining one side of the Patuxent Naval Air Station—appears to be the commercial center of the county.

A search of public records disclosed the following information.

Birth records of the Saint Mary's County Health Department begin in 1898. Prior to 1898, records of birth are to be found in the baptismal records kept by the individual parish churches. Saint Mary's County Historical Society provided a handwritten slip of paper labeled "Copy of Baptismal Record of Samuel Dashiell Hammett." This document read as follows:

BORN: May 27, 1884(sic)

BAPTIZED: July 5, 1894 at St. Nicholas' Church.
PARENTS: Richard Thomas Hammett
            Anna Bond Dashiel(sic)
SPONSORS: David and Henriett(sic)Hammett
PRIEST: J.M. GIROUD, S.J.

Saint Nicholas's Church no longer exists, all its records having been moved to Saint Michael's Church some time ago. A notation at the bottom of the slip indicated that the information it contained was drawn from the baptismal record on file at Saint Michael's. Since the birth date and spellings of "Dashiel" and "Henriett" appeared to be incorrect, a call was made to Father Cooney of Saint Michael's. Father Cooney exploded as soon as the name "Dashiell Hammett" was mentioned. He stated he had been bothered enough about Hammett, that approximately a year previous a New York lawyer writing a book on Hammett had bothered him, and that other people had been asking "stupid" questions about Hammett. Father Cooney hung up before it was possible to tell him the purpose of the inquiry. Mrs. Palmer of the Historical Society said she would send one of her researchers to Saint Michael's to check Hammett's baptismal record and report the results to this office.

My report went on to describe what I'd found in the *Death Records* and in the *General Index to Land Records*. But something had been bothering me as I described Father Cooney's response. It was the awkwardness of the Report of Investigation format. Not only were all opinions and editorial comments to be kept out, but the writer was never to use the pronouns *I* or *me*. At one point I'd wanted to say, "I called Father Cooney and . . ."; instead, I'd had to rearrange the sentence in the passive voice. In earlier reports, I remembered, I'd written myself into corners where the only way out was to refer to myself in the third person ("This investigator challenged Miss Fellman's opinion that he was not entitled to see the document . . ."). I'd seen the third person used in many reports by other detectives. Why did the Report of Investigation seek to remove the writer from the document at the price of such awkwardness?

After describing my visit to the house where Hammett was born, I leafed through notes of my interview with his second cousin. She was the owner of the Milestown Beauty Salon. We'd sat on adjoining green vinyl chairs as her customers eyed us from under their hairdryers.

Jane Fish Yowaisky
Old Annapolis Wharf Road
Maddox, Maryland 20621

Yowaisky was interviewed at her workplace on the morning of August 12, 1977. She is the second cousin of Dashiell Hammett. Her mother, Effie Marie Miles Fish, is Dashiell Hammett's first cousin, and was a secretary to many business and community organizations in the area. Yowaisky believes that Effie Fish may be a model for "Effie Perine," the fictional secretary to Sam Spade in The Maltese Falcon.

Yowaisky stated she attended Hammett's funeral at Arlington Memorial Cemetery in Arlington, Virginia, on January 16, 1961. According to Yowaisky, six people attended the funeral: herself, her father, Riba Hammett (sister of the deceased), Charles Mattingly, Agnes Mattingly (first cousin of the deceased), and Lillian Hellman. She recalled it was a simple military funeral. Lillian Hellman, she said, wore a fur coat and shivered noticeably at each volley of shots from the honor guard. Hellman was given the flag covering Hammett's casket but exchanged only a few words with the rest of the mourners. Richard "Dick" Hammett, the deceased's brother and a Standard Oil executive, had been expected at the funeral, but failed to appear. At the conclusion of the service, said Yowaisky, all the mourners went their separate ways with scarcely a word to one another.

Yowaisky had a sharp recollection of visits Hammett's father made to her family home in the 1930s. He would come as "the King," she recalled, to visit his sister, Yowaisky's grandmother. Yowaisky gave up her room to accommodate him and regularly brought him a basin of water in the morning for shaving. She recalled him as a big man—six foot three or four and well over two hundred pounds—with the beginnings of a potbelly, snow-white hair, and dark black eyes. On these visits, Richard Thomas Hammett often wore formal clothes and, according to Yowaisky, "looked just like the governor of Maryland." He had a reputation around Baltimore as "quite a ladies' man" and often would appear in Saint Mary's

County in cars driven by attractive women in their midthirties. He would introduce his companion of the moment as "so-and-so, my friend," said Yowaisky.

It was well known in the family, said Yowaisky, that Hammett's father did not like the people Dashiell Hammett was socializing with in Baltimore. On one occasion in 1940, Yowaisky heard Richard Thomas Hammett say, "Well, I always did think these people he [Dashiell Hammett] was running around with in Baltimore were Communists." Dashiell Hammett, for his part, was not particularly close to his father. Yowaisky believed the younger Hammett resented the necessity of his mother working and blamed this on his father.

Yowaisky said Dashiell Hammett was devoted to his mother, who was known in the family as "Aunt Annie." She suffered from tuberculosis for some time, but Yowaisky does not know if she finally succumbed to that disease. Dashiell Hammett was not a devout Catholic, said Yowaisky, and went to church only when his mother made him. As a boy and later as a young man, he was known to love detective stories. "Aunt Annie" was known often to spend most of a morning getting her son out of bed after a late night of reading. Consequently, he was chronically late for work during his years in Baltimore.

The family, said Yowaisky, considered Dashiell Hammett "very smart." Her mother taught her that Hammett was a relative "to be proud of." She said family pride in Hammett continued unabated through the witch-hunt years of the 1950s. Little was known in the family of Hammett's later years—only that he had tuberculosis, married his nurse and had two children by her, then went on to become a famous writer. No one in the family knew Hammett's wife or his two children.

Yowaisky expressed an interest in learning the addresses of Hammett's wife and daughters in Los Angeles. She stated she would be willing to answer additional questions and supplied the above two phone numbers for that purpose.

The interview with Yowaisky was tape-recorded with her knowledge and permission.

Investigation is not continuing.

(SIGNATURE)

JT/gs
ENCLOSURES (UNDER SEPARATE COVER)
    tape of Yowaisky interview
    <u>*Yesterday in Old St. Mary's County*</u>
    map of St. Mary's County
    selected pamphlets on St. Mary's County

It wasn't literary. It couldn't be. That was the point of a Report of Investigation: its strictures made embellishment difficult. If written correctly, it was gritty and hard. It put the center of gravity out there in the world, and shrank the subject to a vanishing still point. Its ideal—unrealizable—was to make its author disappear altogether, and that was also the source of its awkwardness, the forced grammar used to bury the *I* in the muffled passages of the passive voice or hide it under a disingenuous third person. Then, too, it also included some seller's puff. It was the basic vehicle for communicating with a client, and for that reason was designed to reenforce the client's expectations. The client wanted information—objective, uninterpreted, unskewed facts. The client had hired not a "private I" but a "private eye." He or she wanted to know what that *eye* had uncovered, not how the *I* behind the *eye* interpreted what it had seen. The impersonal tone, the disembodied voice of the speaker in the investigative report—all of that was window-dressing. It stoked the client's fantasy that he or she could buy unvarnished facts. It encouraged a fallacy of misplaced objectivity.

There was also another aspect to it. It lay in the modesty of the Report of Investigation, in all it *didn't* say, in the silences that fell between the uninterpreted facts, in its refusal to tell a story. And that, I suddenly understood, was why it was the perfect vehicle for conveying what I'd learned about Hammett.

The week before, I'd interviewed Effie's daughter, but in the days and weeks prior to that interview, I'd often encountered the fictional Effie. It had all started that afternoon on Grove Street when I reread the Flitcraft episode. After that reading, I was hooked; *The Maltese Falcon* became a kind of original text against which I kept comparing my own experience. Packing to fly East, I'd tossed the book into my suitcase. In Boston, in Nonquitt Harbor, in Philadelphia, and in a $12.88-a-night motel near Leonardtown, Maryland, I'd opened its black cover and burrowed into it. I'd underlined passages and written notes in the margins. After a while I'd come to recognize I was actually *studying* it, a fact that seemed mildly embarrassing. Was this what happened to you after fifteen years of making a living studying texts? Do you end up studying detective novels?

But I wasn't studying the *Falcon* out of habit. I was studying it because there was something in it that didn't come clear on the surface. There were meanings to be deciphered in the book, and they weren't the sort of thing you'd expect a literary critic to be concerned with. They were asides, *aperçus*, and references that connected in some uncanny way with my own experience of the last year. Some would remind me of a jam I'd gotten into or of a technique Fechheimer had used or suggested to me. Others were more general and referred to basic features of Spade's experience. A lot of my notes, for example, had to do with what I called "Spade's worldliness."

Actually, these were more than notes. The previous week, the night before interviewing Effie's daughter, I'd sat at a glass-topped desk in the Elmo Motel in Leonardtown, Maryland, flipped to the back of the yellow legal pad I was using for interview notes, and begun to write. At first slowly, and then more quickly as the idea took hold, I'd written about the *Falcon* and about Spade. It was easy to find those pages now, sandwiched between notes of the Yowaisky interview and expense-account calculations:

Everything seems to happen just outside Spade's peripheral vision. Events intrude from out of frame, like the half-dead Jacobi, falcon in arms, stumbling into Spade's office. The novel is built in a series of dialogues; its artistry lies in the fact it permits the world—like the San Francisco fog—to seep through between the lines, rising always from a ground just out of sight.

Spade can never get to a position where clear seeing is possible. He's always too much in the middle of things. When Jacobi arrives with the falcon, Spade must act before he knows who this man is or how he was shot or why he has come to his office. But that's precisely the problem posed by the novel: how to survive in a world where there are no general principles to guide action, where one plays the percentages, follows rules of thumb, trusts hunches, and has to act swiftly—all without any sort of rational comprehension. A world where judgment is often irrelevant and sometimes dangerous.

"My way of learning," Spade says at one point, "is to heave a wild and unpredictable monkey-wrench into the machinery." Like the continental op of the early stories, Spade's strategy is to "stir things up" and watch what happens. In the *Falcon* the things that happen include the death of Spade's partner, Brigid's imprisonment, Cairo's flight, and Gutman's death at the hands of Wilmer. Spade doesn't directly bring about any of these things; he does things or reacts to what other people do, and other things happen. Getting his client (Brigid) arrested, for example, is hardly a successful conclusion to a case.

Some of Spade's actions go beyond their intentions, some fall short, others boomerang on the actor. The point of all this is that actions hardly ever turn out to be what one expects them to be. Spade's wisdom consists in knowing that any action is, inherently, partly out of control, that actions must be herded or ridden but not programmed. The world changes actions, nullifying some, putting "backspin" on others.

In Spade, then, we have a portrait of the detective as fully worldly, as literally awash in the world. Is this what Raymond Chandler (cf "The Simple Art of Murder") meant when he said Hammett took murder out of the drawing room and put it in the alley where it belonged?

Think of the structure of the standard detective novel (cf Steven Marcus's introduction to *The Continental Op*). Think of Conan Doyle or Dorothy Sayers or any of the others. Think of the primacy they give reasoned judgment. The detective judges with heroic incisiveness and power. At the outset, he is presented with a fiction. No matter; he'll figure it out. He'll find that one something that doesn't "fit." A clue, an expression on a character's face, a letter with a wrong date starts his mind churning. He pursues this clue. He investigates, pries, searches for the truth. And finally, at the end of a long process of reasoning, he makes a breakthrough. The case is "broken," the fiction is seen through, and behind it the truth is discovered. Either the butler did it or he didn't. But it is the detective's power of judgment—his reason—that "cracks" the case. The standard detective novel is really a product of the eighteenth century, a celebration of the power of reason.

What of Hammett?

Hammett belongs to a different century.

The Maltese Falcon begins in the usual way. Spade is confronted with a fiction: Brigid O'Shaughnessy's self-serving and fraudulent account of who she is and what she's doing. But from this point the book diverges from the standard model. Spade "stirs things up." From time to time, he even tries to "figure things out." But most of the time he is immune to this temptation, and his figuring never leads to a solution to anything.

It is the other people in the book who try to "figure things out." District Attorney Bryan, for example, hatches a tripartite scheme of possible solutions to Thursby's murder. It's a reasonable scheme, only it has nothing to do with the facts of Thursby's death at the hands of Wilmer. Effie jumps to the false conclusion that Archer's wife, Iva, killed him, because Iva was out on the night of his death. Within the skein of lie and interest that makes up the *Falcon*, figuring things out leads only to error.

At the close of the book we're no closer to knowing the true story of Brigid, Thursby, Cairo, Gutman, and the falcon than we were at the beginning. Events have transpired. People have died. Other people have been arrested. But we're left with only another fiction no more profound, no more revealing, than Brigid's originating one. Who substituted the lead figure for the bejeweled falcon? Was it really the Russian general, Kemidov? Or is Gutman's ready acceptance of Kemidov as villain only a ruse to lull Brigid, Wilmer, Cairo, and Spade to sleep? Might Brigid have sent a dummy falcon with Jacobi while shipping the real one by a more circuitous and secure route? Or might Thursby have double-crossed the lot of them? To none of these questions do we have an answer for by the very nature of Hammett's vision no answers are possible. Any answers will contain more questions.

We haven't moved from illusion to truth. We haven't seen Spade "crack the case." Rather, we've watched Spade participate in a series of events that break up the initial illusion only to replace it with another. There's no truth anywhere in the story, only ambiguous half-truths, only a face seen darkly in a mirror, a figure disappearing around a corner.

And that, I said to myself, is how it seems to be. That was why Hammett was taking up so much space in the back of

my head. Fechheimer knew all this. He knew the detective is
no hero of reason. That's why he'd been so amused by my
early attempts to figure out a case by reading and rereading
the file. He knew the detective's world is not the sunlit world
of the eighteenth-century philosophers, but a nightmare world
where hunch and chance are more important than logical
acuteness.

The Professor was still present in these notes. Here and there
he could be seen reaching for an effect, giving a phrase a poetic
twist, embellishing, embroidering. It was easy to get caught up
in the athletic joy of writing, to become infatuated with the
sound and rhythm of language.

But wasn't the Professor struggling with something real?
Wasn't he trying to identify something in the *Falcon* that would
make sense of what he was doing now in New England? And
beyond that, make sense of what he was doing, period? I ripped
the pages of the investigative report out of the pad and addressed
an envelope to David. On the right lay the Report of Investigation. On the left lay the pad with the Professor's thoughts on the
Falcon.

Those thoughts seemed both familiar and obscure—familiar
in that the rhythms and the voice belonged to an earlier me,
obscure in that I no longer recognized them as mine. They
belonged to another time, to New Haven and Haverford and
Denmark.

By comparison, the Report was modest, even pedestrian. It
risked no conclusions. Its style was matter-of-fact. On this August morning, with the sea breeze stirring the curtains of the
Carvell family home and teasing the papers on the oak table
before me, it seemed more than enough.

THURSDAY, AUGUST 18

The knob for the lights came off in my hand. I'd grabbed for it
when Nancy shut her door, and the round plastic disk had slipped
free. The rod had a knurled end. You could just barely move it
by gripping the tip with your fingers.

"Another triumph of American workmanship," I said, shifting the Chevy wagon into drive and turning left onto the lane.
Another car had its lights on high-beam, blinding me as we

passed the meadow and salt marsh two hundred feet from the house. "Asshole!" I yelled, flicking the dimmer up and down.

We'd been here too long, waiting. It was Thursday night, and there was still nothing definite from Fechheimer. He was "working on it," he'd said at around four that afternoon. The guy who'd hidden the money was in Hawaii, and it was taking time to set up a phone contact. I was to call every afternoon at four until contact was made. We'd already taken all the tours, visited all the shops, and even gone back and photocopied the local papers on the Reynolds bust. There wasn't anything else to do.

"I want to be on that plane Sunday come what may," said Nancy. "That'll make ten days, long enough to have been away."

"OK," I said, turning left now at the shopping center intersection and heading for the harbor. It was nine-thirty. Most of the people going anywhere were already there. Traffic was light on the highway into Nonquitt Harbor. "We can come up with some excuse why you had to leave and I'm staying on."

"You think David's really trying to reach this guy?" she asked. "Something in the back of my mind tells me David's very glad you're here in New England. He sure is taking his time."

"Come on," I said. "The dope world isn't like IBM. It takes a while to find people, especially after there's been a bust." At the same time, I was thinking David had his own priorities, and my hundred a day plus expenses didn't make it to the top of his list.

Something else was bothering me, and I didn't know what it was. Something out of place. I reached into my inside pocket and fished out a pack of Kools.

"Any bets on whether the lighter works?" I asked.

I was taking the first drag on the cigarette when I recognized what it was. The same pair of headlights had been with us since we'd crossed the bridge on the main road. They'd been hanging there, a couple of hundred feet back, for the last mile or so.

"I think we've got company," I said. "The trouble is I haven't the foggiest who it might be."

"What do you mean?"

"From the size of the headlights, it looks like a full-size American car. Back a couple of hundred feet. It's been with us for the last mile or so.

"What're we going to do?"

"Just drive normally for a while. Who the hell could it be?"

"DEA?"

"Possibly. There could've been a tap on David's phone when he told me to take the can as evidence. But if it's them, it's an awfully clumsy tail. You didn't see anything earlier did you?"

"Nope."

I didn't like this at all. Whose movie were we in? Whatever it was, I didn't like the *we* part. This was supposed to be a safe deal, with a vacation for two thrown in.

At the corner, I turned right. The car followed. Two lefts and a right, and we were back on the main drag, mercury-vapor lamps yellowing the roadway.

"I'm going to pull over in about two hundred yards," I said. "I'm going to leave it in PARK with the engine running. If he stops, I'll get out and walk back there. Slip into the driver's seat and watch me in the mirror. If anything happens—and I mean *anything*—take off. OK?"

"I don't have any money. I don't want to go back to that house. I'm scared."

"Here we go," I said.

The other car stopped, with its headlights on, under the last overhead street lamp. It was a late-sixties Mustang with a Massachusetts license—DRM 658. "Dream six-fifty-eight," I said aloud to fix it in memory. It was quiet. My boots tapped on the roadway.

The light from the street lamp left the interior of the car in full shadow. I couldn't see who it was until I'd passed the front bumper.

"Hi, Briar," I said, leaning down to talk through the open driver's window.

"Evening, Tink. I'd like you to meet Estelle Buchman."

He nodded toward the dark-haired woman in the passenger seat. She looked like a younger Barbara Walters, features sagging a bit but still attractive, even exotic-looking. I mumbled the usual to her and then turned back to Reynolds.

"Sheila called just a bit ago," he said.

He was wearing a patterned yellow bow tie and an expensive sport coat. They were going out.

"We were talking," he went on, "and Sheila mentioned that Fechheimer wanted to talk to you. So I told her I'd stop by your place on the way into town. Hope I didn't spook you."

"No, just didn't recognize the car. Hadn't seen it before."

"It's Estelle and Kurt's. I'm staying with them. You remember the place. Estelle and I were on the lane near the Carvells' when you pulled out. We figured you were probably going to town too. I'd say let's have dinner together, but Sheila seemed to think it was fairly important you call San Francisco."

"Thanks a million, Briar. I'll take care of it right away."

"What was that all about?" asked Nancy, a few seconds later.

"That was Jamie's brother, Briar. I told you about giving him the ten thousand—really the nine thousand, nine hundred. He was just relaying a message to call Fechheimer. Why don't you make a U-turn and go back to the shopping center."

By eight-forty I'd made the call and we were driving back to the house.

"Will we have to pull up a lot of boards?" Nancy wanted to know.

"None. The guy in Hawaii said he just laid the bag under the edge of the floor. Remember that railing at the top of the stair?"

"Yeah."

"That lines us up. We go up the stairs and turn a hundred and eighty degrees. That railing will be right beside us now, on the right. We walk straight to the end of the attic, reach under, and the bag ought to be there."

I was thinking now that the cops must have found it. The attic had been searched. If the money was just shoved under the boards at one end, they must've found it. They couldn't have missed something that easy.

Either way, though, we'd be out of here the next day.

I felt for the light switch to the right of the attic door. The hundred-watt bulb in the ceiling seemed almost too bright. Nancy stood off to the side, watching.

I felt the top of the railing and then cast off, walking directly to the far end of the attic. I reached under.

"Nothing," I said disgustedly. "There's a goddamn two-by-twelve that probably runs the whole width of the attic. You couldn't hide anything here if you wanted to."

I started feeling all the way to the right and left along the two-by-twelve. There were two seams where similar planks joined the center section. But no cavities, no interruptions in the rough, blank faces of the boards. Discouraged and nervous, I walked back to the center.

The air, heated by the late-afternoon sun beating on the roof, was warm and close. A single fly was buzzing near the naked light bulb. My nervousness grew. I turned at a right angle to the railing, walked to the middle of the northwest side of the attic, and reached under.

My hand hit something. Something that rustled to the touch. Not a newspaper. A bag. *The* bag!

I pulled it out—an ordinary supermarket bag—and reached inside. There were several packets bound with rubber bands. I knew it was money even before I'd pulled out one of the packets and looked at the *100* on the bill.

"I've got it!" I yelled. "I've really got it. It was here all along."

We took the bag downstairs to the master bedroom. Nancy pulled the curtains, and I dumped the packets out on the bed. There were six in all, two larger than the other four. She took one of the big packets and peeled off the rubber band. It contained one hundred fifty-dollar bills—all pretty old. I did the same thing with one of the smaller packets. It contained fifty hundred-dollar bills—some new, some old. We looked at thirty thousand dollars in six packets of five thousand dollars each.

"Great," said Nancy. "We've got the money. We can leave tomorrow. Job's done. Let's get to that restaurant before it closes. I'm hungry. All this hugger-mugger stuff does that to you, doesn't it? I mean, gives you an appetite?"

At the restaurant, I excused myself from the table and called Fechheimer to let him know we'd found the money.

"I can't steal it," I told Nancy abruptly when I got back. "It's real. It's in the trunk of our car. Before we had it, I was tempted. But not anymore. It's too real. I'm sorry."

"Are you really?"

"What?"

"Are you sorry?"

"No. I guess not."

"Who just said that? The professor or the detective?"

"I don't know which one."

"I think," said Nancy, "I'll have the pound-and-a half lobster. Stuffed with crabmeat."

SUNDAY, AUGUST 21

Logan Airport, Boston. I saw Fechheimer's bag before I saw him. There was a crush of people at the gate meeting TWA

Flight 478 from San Francisco. I was getting nervous. Had he missed the plane? Or had *I* missed *him*? Then, behind a seven-year-old carrying an inflated crocodile, I saw the leather top of David's bag sitting on the floor. It came from Hunting World in New York and cost $750, an incredible sum for a bag that was little more than an overgrown briefcase. Sumptuously made of saddle leather and a nylon exotic called Battue Cloth, it had innumerable pockets and a shoulder strap. I'd long coveted it and promised myself when I got my detective's license, I'd splurge and buy one like it. A black umbrella was cuffed against the leather top, just below the handle.

David was beyond the bag, talking into a pay phone. He had on a blue blazer, Italian shirt, and jeans. Under his cropped beard, his chin made a kind of V, matching the V above formed by his thick brows and tousled brown hair. His face was tanned, his eyes bloodshot. He looked tired. When I picked up his bag to move it against the wall, he glanced over and signaled he'd be off the phone in a second.

"Have a good vacation?" he asked a moment later as we shook hands.

"Profitable," I said.

David was scanning the crowd over my shoulder.

"I kept the station wagon," I continued. "I'll bring it up to the arrivals curb while you pick up your other bag."

Twenty minutes later we joined the sparse flow of traffic into Sumner Tunnel. David navigated us south through a maze of freeway signs until we were on I-93, heading for Rhode Island. Quickly, he filled me in. I knew he'd come East to help arrange Reynolds's $1,250,000 bail. But why were we heading for Rhode Island?

"When all this blew up, Reed was vacationing with friends of his parents on the Sound below Fall River," explained David, and then, inexplicably, he fell silent.

We passed Brockton, and the evening light began to fade.

"You turn right there, where the sign says Route 104," he said, looking up from the map. "Then there'll be some more turns."

As the car swung onto the new route, David leaned back against the door and continued to fill me in.

"Briar will go to Paris to meet with some family who will end up fronting the money. But it's going to be complicated with the wire transfers in and out of Zurich. I thought it best we all meet down here while the deal is being set up. Briar sailed the yawl over and should be waiting for us. Sheila and Cathy are with him on the boat."

"Sheila I know," I said. "But who are the rest of these people?"

"Cathy is Briar's girlfriend. Didn't you meet her up there?"

"Nope. The last time I saw Briar he was riding around in a 'sixty-eight Mustang with someone called Estelle."

"Cathy's got short, dark hair. Good body. Probably mid-thirties."

"That wasn't Estelle. But go on. Reed Collins I've heard you talk about. Some kind of lawyer, right?"

"Yeah. He got out of Boalt Hall in the late sixties and hung around the prison movement for a time. I met him in the San Quentin Six case. Then he moved back East to New Haven. I thought you knew he handled the bail hearing in Boston?"

"Terrific job. Only a million two hundred fifty thousand."

"That wasn't his fault. The DEA had the magistrate wired. Oh, speaking of money. That thirty grand you picked up turns out to be more a pain in the ass than anything else. You can't legally take more than five thousand in cash out of the country, so neither Briar nor I can carry it with us. You'll have to take it back to the West Coast with you. Got a safe in Bolinas?"

"A professor with a safe? You kidding?" I hesitated, pushed in the cigarette lighter, and looked at David. "I should have saved everybody the trouble and ripped it off."

"Rent a safety deposit box, then," he went on. "A big one. Can you hold on to it till I get back?"

I nodded.

I'd rigged a nice glow by electing myself hero of the month. But it wasn't turning out that way. Jesus! I bust my ass to get the thirty thousand, and it turns out to be just a bother to have around. And if I lost it?

"Briar," said David, reading my mind, "told Sheila he got only nine thousand, nine hundred. That right?"

"Yeah. I don't know. I must have miscounted back in San Francisco."

"OK, I'll eat it this time. But double-check your count in the future. Those are the rules. Did you really offer Briar a receipt?"

"Yeah."

Silently, the small Rhode Island towns drifted by: Tiverton,

Adamsville, Little Compton. Neither by name nor sight could they be mistaken for their California counterparts.

Inwardly I was steaming. I'd succeeded brilliantly. And what did I get? A ration of shit. This was the toughest job Fechheimer had ever given me, and . . .

"I know you're angry," he said, "but you seemed nauseatingly pleased with yourself at the airport. The Greeks have a word for it, Professor. Not *kairos*, but *hubris*. It never hurts to be reminded of one's failings."

"Did you ever hear from Irene Kuznetzov again?"

"Yeah. Her daughter was picked up for speeding in Ashtabula, Ohio. They're in contact and by now have probably met. She told me she liked your touch. You go see a detective, and end up being told about *kairos*."

"That's nice," I said, thinking to myself that Fechheimer was playing me like a violin.

We were silent now as the light faded. I flipped off the air-conditioner and opened the window. Immediately the heavy scent of the sea blew into the car, and with it memories of Virginia Beach, Pensacola, and St. Thomas. Even on Fisherman's Wharf in San Francisco you can't really smell the sea. Fish and crabs, yes, but not the sea. It must have to do with the water temperature. But even in February you could smell the sea in Norfolk, or in Pensacola, at that little cove and beach near the Officer's Club. I remembered swimming there in late afternoon. It'd been September—hurricane season—and there'd been other smells. The chemical odor, for example, that oozed up near the seaplane ramp. Now, years later, whenever I ran into that smell, Pensacola in September 1957 would stream back. The mnemonic power of smell. Like tonight. Here in this car. Smelling the sea.

"Take your next right," said David.

I nodded and turned into a long driveway that wound through woods and then curved along a spit of land. The estate was huge.

"Where's the house?" I asked.

"According to Reed's instructions, you still have a couple of curves to go. The main house should be out on the end. There are a couple of other—what would you call them?—large guesthouses. I don't know if anyone's living in them now. We'll be in the main house. By the way, our hosts are named Haddon. Their first names are Woolrich and Charlotte."

"I think I'll just settle for Mr. and Mrs. Haddon, thanks. He's not a doctor or anything like that?"

"No Dr. Thompson, he's not a doctor. Should I introduce my prized operative as 'Doctor'?"

"That would be tacky. The Ivy League shuns that sort of thing. And we're going to be so Ivy, vines'll be growing out of our pockets, right?"

"You got it," said David.

Turning the last of the bends in the driveway, we could see part of the Sound to the northeast. There was a light bobbing in the waves about a quarter mile offshore. I thought of the yawl.

"That them?"

"Most likely. They were supposed to get in early afternoon today."

I pulled the station wagon into a diagonal parking space near the front door between a Toyota with Connecticut plates and an older-model Plymouth. The Toyota was probably Reed's. The Haddons must be driving the old Plymouth. That figured. The reverse ostentation of Eastern money. In California the old Plymouth would have been a new Jag.

We met everyone on the front steps, which led to a broad shingled porch. A friendly Alaskan husky bounded up to the car before we got out. Reed took the dog by the collar and then extended his hand. He was in his early thirties, blond and angular with horn-rimmed glasses. He had the bone structure and speech rhythms of the East Coast; even tanned and jeans-clad, he'd never be taken for a Californian. Woolrich Haddon gave us a hearty welcome, bantering with David about us being private eyes. He had on plaid pants and a tan Shetland sweater and was holding a Meerschaum. Charlotte Haddon was gracious but a bit preoccupied, as if something was bothering her. Us?

After twenty minutes of chitchat on the porch, David and I carried our bags to rooms on the third floor. The hall was painted white, its dark floor punctuated by hooked rugs in pastel shades. The bedrooms were wallpapered, each one with matching twin beds and wicker furniture. When I opened the closet, out streamed the aroma of cedar from a sachet hanging on a velvet-covered hanger. The smell brought back Sunday dinners twenty years before at Mrs. James Dwight Dana's house on Hillhouse Avenue. In cold weather, Margaret, always in black uniform with white apron, would hang my coat in the cedar closet. I wondered if uniformed help served dinner here.

David came into the room, and I asked him what the Haddons thought we were doing there. He said Reed had told them that he, David, and I were working on a federal case and that Briar was the client's brother. We were all meeting here to plan legal strategy.

I walked over to the closet, pulled the can from my suitcase, and tossed it to David.

"Here you go," I said. "All complete except for part of a Thai stick Nancy and I smoked last week."

He walked to the door and turned the metal key in the latch. Then he poured the can's contents on the bed. He riffled quickly through Sheila's diary and dropped it in the pocket of his coat. He was unrolling the chart when I asked, "Did you tell me to keep this stuff as 'evidence' just to cover me?"

"Partially. If you got popped I wanted to be able to get you out fast. But it really is evidence, you know."

"The kind that'd get Reynolds twenty years."

"Look a bit more closely at the chart, Professor."

I moved closer and looked over his shoulder.

"You see those crosses with latitude and longitude numbers and dates?"

"Yeah."

"Look more closely at the route they plot. The ship was on its way to Halifax. It never touched U.S. territorial waters or ever intended to. It was on the high seas heading toward Canada."

"So what?"

"So a crucial legal point. If the Coast Guard found her, they would've had no legal authority to board and search her. This would've helped prove the search was illegal."

He folded the chart back up and rolled it into a cylinder before sliding it into his inside coat pocket.

"You gonna keep that?"

"As a great legal mind once said: Never destroy evidence. Bury it—you never can tell when you'll need it."

While I was trying to figure that out, he took the can and Thai stick into the bathroom and I heard the toilet flush.

When he came back, I pulled out the grocery bag and poured the bundles on the bed.

"Like in the movies, Chief—first the drugs, then the money."

He glanced at the packets on the bed but didn't pick any up.

"How about you taking custody of it now?" I asked. "I've got no way to safeguard it here."

"OK," he said, scooping the money up from the bed.

"You didn't count it," I said as he got up from the bed.

"It doesn't matter," he said with a tired grin, then unlocked the door and left.

The room seemed stuffy. I opened the window, switched off the light, and lay down on one of the beds. The sea air flooded in and mixed with the odor of cedar. I closed my eyes and didn't know where I was.

MONDAY, AUGUST 22

I heard it before I saw it. We were out beyond the point, swimming in a mild chop beyond the end of the spit that was the Haddon estate. David, Reed, and I had left Woolrich on the back patio. It was screened from the wind and not a bad place to read the travel section of the Sunday *New York Times*. That was what Woolrich had been doing when we'd left, his pipe on the glass lawn table in front of him, Abraxas the dog rooting under a nearby bush.

Reed had disappeared for a few moments, returning with three huge beach towels. He'd led us, then, over shale ledges to a rocky beach on the south side of the point. We'd entered the water hesitantly, testing its coldness, and then Reed had dived under and headed out in a strong crawl. The yawl was too far out to reach on this swim—especially with the wind against us—and I had to strain to see it. David had spent the morning out there with Briar and then an hour on the phone to Europe. I was superfluous, but who cared? It was a great day for a swim, and the wind was now at our backs as we rested for a moment and then headed back to the ledges.

At first there was only a low hum. Then the hum got louder. Beyond Reed's bobbing head, this side of the thunderheads building in the northwest, I could see the storklike shape of the seaplane dropping the last twenty-five feet to the bay's surface. Its pontoons sliced the water in great waves less than four hundred feet beyond David, who was furthest out. The noise of its engines dropped to a rhythmic throb, and it taxied to a dock on the neighboring spit. I was too low in the water to see who got out.

Twenty minutes later we were all back on the rocky ledges, wrapped in beach towels, shaking the water out of our hair.

"Somebody coming for dinner?" I asked Reed.

"Yeah," he said. "That's Uncle Webb and Aunt Carol. Actually they're not my real aunt and uncle, but I call them that. He has to be in Providence on business, so they decided to stay overnight here."

"What kind of business?" I asked.

"I don't know," Reed said, smiling. "He was in the OSS during the war and then became a diplomat for a time. Now he's working for some alphabet-soup outfit in the Pentagon. A long time ago I learned not to ask him about it."

I looked over at David. There was a mischievous smile on his face. Here we were in the lair of the Eastern establishment, raising bail for a jailed dope dealer. And who should pop in for dinner?

Dinner was served not in the high-ceilinged room with the twenty-foot polished mahogany table but in the cozy alcove between kitchen and patio. The table was set for seven, with a cotton tablecloth and colorful Quimper ware from Brittany. With characteristic understatement, the Haddons did not employ uniformed servants. Their "help" was a couple who dressed like young professionals on vacation. Jim wore penny loafers, khakis, and either a blue or white button-down shirt (no tie); Julie wore sandals, a skirt, and (apparently always) a white blouse. He cooked and she served.

Sitting down at the table, I expected something odd—even hilarious—to happen. Midway through dessert, I was still expecting it.

The first surprise was Webb Stryker. I liked him. He seemed charming, intelligent, and modest. With his compact build, very clear blue eyes, and close-cropped white hair, there was nothing inefficient, sloppy, or down-home about him. He was—if one could strip all the negative connotations from the word—sleek.

His wife, Carol, was cut from a similar mold. She was Charlotte's younger sister, and her clothes emphasized what it meant to be a handsome woman of fifty with money and style. Apparently Reed's parents had died years before in a plane crash, and he'd been befriended by the Haddons. They'd no children, but the Strykers had three in their twenties, the youngest of whom had just graduated from college. When Reed asked about their recent exploits and achievements, the Strykers replied with wit and modesty. Their account of a visit to Pamplona provoked a discussion of Hemingway. This, in turn, led David to talk about Jack Spicer and Bukovsky. Everyone was polite and animated, but the conversation lacked bite. It was as if Stryker, David, and I knew our roles too well and were wary of falling into the clichés those roles assigned. The others too were wary, not wanting to start a conversational lead that would bring discomfort. Thus the table talk labored under a brittle restraint, like the Irish lace napkin covering the Parker House rolls. It was almost as if Stryker, David, and I were all known to have served time in disparate penitentiaries, detox centers, and funny farms, and no one wanted to mention the fact for fear where it might lead.

After dinner we strolled into an interior sitting room. David and Stryker started talking about trans-Sahara Africa, where David had traveled and Stryker had lived, both in the early sixties. The two sisters huddled in a corner, talking family business, leaving Woolrich, Reed, and me to make do.

A band of lightning advanced eastward across the bay. Occasionally we heard the rumble of thunder.

The Strykers slipped off to bed first. Reed yawned, and soon David and I were left alone, sitting at the kitchen table.

"So tell me what Effie's daughter was like," he said.

"Her name is Yowaisky," I said. "A cheerful lady. Solid middle class. Runs a beauty shop in a village called Milestown. Said the family didn't like Hammett's father much. Apparently he was a bit of a skirt chaser. But they still admire Hammett—didn't buy any of the red-baiting stuff from the fifties.

"One thing was new. She told me Hammett loved mysteries and would stay up all night reading them. When he was still living at home in Baltimore, Mama Hammett had a hell of a time getting him up for work in the morning. You really think Yowaisky's mother was the model for Spade's secretary?"

"Yes and no," said David, finishing off the Cuervo in his glass. "Hammett undoubtedly got the name from her and thought it'd be fun to use it for another secretary. The character? Probably not."

"When I picked you up at the airport today I was thinking of Hammett's description of Spade—the V's of his chin, mouth, and brows," I said. "Anybody ever tell you they issued an APB for Spade the cops'd probably pick you up?"

"Yeah," he said wryly, "except for minor differences like body build and height."

"OK," I agreed. "I had in mind that first paragraph where he talks about the V's and where he says Spade looked something like 'a blond Satan.' You'd pass."

"Maybe. I don't know. What does it matter anyway? Spade's a dream creature. Of course, all of us gumshoes'd love to be Spade. Who wouldn't. But he's a dream. Hammett made him up. Made him up to be the ideal detective. And Hammett knew what he was doing. He wasn't like these dickheads who think you learn what it's like by reading other dickheads."

"Fair enough," I said. "But how come you're so sure Hammett meant Spade to be the ideal? Why isn't he just another one of Hammett's detectives? Like, you know, the continental op, Ned Beaumont, or even Nick Charles?"

"Why?" said David. "Because he *says* so, Professor! I think the Haddons have the book. I spotted it this morning in the library. I'll show you the goddamn text so you can footnote it in your next report."

While David searched for the book, I looked around the kitchen at the commercial dishwasher next to the sink. The quasi-institutional kitchen was a fixture in these homes. The commercial-grade gas stove was here not because someone thought it'd be fun to cook omelets on but because the staff might have to prepare dinner for sixty. It reminded me of the kitchen in the basement of my Yale secret society. In both, the stainless-steel work surfaces and refrigerators contrasted with the seventy-year-old wooden cabinets and light fixtures. Recently my mind had been drifting back a lot to New Haven twenty years before. The reason was similarity. This house, for example, was the clone of a post-Victorian I'd stayed in on the Cape after classes let out in May 1957. Had that been the last time I'd felt comfy all nestled down in the bosom of privilege?

The breeze blew the curtains over the sink. Once again the smell of the sea crept up my nose. The lightning flashed closer, and I heard David's steps in the corridor. He was holding a cheap, Modern Library edition of something and the bottle of Cuervo Gold.

"Hammett wrote the introduction to this in 'thirty-four," David was saying as he sat back down at the table. "Look what he says about where Spade came from."

He handed me the *Falcon*, open to a page in the Introduction. I began to read aloud:

> The Cairo character I picked up on a forgery charge in 1920. Wilmer, the boy gunman, was picked up in Stockton, California . . . a neat small smooth-faced quiet boy of perhaps twenty-one. . . .

"No, not there," David said, at the same time pouring himself a good-sized belt of tequila. "Farther down the page, where he talks about Spade."

I shifted my eyes lower and continued to read:

> Sam had no original. . . . He's a dream man in the sense that he is what most of the detectives I worked with would like to have been and what quite a few of them, in their cockier moments, thought they approached . . . a hard and shifty fellow, able to take care of himself in any situation, able to get the best of anybody he comes in contact with, whether criminal, innocent bystander or client.

"OK," I said, "But that makes the whole thing silly, just a stupid macho game of who can get the best of whom."

"Whoa, Professor!" said David. "Slow down. The interest is not in the *fact* Spade takes care of himself—even Mannix does that. The interest is in *how* he does it. But you're the philosopher."

David took another drink and then—very deliberately, very slowly—slid the glass away with arms extended, elbows locked. He was talking now as much to the glass as to me.

"Did you ever think lying is just a style of communication?" he asked. "I mean, no one describes papal encyclicals as lies. Just the Catholic style. Different only because more people go along with them than with your usual fib. You think maybe Spade knows this? Could that be why he doesn't get mad when Iva or Brigid or Gutman lies to him? Because he sees it as just their style? But it's not Spade's style. Sure, Spade lies from time to time. He doesn't tell Brigid he's tossed her place looking for the falcon. He lies about it, and he lies a couple of other times too. But if you check, you'll see it's the other people in the book who are doing the lying, and who are also talking all the time about 'trust' and 'truth' and those other big words. There's that one place where Spade tells Brigid, 'You don't have to trust me as long as you can persuade me to trust you.' That pretty well says it—at least from Spade's point of view.''

The sound had started, imperceptibly, about the time David handed me the book. First a few muffled drops, then louder, until it became an insistent clatter. I went to the window. The rain was coming in sheets from the northeast. The lightning, too, was much closer. There was the smell of ozone. I shut the window.

"Remember a long time ago, when I told you about paying attention? The only two places in the book where Spade gets taken—when Gutman gives him the Mickey Finn and when Gutman palms the thousand-dollar bill—are places where Spade hasn't been paying attention. OK, no one does it perfectly or *can* do it perfectly. We'll go on making those sorts of mistakes. So Hammett has it right there. But he won't let Spade make the lethal mistake. You know what that is?''

David was both drunk and not drunk. He wasn't slurring his words. He was speaking with urgency, as if this was an idea he'd had for a long time but never expressed directly. He was still staring at the glass, but hadn't moved to drink any of the liquid.

"To trust Brigid," I said. "To give in, to 'play the sap' for her.''

"I don't know, Thompson," he went on, "whether you're a better detective than you were a professor. But you're not a bad reader. Yeah, the lethal mistake is *to believe*, to play the sap. . . .'' His voice trailed off. He was still staring at the glass.

"What's the matter?" I asked.

"I was just thinking about blood. Or really about bleeding, I should say. The first thing you notice about it, even before the wetness, is that it's warm. Ever notice that?''

"No, I guess because I can't remember any time when I ever bled a lot. What were you thinking of?''

He ignored the question and continued staring at the glass.

"In circumstances that are indifferent''—he now spoke very precisely, almost as if he were reading from a text only he could see—''honor can be invented and a private scaffold of meaning can be raised around an unbuilt center. Hammett built his scaffolding well but apparently had little stomach for examining its supports. Or''—he paused for a moment, slowly turning the glass in his extended hands—''the lack of them.''

"David," I asked quickly, "did you send me East because you knew I wouldn't steal the money?"

He looked at me, an expression of mild amusement lifting his brow.

"I thought about it," I went on. "Nancy and I both thought about it. We did more than think about it. We talked about it. But when I actually had the money, up there in the attic when I held it in my hands, I couldn't steal it. I didn't even want to. I can't explain it. It was just too *real*. Did you know I'd feel that? Is that why you decided to send me—of all the people you could send—after it?"

"You haven't figured it out," he said, "have you?"

"What do you mean?"

"You really haven't figured out why I sent you East?"

"I was just asking you that," I answered. "Was it because you knew I wouldn't steal the money?"

"Look. The money was beside the point. Nobody ever cared about the money. It was nice to get it, and even nicer to know the cops hadn't gotten it. It was nice to get the can. It was nice to get what you picked up about the bust. But the real reason I sent you East had nothing to do with those things. I wanted to get you out of the way. Sure, it was a kindness to you. Protection for you, if you will. But also protection for me. I didn't want you around. I wanted you out of it. New England was just a sideshow; center ring was back in San Francisco."

"What?"

"Remember the Seville at the airport? Reynolds's Seville?"

"Of course."

"That was close as you came to the main event. And even that wasn't real close."

"What?"

"Let's just put it this way: a suitcase was supposed to get itself left in the trunk of that car. Somebody had an extra set of keys and was supposed to use them on arriving in San Francisco. Then the keys were supposed to get dropped in a mailbox to us. When I didn't get the keys, I figured somebody had screwed up and nothing was in the car. But I had to know for sure. That's why the Professor and the hippie locksmith made their little trip to the airport. When the deputy called, I thought the balloon had gone up. But still, it would have made no sense to lie about who you were. I checked the car that night at the garage, and the suitcase wasn't in it. It took two and a half days longer to find out what had happened.''

"What was that?"

"The somebody I was talking about did a little sampling from his personal stash in the lavatory on the plane. By the time the plane got to SFO, paranoia is too delicate a word to describe that somebody's state. The suitcase got left on the plane. And for the last two weeks I've been working out a scam to get it back at minimal risk. We got it last Wednesday, so I let you go after the money on Thursday. And here we are the following Monday. Or"—looking at his watch—"is it Tuesday?"

"Is that why you were looking around at the airport," I asked. "and also later, on the road?"

"You saw that?"

"I thought so."

"Yeah," he said, tossing off what amber liquid remained in his glass. "Given the fact the suitcase came to me personally last Wednesday, if I didn't get any heat on a trip like this, it'd mean the scam had worked. That's what I was checking. Come on, let's go to bed!"

"No shit!" I said, stunned. "No shit!"

"Don't take it so hard," he said, flicking off the kitchen light and smiling. "I might've made the whole thing up."

PART TWO

FIVE

KRIEGSCHMERZ

THURSDAY, OCTOBER 12, 1978

Columbus Day. There had been a parade in downtown San Francisco, so the cabby had taken an alternate route to the airport. It was now almost four o'clock San Francisco time, and we were somewhere east of the Rockies. With the clouds below, I couldn't tell where. It didn't matter.

Painfully, I turned toward Phillip Green. He was sitting six rows back, next to a young sailor's wife with a colicky baby. The kid had already slobbered over the arm of his gabardine suit. The seating arrangements couldn't be helped; we'd gotten the last seats on this flight to Cleveland.

Turning forward, I felt a twinge from the cracked rib on my right side. After five days, the adhesive tape was loosening and the skin underneath starting to itch. I poured the second can of Mr. & Mrs. T's Bloody Mary Mix into the plastic cup.

"So anyway," the woman next to me was saying, idly stirring her bourbon and water with the swizzle stick, "we thought we really had to get the agreement finalized before we started distributing test samples."

We hadn't exchanged names yet. She had a pert nose, but her makeup didn't completely hide the ravages of an oily-skinned adolescence. Her strawberry-blond hair was drawn up in a bun, and she was wearing a blue suit with a white ruffled blouse. The suit was too severe and the blouse too frilly; the total effect was of someone wearing the costume "businesswoman." She worked for a small market-research firm in San Francisco. We'd

135

struck up a conversation when the drinks were served, and now I couldn't shut her off.

"Do you fly to Cleveland often?" she asked.

I knew it was coming. Where was I on the scorecard? Back in June, Fechheimer had been three ahead of me, with seventeen. There'd been the one score on the plane back from Washington, so I figured she'd be number sixteen.

"No," I said carefully. "Actually, this is my first time."

"A business trip?"

"Yeah, I have a case there. I'm a private investigator."

"Really?" she said, hesitating for only a moment before giving me the score. "That must be very interesting."

She looked uncertainly at me, wondering what I was smiling about.

"Sometimes," I answered.

A year earlier, Fechheimer and I'd started a contest based on a remark of Hammett's. *"In 1917 in Washington, D.C.,"* he'd written, tongue-in-cheek, *"I met a young woman who did not remark that my work must be very interesting."* We'd turned it the other way round, keeping score of the people who, learning for the first time either of us was a gumshoe, observed that the work must be "interesting." Now I was nearly even with him. But then again, I hadn't seen him since August. There was no telling how many he'd chalked up since then.

She was chattering on about her boss. I paid no attention; my thoughts were on Fechheimer.

All through the earlier part of the year, Fechheimer had been quietly unraveling. When we'd last talked, a couple of months before, he'd stopped working as a detective and was going to New Zealand. A vacation, or something more permanent? He didn't know. Why New Zealand? He hadn't replied. Perhaps his thoughts had been drawn there by the serenity of that late-nineteenth-century landscape hanging in his apartment, the oil painting I'd shown Irene Kuznetzov. I didn't know, and perhaps he didn't either.

That night in June had forecast what was coming. He'd been drunk, sitting down on the curb of Washington Street after breaking off nine car-radio antennae as I, Boswell-like, followed along, steering, cajoling. "I don't wanna do anything," he'd said to no one in particular, looking off across the street. "I wanna quit."

As a detective, he was the closest thing to a genius I'd ever met or ever hoped to meet. Yet after twelve years of work that earned him a national reputation while still in his midthirties, he was burned out, setting out for New Zealand with the trammeled dream of a new life. Why?

I chuckled, remembering some of our adventures: that crazy two-car chase through the slums of Oakland after Huey Newton's tailor, the six-month failed attempt to trap a murderer in Alaska, all the characters who'd brought their problems and eccentric lives to Laguna Street.

After the trip East, our relationship changed. With that case, my apprenticeship had ended, and thereafter he'd treated me as a detective who, if not yet gifted, was at least serious and dependable. A loose camaraderie developed. Standing in his kitchen at the end of the day, we'd share vignettes from the day's work or stories from the past, each illustrating in its own way the variety of human frailty or the propensity for weirdness in even the blandest of individuals. Working for him had been like a tutorial in the human comedy.

Those years had been filled with good times.

But now I was thinking of something else: the undercurrent of self-destruction that also ran through them. I'd watched that current work on Fechheimer day after day, undermining the bulwarks a simpler mind would have erected to the exigencies of the detective's life. It wasn't just that his health and mind had been strained by too many cases, too much peril, and a marriage the ending of which he'd not been able to accept. All of those things were factors, but there was something more. I'd watched his eyes redden and his hair become flecked with gray, and the spring before I'd been there when he started coughing blood. I'd seen him become more and more combat-weary, until, finally, nerves frayed and energies depleted, he ground to a halt. Much of it could be chalked up to what, for lack of a better understanding, we call stress. But part had been self-inflicted, the consequence perhaps of a judgment about the world in which we operated. He wanted to be free of it.

For me that was out of the question. Unlicensed though I still was, the die had been cast. The February before, I'd flown east to Haverford and formally delivered my letter of resignation. The president and I'd chatted amiably, and then I'd gone off to a retirement dinner given by the philosophy department. The next morning I'd left for work on a case in Washington, returning in July to clean out the house on College Lane and ship our furniture to California.

It was only a week or two after that when Fechheimer told me he was pulling out, closing up his practice and moving to New Zealand. Characteristically, he was considerate of my interests, proposing another detective from Santa Cruz as a potential partner under whose license I could work. We could take over the rent on his Laguna Street office/apartment and his phone number. When clients called, we could tell them he'd gone to New Zealand. The majority, he suggested, would hire us.

Fearing this a route to bankruptcy, I'd chosen another option. Two former Lipset operatives, Jack Palladino and Sandra Sutherland, ran a small detective agency. They'd met years earlier in the Nassau County, New York, Jail, where both were working undercover as part of a jail-corruption investigation being run by Lipset. All three of us were members of a cadre of overeducated operatives Fechheimer had brought into the Lipset Service in the 1970s. Two years before, Jack Palladino had run the Oakland strike investigation; during my first days as a hapless surveillance man, he'd been my controller. After getting a degree from Cornell, he'd done graduate work in political science at Berkeley before getting a law degree from Boalt Hall. His wife, Sandra Sutherland, was attractive, Australian, and an accomplished poet. In the preface to a selection of her poems, she'd written that being an investigator "exemplifies that 'genius for lying and adoration for the truth' Denise Levertov has attributed to the poet."

"Excuse me," said my neighbor.

I eased up out of the seat, protecting my right side, and let her pass on the way to the lavatory.

That cracked rib, the result of a karate kick when I hadn't been paying attention, was among the first consequences of the formation of Palladino, Sutherland & Thompson. On October 1, we'd moved the office from Jack and Sandra's home in Oakland to a long railroad flat on Union Street in San Francisco. It was large enough so I could dispense with the Grove Street apartment.

Jack's brother, Paul, had helped me move my things to the new office the previous weekend. A passerby had kindly held the door open as Paul and I carried the rug from the Grove Street lobby to the Volvo at the curb. Only after dumping the rug in the trunk of the Volvo had we realized the good samaritan had disappeared into the building. We'd found him in my bathroom, glassy-eyed, going through the medicine cabinet. He'd grabbed a screwdriver lying on the sink. When I'd started for a table lamp, his foot had snaked out in an artful kick, flooring me and cracking a rib. He'd fled in a welter of shouting, leaving Paul and me feeling foolish.

"I'm back," I heard now over my right shoulder. Easing into the aisle to let her slide by, I nodded to Green. She picked up *New Woman* and began leafing through it. I wasn't ready to attack the three file folders in my briefcase; the question mark of Fechheimer still hung in my mind.

Why, finally, had he needed to break free of the detective world? What was it about that world that seemed so—how to put it?—spiritually hazardous? "Sometimes," Hal Lipset once told a journalist, "it doesn't seem fair that people pay us to have this much fun." High jinks, eh, Hal, being able to play the games and enjoy the scams other people only dream about? Is that the way it is, Hal? We both know it isn't. Fechheimer is the proof.

Over the last weeks and months, especially in moments of disappointment or exhaustion, I'd begun to wonder what I was doing and where I was going. Underneath the gathering of new energies and learning the skills needed to survive in a new world, I'd come to wonder where it was leading. An uncomfortable suspicion about the nature of the profession had begun to tease the back of my mind.

It started a few weeks earlier, on a flight back to San Francisco from Los Angeles. I'd just worked a competent ruse to get into a guarded residential development to learn the whereabouts of a drug dealer. Everything had gone extremely well. No fuss, no bother. But on the way back, I'd begun to wonder what would happen to the man I'd fingered. The attorney I'd worked for wore a gold chain and assured me it had been only a minor burn; no one would get hurt. Only "some money would change hands," was how he'd put it. Could I believe him? Even if I could, was his client lying to *him*? Would I read about a murder in the paper a week or two later and know I'd helped set up the victim? Sitting on that other airplane, it had struck me the private detective might be simply a closet criminal. Or if not a criminal, something even less—the hired hand of criminals.

There was, to start with, the point about memorability. When I sat back and tried to remember past cases, they fell out on a line of memorability roughly corresponding to how close we'd come to the line: the house with the thirty thousand dollars in the attic; the trip Nancy and I took to Tijuana; the flight to Frankfurt, Germany, on twenty minutes' notice; the electronics job; all those meetings in airport coffee shops where only first names were used. It sometimes seemed as if danger, heightened senses, general weirdness, and extraordinary satisfaction all lay on a graph where something like criminality was the ordinate. However you cut it, the detective and the criminal shared many things. They shared an affinity for keeping secrets, paying attention, acting evasively, and seeing the noonday, public world as danger, as "other." Did they also share that affinity for things dark the true criminal harbors in his heart? Had I traded Haverford for a column in the police gazette?

On the other hand, there were cases like *Cutler* vs. *Cutler*. Clifford P. Cutler was no criminal. Nor, in serving his interests, were we. In pursuing those interests, we'd all treated his wife as an object to be manipulated. But there was nothing criminal or even surprising in that. After all, he'd been trying to divorce her because she'd already abandoned him. It was also true the only difference between stealing the Continental and "repossessing" it lay in a piece of paper. But that piece of paper made all the difference, since it proved the car was Cutler's.

In August of the year before, Jamie Reynolds had had every right to hire us to construct a defense to the charges against him. Along with his attorney, we'd functioned as his constitutionally guaranteed defenders. The police had had an opportunity to search the house and its grounds; if they'd botched it, that was their failure, not ours. Reynolds had paid us to retrieve his property, and that we had done. The suitcase from the airplane? I wasn't even sure it existed, but if it did, Fechheimer had done only what I'd done in New England—retrieve someone's property.

You could even see the Los Angeles drug job the same way. No criminality, just a service performed by the detective-as-small-businessman, duly licensed by the state of California to perform investigations of a private nature.

This was beginning to sound like a speech to the California Association of Licensed Investigators. It was also missing the point. It wasn't that the detective sometimes served criminals. Accountants, lawyers, and chauffeurs may all serve criminals without themselves becoming criminal. Nor was it that the nature of our work often led us into a boundary zone where the line between legality and illegality became smudged; the distinction between the criminal and the noncriminal was the wrong distinction. If the criminal life is defined as inherently predatory, as viewing the world as made up of objects to be manipulated or, more forcefully, as prey to be taken, you don't have to be a Marxist to see that such a definition also includes the Avon lady or even the corner druggist. Any system based on private property inevitably produces a Hobbesian universe where predation becomes the norm independent of the success or failure of the latest United Fund campaign. Criminality wasn't the problem; power was.

The world of power and the world of love: they stand one against the other. In the world of power, individual interests contest in a domain of scarcity. To be a cogent actor in that domain requires craft and guile, whether one is an Ivan Boesky or a lowly detective. That was what made Hammett's Spade such an archetype—*"a hard and shifty fellow, able to take care of himself in any situation, able to get the best of anybody he comes in contact with, whether criminal, innocent bystander or client."* Fechheimer had showed me those words the year before, in Rhode Island. Now, for the first time, I thought I understood the problem they concealed.

"Getting the best of" is the *telos* of that world. It is also, lethally, the psychic obstacle that blocks one's entry into the world of love.

In love, all the skills of the cogent actor become disabilities. In order to love, one must put off hardness and shiftiness. "Taking care of" becomes directed toward the other and not oneself. The ability to lie effectively, to appear different than one really is—all the disguises essential in the world of power—become, in the world of love, temptations, artful excuses to avoid the nakedness love requires, to avoid love.

Hammett knew all this. He'd distilled it from his bloodstream. That's why in the last line of *The Maltese Falcon* he makes Spade "shiver" as Spade looks down the cold barrel of his future. I'd always liked that last line, and now I thought I knew why.

Had something like this sent Fechheimer flying off into the sunset? I didn't know. I did know that he'd left the gumshoe world not simply because he was worn out by it but because he was looking beyond it, wanting something better—something richer and warmer—than it could provide. Perhaps, in a parallel way, I was feeling the same thing. Not *Weltschmerz* but *Kriegschmerz*, the weariness of the mercenary.

I picked up the briefcase and pulled out the papers I'd been given in San Francisco. Most of them were legal documents, filings in the case of *Wylie vs. Green*. Green was a no-nonsense gay businessman whose ex-lover, "Junior" Wylie, had become so enamored of the possibilities opened by the *Marvin vs. Marvin* palimony decision that he'd sued Green for half of Green's assets, about $250,000. Green had mounted a vigorous defense, hiring the attorney who'd contacted me this morning and who'd earlier obtained Wylie's bank records under subpoena. Those records showed Wylie had deposited a check for twenty thousand dollars on April 16, and three days later had paid just about that amount for a Cadillac Seville. Some fast footwork by Green's attorney had obtained the purchase order for the car and the handsome eight-by-ten color photo of it that now stared out from the file folder. We were going to see the person who'd written the check, a gay podiatrist in Cleveland. Green was convinced Wylie was bilking the foot doctor, who would become our ally once Wylie's deceit was disclosed. I didn't know whether that was likely or not. I was going along to keep things kosher if it turned out the foot doctor really had been bilked. Green would have preferred a gay investigator for the task, but was mollified, for some reason, by the attorney's explanation that I used to teach philosophy. At most, the case would take two or three days. I liked Green, and the case had its touch of weirdness.

Leafing through the documents, it wasn't long before I was sucked into the case. Soon I was figuring out how to work it. My earlier questions quickly became sodden, left behind with the ice melting at the bottom of my cup. As had happened so often in the previous two years, the exigencies of action overwhelmed reflection.

And Fechheimer? Good luck to you, David, wherever you are. And thanks.

In the airport lot, I automatically started to peel the Hertz sticker from the windshield of the Ford Escort when Green asked, "Why are you doing that?"

"No reason," I said, fumbling. "Just habit. I forgot there's no reason we shouldn't be driving a rental car."

The car oversteered badly coming out of the parking lot. Down the freeway, rain was sweeping in great sheets from left to right in the high-beams. Soon the airport, familiar like all airports in its generality, was left behind, and we met the particular: Cleveland, Ohio, at 9:12 P.M. on Thursday, October 12, 1978, a freeway curving to the right, everything beyond the burrowing beam of the headlights obscured in curtains of rain.

The map only partially corresponded to what was passing by the windshield. I overshot the exit and missed the turn onto Central Parkway. Doubling back, I looked for a street sign. The one on the right said Allison Avenue. But Green couldn't find it on the map. Terrific. Lost after half an hour in Cleveland.

Green was getting mildly irritated. "Good thing I'm on a daily rate," I said. "Otherwise our getting lost would've cost you money." We were on our way to the good doctor's residence on Bywater. Green had called his office from San Francisco and learned he was at home, convalescing from "major surgery." Neither of us knew what that meant, but it suggested we'd find him home the next morning. Right now I just wanted to see what his place looked like.

Twenty minutes later we pulled to the curb in the 1800 block of Bywater Boulevard.

Leaving Green in the car, I stuffed the Sony recorder into my jacket pocket. Twenty feet from the door, the number 1820 embossed on it in digits fifteen inches high, I met a couple on their way out. I played with their rambunctious German shepherd, glancing inside to check that there was no guard in the lobby. Inside was a bank of mailboxes with the usual buzzer/intercom system. Fourth from the top was *20T Dr. P. Walker*. That must be Dr. Pierre Walker, healer of the human foot. Walking down the asphalt path, slippery from the rain, I looked up at the building, counting fourteen floors. I clicked on the recorder: "Eighteen-twenty Bywater Boulevard has fourteen stories. Dr. P. Walker is in Twenty-T. Time ten-fourteen P.M."

By the time we reached the Travelodge a mile and a half away, it was past ten-thirty. In the room, I hung up my three-piece suit and called San Francisco. There was one message: Len Weinglass had called from Los Angeles. I left a contact number with the answering service and on Len's machine in L.A. I unpacked a half-pint of Wild Turkey and poured a glass.

I'd never worked in such close proximity to a client before, and didn't like it. I was largely superfluous. Green would make the crucial move while I just looked on; that much had already been decided in San Francisco. Green, because he was gay and fighting a lawsuit from Wylie, would have a better chance of recruiting Walker.

The logistics were becoming sticky. It would be better to encounter the doctor at his door. As a rule, you have a better than 90 percent chance of getting someone to talk to you if you show up at the door. If the initial contact is by phone, the odds drop to below even money. Furthermore, we had the photo and purchase order to show Walker, and we could only do that face to face. But how do you show up at someone's door when he lives in an apartment building with a buzzer system? Even worse, the mailbox labels in the building (20T for Walker) didn't correspond to floors (there were only fourteen) Sticky.

FRIDAY, OCTOBER 13

The next morning I called Walker's office at 9:15 to make sure he hadn't made a miraculous recovery and returned to work. He hadn't. I loaded the recorder with fresh tape and put it in the left inside pocket of my suit. To avoid carrying a briefcase (many people suspect that briefcases conceal tape recorders), I stuffed legal papers, the purchase order for the Seville, and the color photo in a manila file folder. Leaving the lobby, we could see our image in a wall mirror. We looked like mutual-fund salesmen.

The skies had cleared, and it was chilly. After thirty seconds of cranking, the Escort started, and ten minutes later we were walking up the path to 1820 Bywater.

Pushing open the glass door, I noticed a middle-aged woman with well-coiffed auburn hair clutching some junk mail in one hand. She could have been a model in a Sears catalog, the one who looks out at you so clear-eyed, so obviously trustworthy, reaching for the small pile of freshly laundered, clean-smelling towels on the new washer/dryer. With the hand not holding the junk mail, she held the inner door ajar.

"Twenty-T? Dr. Pierre Walker?" I asked pleasantly.

The suits and the directness of the question did it. There was no suspicion behind her eyes, only mild puzzlement as she tried to figure out an answer. Just as two weeks ago the "passerby" had scammed his way into the Areola Apartments, so were we scamming our way into 1820 Bywater. Still smiling, we passed through the door with her.

"I think that would be Four," she said.

"Are you also on Four?" I asked.

"No, I'm on Six."

Smoothly, Green punched buttons 4 and 6 on the stainless steel elevator control panel. I mumbled something about the junk mail in her hand, but quickly, before the conversation became cloying, the door opened on Four, and Green and I strode out.

To the left was a door marked 18T, with a peephole and a knocker. Beyond it was a door with no peephole and no knocker, marked 19T, and beyond that an identical door marked 20T. We stopped before 20T. I reached into my pocket and pressed the red Record button on the machine, at the same time checked my watch (10:11 A.M. meant I had till 11:10 before the tape hit the end and clicked) and giving Green a *This is it* glance. I knocked three times, moderately hard.

Nothing. No sound came from within. He must be there. According to Green, he had only gotten out of the hospital two days earlier. I knocked again. Again nothing. After twenty seconds I nodded to Green and we walked toward the end of the hall.

What's going on? We got inside by exploiting the chance meeting with Mrs. Washer/Dryer. We're probably on the right floor. But something's wrong. The peephole and the knocker were missing on those two doors. The doors themselves were close together. Could they be storage rooms for apartments on this floor? My breathing steadied. At the end of the corridor we turned around and started back toward the elevator. We passed it and kept on walking. I was getting embarrassed. Suddenly, there it was. The door to 20T lay beyond the elevator to our right; there was a peephole and a knocker just under the numbers. Green looked relieved. His mind must have flown a trajectory parallel to my own. I knocked, and from within came the sound of slow footsteps.

It was awkward at first as Green tried to convey who we were and why we were there. I was introduced as a friend who had been assisting Green in his lawsuit with Wylie; Walker, I think, suspected I was Green's attorney. But it was Green who carried the day. He had an intuitive sense of the moves that would work with Walker. After making his pitch, Green asked me to show Walker the purchase order and photo of the Seville. Walker examined them carefully and then said, "All right, what do you want me to do?"

Green had been right on the money. The check for twenty thousand dollars had been Walker's payment for his part of a real-estate deal. For three months Walker had been asking Wylie for a copy of the deed of trust to the property, and been stalled repeatedly. Walker was readily convinced he'd been bilked; he only wanted to know what we wished him to do.

While Green chatted with Walker, I called his attorney in San Francisco. Twenty minutes later the attorney had managed to persuade a homicide inspector, a friend of his, to wire up Walker with a radio transmitter to gather evidence of criminal fraud. Walker expressed some reluctance at traveling to San Francisco (he'd just had a hernia operation), but after calling his psychic and getting a "go" signal, he agreed. While I made the plane reservations on the living-room phone, I heard Green and Walker exchanging stories about Wylie.

Two jobs remained for the next day: surveillance of Wylie to assure that he and Walker could be brought together, and coordination with SFPD to wire up Walker and move a car into position where it could monitor and record the conversation between Walker and Wylie. This was a job for two men. Later that night, in San Francisco, I suggested that an associate of mine take care of the surveillance while I coordinated things. Green's attorney rejected this and said he'd handle the police while I did the surveillance.

SATURDAY, OCTOBER 14

The alarm clattered at six-thirty. Familiar sensations: tobacco taste in the mouth and weariness everywhere else. I was to be on station by seven. The corner grocery was open, so I could start with a Styrofoam cup of coffee and a miniature six-pack of V-8 juice. On the Formica counter, waxy doughnuts nestled under a plastic cover that preserved their staleness.

After unlocking the Volvo, I loaded the camera with Tri-X and attached the power-winder and the 70-210mm zoom lens. The camera went into the blue climbing pack, along with my father's binoculars, and the pack went on the floor with the rolled-up sleeping bag. The tape recorder fit into the groove between the two front seats. The car was filled with gas from the night before; with the choke all the way out, it coughed twice and started.

Eight forty-nine Alpine Terrace. The steel-blue Cadillac Seville was nestled in the ground-level garage under the three-story apartment building. "Six fifty-seven *a.m.*, October fourteenth, nineteen seventy-eight," I said into the recorder, steering with my left hand, "CVO eight-one-six, that is Charlie-Victor-Oscar-eight-one-six, is under building at Eight forty-nine Alpine Terrace. Beginning surveillance."

It was a dull autumn morning, cold enough so all the pets in this upper-middle-class neighborhood were still inside. I undid the sleeping bag and pulled it over me.

I'd been listening to KKHI on the way over, Glenn Gould playing the Goldberg Variations. I left the ignition on, the volume on the radio turned down. A heavy man with thinning brown hair jogged along the opposite sidewalk, puffing hard to manage a barely respectable pace. Lost in the shuffle last night had been the obligatory call to SFPD to report the general location of surveillance along with my name and the license-plate number of the car. As soon as Wylie got up, we'd be out of here; probably no neighbors would have squawked by then. Everything was quiet, wet, and chilly. I shivered and pulled up the bag.

This parking spot was the best available, but it had its problems. It was four hundred feet from the driveway entrance on the opposite side of the street. If Wylie turned the Caddy around in the garage area and headed away when he hit the street, I'd get only a glimpse of the car. The apartment ought to give off signs of his getting up, but I couldn't count on it.

By 9:15 I'd finished the coffee and one can of V-8. It was still early in the surveillance, but I was feeling edgy, wanting some action. That's the way it always is: first quiet, and then everything happens in a few seconds.

At nine-thirty there was movement behind the translucent blinds of Wylie's apartment. Two minutes later the Caddy backed out of the driveway. I reached for the morning's *Chronicle*, lying on the passenger seat. If he went north, I'd have to go right after him; if he went south, I'd have to wait until he rounded the curve behind me before making a U-turn. I pulled the *Chronicle* up to eye level and waited.

South. Over the top of the paper, I could see the Caddy coming toward me, two people in the front seat. After it passed, I turned the key, then forced myself to wait five seconds before making the turn. Engine racing, the Volvo wound through the gears.

Two hundred yards ahead and just beyond a white Ford, the brake lights of the Seville flashed as it turned right. "Leaving Eight forty-nine Alpine Terrace at nine thirty-two," I said, hitting the Record button with my right hand. "White male with beard in passenger seat, Wylie driving." Then, a few seconds later: "Turning right on Price Street."

The Caddy bounced over an intersection a block ahead and disappeared from sight. I sped up. When Wylie slowed for a left onto Turner Street, I braked sharply, then slid up Turner in the right lane. His right turn signal flashed. He waited for a car to pass and turned onto Divisadero. I sped up again. As he turned onto Market, there were two cars between us. I hesitated, then pulled into a red zone at the corner.

A hundred and fifty feet ahead, he pulled into a parking place. "We're at the travel agency," I said into the recorder. "Time is nine thirty-seven."

Wylie got out, locked the car, and fumbled for change. He was just what I'd been expecting—the con man in his element, black, well dressed, and suave, still impressing his date from the night before, all velvet and gold. It showed in the way he walked, his mannerisms so under control, so compellingly *smooth*. And his date: white, midthirties, close-cropped salt-and-pepper beard, round dark eyes. Talking amiably, they entered the building.

I could only park in the red zone temporarily. Four hundred feet up the street, on the opposite side, were three pay phones and several parking places. If he took off in the car and I was across the street, it would mean a U-turn in heavy traffic. Not good, but better than anything I could see on this side of the street.

After sliding into one of the parking spaces, I went to a phone, still watching the travel agency's door, and called Green. The police inspector hadn't gotten there yet; it would be several hours before they had the doctor wired and ready to move. We tentatively decided to use the travel agency for the initial contact. I said I'd call in every hour.

Ten minutes later Wylie and his companion left the agency and crossed Market Street, turning left on Castro. I followed on foot, lagging forty feet behind on the other side of the street.

Castro Street is the heart of gay San Francisco, and its side-walks were crowded with men. They turned right onto Twenty-first Street, briefly visited a post office, and came back to Castro before going into an Italian café. Across the street, I window-shopped, keeping out of sight of the café's windows.

As usual at times like this, I envied the FBI. The situation was getting tenuous. My car was two blocks away. If Wylie hailed a taxi or got a ride from a friend, I'd lose him. The FBI, if they were doing this, would have that covered. They'd be using three cars, with two men to a car—one to drive, one to spot. In a moving surveillance, two of the cars would be on parallel streets, coordinated by radio and echoing the movements of the primary chase car. In this situation, they'd bring in a car as close as they could and put two agents on foot on the street, all hooked in by walkie-talkie. We never have resources like that; that was why I was out here alone, hoping these turkeys would get their act together before Wylie got away. Because of money con-straints, private detectives almost always work alone, one man in a car trying to anticipate what the quarry will do, finding phone booths catch-as-catch-can. Was the hunt any more intense because the resources were limited? I didn't know. But it *was* a hunt—I felt sure of that as I watched the door of the café in the reflection of a wallpaper shop's window—a hunt carried on in the midst of the human world, the city, with binoculars and camera and tape recorder.

Thirty minutes later I made a second call. Wylie had left his companion in the café and returned alone to the travel agency. This was the perfect time for the doctor to meet him. But they still weren't ready. The inspector with the transmitter had called from the Hall of Justice, but he hadn't yet arrived at Green's apartment. As soon as he did, they'd wire up Walker and ren-dezvous with me near the travel agency so my miniature re-corder could be placed on Walker as a backup. It was a clumsy, inelegant plan. The waiting had to continue while our best op-portunity slipped away. I put a dime in the parking meter and took up the watch again.

Market Street was a passing parade. Clothes are important here, as they signal identities and preferences. The "construc-tion worker" look was much in vogue: tight jeans, short haircut, plaid shirt with sleeves rolled to the elbows. Out of a stereo shop across the street came a good example wearing an immaculate yellow hard hat. Behind him, a man of about fifty in morning coat and homburg made his way toward the corner. In the rear-view mirror, I watched an elegant young man and woman in a Porsche pull into a parking spot four spaces back. She stayed in the car with a jittery Russian wolfhound. A few moments later she moved the car into the next parking spot, put the dog on a leash, and crossed the street. In the travel agency, Wylie was dusting the venetian blinds.

My tiredness was receding, and I was starting to enjoy the morning. I took the binoculars from the climbing pack.

Wylie had raised the blinds and was now standing at his desk, phone in hand. The glasses carried me right into the room. It was as if space had been twisted and I'd been brought into Wylie's zone, just as thirty years before I'd been brought into the zone of the beaver, nose upturned, sniffing the air. Watching Wylie, I felt the familiar rush. It was almost sexual, a sense of unfettered power, of the other as pure object for my gaze.

Most detectives see surveillance as an onerous but rudimentary task, to be assigned to subordinates whenever possible. I didn't. I enjoyed it not only for the exhilaration of the chase and the chance to polish my skills but also for the voyeur's rush. The night before, I'd wanted to assign the surveillance to someone else. But the reason for that was simple: the whole thing would have been easier with someone else doing the shadowing, and I wouldn't have had to get up at six-thirty after four hours' sleep. But now that I was doing the surveillance, the old emotions came back, and with them all the old questions.

In a fundamental way, surveillance is the detective's paradigm activity. The human eye was Pinkerton's original logo, and it survives as a graphic symbol for the gumshoe fraternity. The investigator's should always be the private eye, the eye that sees but is not seen. Was that the origin of the surge of power I'd felt a moment before, watching Wylie through the glasses? Traditionally the eye that sees and is not seen is God's eye. Is that what the surveillance man seeks? Does he wish to become God? The closing section of Sartre's *Being and Nothingness* flashed to mind. All human projects are doomed, wrote Sartre, because they share a contradictory desire, to become the *ens causa sui*—that is, God. Could it be that the humble surveillance man—his car's ashtray overflowing, the detritus of his waiting collecting under his seat as empty cans, Styrofoam cups, crumpled paper napkins, and an unrolled sleeping bag—could it be that he is

God-struck, that through all his activity courses a single aspiration, to be pure subject, always seeing, never seen?

· From behind came a heavy thud.

A glance in the side-view mirror showed the weathered hood of an old Ford station wagon that, just now, had backed into the Porsche's grille. The driver, a middle-aged black man, got out and walked up Market Street. Looking at the image in the mirror, I began to chuckle. The mirror, I thought, the side-view mirror! Hanging there on the door, it tells me I can become object for another subject, that I remain hunter only so long as the hunted does not appear in that oval surface hunting *me*. The surveillance man, playing out his fantasy of incipient divinity, forgets the mirror at his peril. It should remind him of his limits, of his finitude.

Chuckling over my "notes toward a phenomenology of surveillance," I left the car and walked to the pay phones.

It was 11:45. Wylie had been inside for ninety minutes now, and we'd been unable to move. My voice showing only part of the irritation I felt, I told the lawyer where Wylie's car was parked and gave him my location across the street.

Five after twelve. The young couple returned. He was carping at her because she'd moved the car.

"You dented the fucking grille," I heard him yell. "You got any idea what a Porsche grille costs?"

They argued, she with arms folded in front of her, he pacing back and forth. I could have bailed her out by telling them both what happened. I could have, but I didn't; like God, I remained silent, watching Wylie's window.

Twelve fifteen. I called Green again, urging speed. The attorney said they were just leaving in the police inspector's car. If Wylie held still for a few moments more, we'd have him; the con man would be conned.

Twelve twenty-three. Wylie came out of the agency and got into the Seville. I turned the key in the Volvo's ignition, then waited for him to clear the stoplight before making an outrageous U-turn in heavy traffic. I keyed the recorder while working the wheel: "Leaving the agency at twelve twenty-three. Wylie alone, heading south on Market." Ten car lengths ahead, Wylie turned right on Price Street. Good: he was going home. Three minutes later he pulled into his garage. Roosevelt Hospital, a quarter mile distant, had pay phones.

Twelve thirty-two. I talked with Green's roommate. They'd left. I gave him Wylie's present location and hung up.

Given the route Wylie usually followed to the agency, I should park north of his apartment. I pulled in, partially blocking the crosswalk just north of his building. Through some bushes I could make out the entrance to his driveway.

Twelve fifty-four. Wylie left the driveway and retraced his earlier route. Since I knew the turns he'd make, it was an easy tail.

Back on Market Street, I couldn't spot the inspector's car. It was supposed to be a yellow two-door Plymouth. The attorney should be sitting in it, along with Walker and the inspector. Where were they? From across the street I could just make out the doctor's balding red head in a corner of the agency. Where was their car? They have to be within a quarter mile to receive the signal. What to do?

Since I still had the recorder, Walker must be in there with only the transmitter. Transmitters are notoriously unreliable, and I didn't know how close the receiver was. Building construction can affect transmission; if that building was reinforced concrete with lots of I-beams, the signal wouldn't get through. It had been nuts to send him in there without a recorder. If he hadn't begun talking to Wylie, I might be able to slip him the recorder or, failing that, get close enough to catch part of their conversation and be able to corroborate Walker's eventual testimony. Was there a legal problem? The travel agency was a public space; someone talking there couldn't have an expectation of privacy. Then, too, this was already a law-enforcement matter; we were trying to gather evidence of criminal fraud. The foul-up wouldn't have happened if they'd listened to me the night before and authorized another man.

I climbed the stairs to the second-floor agency. Walker was off to the left, talking with Wylie, who was sitting behind a large rosewood desk. A speaker in the ceiling broadcast easy-listening music. The clerk at the desk was wearing a white shirt and narrow tie, with no sport jacket. He asked, "May I help you?"

"Yes. My wife and I've been thinking about a trip to Hawaii after the holidays. Maybe ten days in the middle of January. You have any good package deals for hotels and airfare combined?"

He went to a rack and pulled out eight or ten brochures. While he described the various tour packages, I strained to pick up what was happening between the doctor and Wylie. After a few minutes another customer came in and stood beside me at the counter.

"I'll sit down and look these over," I said. "Maybe I'll have some questions."

As the clerk turned to the other man, I moved off to a couch midway between the clerk and Wylie's desk. Only intermittently could I overhear their conversation. The doctor's voice was sharp and high-pitched, while Wylie's was low and mellifluous. The doctor was asking for his money, and Wylie was soothing him, saying he'd get it after the first of the year and this would benefit him "taxwise." Walker said he wanted to drive over and see the house he'd invested in. I laughed inwardly when Wylie said the house was in Los Angeles (earlier, he'd told Walker it was a San Francisco Victorian).

After twenty minutes Walker made ready to leave. I hoped he'd be savvy enough not to accept a ride from Wylie. If he did, the inspector would have to tail them to the hotel in order to pick up the rest of the conversation. Since the inspector's car was out of sight of the agency, that would be impossible unless the transmission was clear enough to alert the inspector to what was going on. I made my excuses to the clerk, kept the brochures, and left.

Back in the car, I had only a seven-minute wait before Walker and Wylie came out and got into Wylie's car. My job was really done, but I followed on the general principle you don't let a wired informant out of your sight: he could get hurt.

It was tricky crossing town behind the Seville with all the stoplights. I followed four or five cars back and then, after half a mile, moved in closer, with only one car separating us. I could see them chatting in the front seat, but the inspector's yellow Plymouth was nowhere in sight. As we swung together through downtown traffic, a rhythm was set up. Right, left, right again. I thought back to my first tail jobs two years before, how often I'd lost the quarry, how I'd always believed he was watching me in the rearview mirror. And I remembered too how I'd felt then there was something vaguely off-color about tailing someone, as if it were a private vice. Maybe it was, but it was also a way to make a living. Right now I just wanted to avoid getting burned in the last few minutes on the job.

Finally Wylie broke the rhythm by pulling up in front of the Mark Twain Hotel on Taylor. Sitting at the curb watching Wylie's taillights disappear, I dictated a conclusion into the recorder: "Two forty-eight. Wylie dropped the doctor off at the Mark Twain Hotel. Surveillance terminated." I went to a pay phone, dialed Greens' number, and asked his roommate to tell them the doctor and their wire were at the Mark Twain Hotel. Then I headed for Bolinas.

Outbound traffic over the Golden Gate Bridge was sparse. Rolling down the Waldo Grade to the Stinson Beach exit, I slipped into the right lane near the spot where, on that July morning more than a year earlier, I'd left the highway and bushwhacked down the slope to Karin Cutler's townhouse. If I were doing that job now, I thought, I'd stay farther up the bank in deeper cover and use a more powerful lens to photograph the boyfriend leaving. Later, I might still have tailed him over the bridge, but I'd stay three or four cars back, in another lane, never giving him the chance to pick me up. That wouldn't do much good, though, if he'd spotted the Volvo when he pulled out of the townhouse. Who knows? We hadn't heard a word from Cutler or his lawyer in sixteen months. Cases are like that; you work hard for days or weeks or months, and then the work is finished and you never learn the outcome. The same would probably happen with Green's case. It had never amounted to much—a few days' pay, some travel, a bit of excitement. I was glad it was over.

The freeway reached sea level near Richardson's Bay. I slipped off it and followed California Highway 1 upward through groves of eucalyptus to the Marin Headlands. The road curved down to Muir Beach and then up the other side to a ridge that dropped off on the west to the Pacific. Between there and Stinson Beach lay some of the most spectacular sea-swept scenery in northern California, but on this overcast Saturday afternoon it was just the road home. Scratching gravel, I pulled hard right into our driveway a little over an hour after leaving the hotel.

In the silence after the engine stopped, I heard the race of skateboard wheels and laughter. "You ate it, Ev," a boy yelled, laughing. "You really beefed that time!"

I walked down the bank to where Ev and his seventh-grade friends had built a skateboard ramp from scavenged plywood and lumber scraps. Ev carried his board to the top of the ramp, where a narrow platform made of plywood and two-by-fours was nailed together under an overhanging Monterey pine. He was wearing an Ocean Pacific T-shirt and droopy shorts.

"Watch this, Dad," he yelled over at me. "It's a tail tap. I just wiped out on it."

He hopped on his board and started down the runway. Hitting the plywood ramp, shoulder-length red hair streaming behind as his feet came up and body stretched parallel to the ground, he tapped the coping at the last possible instant with the tail of his board and twisted round to shoot down the ramp with knees bent, ending his stunt partway up the makeshift runway.

"Hot move, Rev!" said Ethan Okamura.

"All *right*," added the other boy. "That was radical!"

"Far out," I said, feeling old and silly. "You guys gonna be doing this for a while?"

"Naw," said Ev. "We're goin' down to the school to shoot a few hoops as soon as Ethan can figure out how to do the elevator drop."

"I already did it, Reverend," said Ethan. "You must've hit your head on the wipeout so bad you can't remember."

"Where're Nancy and Lis?" I asked. "The Chevette's gone."

"Lis and Mom took Toots over to Lagunitas," said Ev. "Horse show or somethin'. They were over in her stall last night braiding her mane. There's a note for you on the table."

"Thanks, man," I said. "We'll be eating 'round seven."

"OK." Ev turned away to watch Ethan, who was just starting his run.

I walked back to the car. I picked up the recorder, rewound it for a second or two, and then clicked it on. I heard the engine whine in the background, shifting up through the gears, while my own voice, breathing hard, said, "He's two blocks ahead, going east on Bush." The sound level seemed fine; tomorrow I'd have to write a report.

On the kitchen table was a note from Nancy:

Tink:

We're at a show in Lagunitas and should be back by six. Len Weinglass called last night and said to call him. He said you knew the number. Hope your guy didn't get on any buses; they can really be a bitch!

Love,

N.

The double-bus fiasco in Berkeley had become a family joke by then. I walked out on the deck and lit a cigarette. The clouds were skidding low over Bolinas Ridge. I felt lonely and drained.

SIX

"ODD MAN OUT"

WEDNESDAY, OCTOBER 18, 1978

A reporter once described Len Weinglass as "leonine." I was thinking of that when I saw him through the steamed-up glass of the café on Fourth Street. He was in a booth, studying legal papers through half-lensed reading glasses. A year ago he'd had a beard; now he was clean-shaven under a rich shock of dark red hair, and had on a loose-fitting Shetland sweater over a polo shirt. His sturdy face and fresh tan could have belonged to a yachtsman checking a list of equipment from the ship chandlery. That was rich: Len Weinglass, attorney for the downtrodden and forgotten, hired gun of the Left, looking like a yachtsman! It was seven-thiry; the sweater meant he wasn't going to court later in the day.

When I slid into the booth, he looked up and smiled. We shook hands and talked of mutual friends in Los Angeles and of Paul Skyhorse and Richard Mohawk. It was through them we'd met almost two years before. He'd come to their case with the fresh notches of the Chicago Seven and Pentagon Papers cases on his belt. Skyhorse and Mohawk were members of the American Indian Movement charged with the torture murder of a cabdriver. Their case had had the longest pretrial run in California history, and the trial itself had lasted fourteen months before ending in an acquittal the previous spring. Fechheimer had seconded me to Los Angeles for nearly four months to work under Weinglass's direction. The defense team had occasionally met in Len's nondescript house in the West Los Angeles hills.

157

It carried a mortgage of eighty-seven dollars a month, he'd once told me, and that fact revealed something important about him. He was a gifted criminal attorney with a national reputation, but had never made any money. Why? I'd asked him about it once, and he'd said he never defended anyone he didn't believe was innocent.

"You really think this mother's done five years for a murder he didn't commit?" I asked him now.

The waitress slid English muffins and coffee in front of me before Len could reply. Ten minutes earlier he'd begun describing the case, the reason for our meeting. As he'd explained it, the present chapter had begun a year earlier, when a young Korean named Chol Soo Lee killed another prisoner in the yard at Tracy. Because Lee was already doing time for first-degree murder, the second killing was charged as "murder with special circumstances" and carried the death penalty. At that point, both the press and the Korean community began to take an interest in Lee's predicament. Articles appeared in the Sacramento papers, and a defense committee was formed. That committee had hired Weinglass about a month earlier, and now he was hiring me.

Oddly enough, we weren't going to defend Lee in the prison killing. That was being handled by a senior attorney in the San Joaquin County Public Defender's Office. It was a straightforward case: Lee had killed the other prisoner in a fight and had been arrested on the spot. Lee's lawyer would argue it was self-defense. The track record of San Joaquin juries in prison killings was mixed; the outcome was uncertain.

Our focus would be the first killing, the one that had landed Lee in jail in the first place. If we could overturn that conviction, we could keep him off death row, since convictions in both cases were necessary to sustain "murder with special circumstances."

Why, now, did Len think Lee was innocent of the five-year-old gang killing in Chinatown?

"First, there's the polygraph. Lee kept claiming to his public defender that he'd been framed for the Chinatown killing. The public defender, Len Tauman, is a good man. By the way, he's expecting a call from you. Anyway, Tauman ordered up a polygraph from Cleve Backster's office in San Diego. Backster's people came to Tracy and ran Lee on the machine for two days. He came up completely clean."

"And how many people do you and I both know, Len, who've beaten the polygraph?" It wasn't I was more cynical than Len; it was just that he was already in the case, and I wasn't.

"If it were only the polygraph, I wouldn't be sitting here. The case has an odor to it. The closer you get to it, the greater the smell. Lee was convicted on the basis of identifications from three eyewitnesses who saw the shooter for only seconds. The trial was a mess. It got moved out of San Francisco. Lee's Sacramento attorney did less than ten hours of investigation, and then had a heart attack in the middle of it. Lee never got a proper defense."

"Getting a proper defense and being innocent are two different things."

"Right," said Len. "But what would you say if I told you people have been telling me for two weeks that everyone in Chinatown has known since it happened the killer was a young Wah Ching named Danny Choi?"

"I guess I'd ask where this dude is. He might have some interest in what we're doing."

"He's not around. A couple of people told me he's in Hawaii. Maybe in law school."

"Law school? Beautiful. The Wah Ching are now training their own. First you learn how to kill. Then, you go to law school."

Len shifted in the booth. He was impatient with the repartee.

"You said last night that a judge granted a hearing on the *habeas*," I said.

"Yeah. That's the news. It's the only shot we've got. All Lee's appeals on the first case were denied long ago, and the second case is probably a loser. Basically we've got the *habeas* hearing, and that's it. It starts next Thursday, so you'll have enough time to go after only the best leads. Can you get right on it?"

"Sure. I'll need the morning to clear up some things, but then I'm yours. Lucky I just wrapped up the case of the gay podiatrist."

"What?"

"Unimportant. You said Raul Ramirez would show us around the crime scene this afternoon?"

"Yeah. We'll meet him at the corner of Grant and Pacific— that's where it happened—at four-thirty. You know Raul?"

"I know *of* him. He and Lowell Bergman worked on that Chinatown story for the *Examiner*. When I went up to Pine

Ridge last year on Skyhorse-Mohawk, Lowell was a lot of help with the people there. How come a Cuban like Raul is wired into Chinatown?"

"You can ask him this afternoon," said Len, gathering up the papers on the table. "Here," he said, handing them over. "The files in Stockton fill ten boxes. But this is the basic stuff. Look it over, Xerox what you want, and give it back to me later."

I skimmed through the papers while Len paid the check. Outside, we stood for a moment by the door. The wind was blowing his hair. Already he looked cold.

"I think this could turn into quite a ride," he said, looking down at the sidewalk. "I know you detectives are supposed to be hard-bitten and cynical. So are lawyers. But something really smells here. I've felt it from the beginning, and I think you will too when you've read those." He nodded toward the documents.

"I'm not cynical, just grouchy. See you at four-thirty."

By 4:15 I was beginning to see it Len's way. Driving the twenty blocks to Chinatown, I was wondering if Chol Soo Lee might be that rare creature found only in bad detective novels: the innocent man put away for a murder he didn't do.

One document seemed particularly noteworthy.

It was the SFPD lab report on a firearms-identification test, what the TV dramas incorrectly call a ballistics test. Dated twelve days after the murder and signed by the criminalist in charge of the lab, it compared a slug fired by Lee into a wall the day before the killing with test bullets from the murder weapon. I'd underlined the last sentence of the report in red: *"Microscopic examination revealed that this bullet was also fired from the S&W revolver J91385."*

The report was extraordinary. Not because it looked any different from hundreds of firearms tests performed by the San Francisco Police lab every year. Not because it drew a noose of circumstantial evidence around Lee's neck. But because it was wrong.

Firearms identification is a strict science. The criminalist first checks the caliber of the weapon, the number of lands and grooves in the riflings, and whether they twist right or left, and then he compares the two slugs for the small irregularities unique to a particular weapon. He puts both bullets in a comparison microscope and turns the knob until similar segments of lands and grooves line up. Either they match or they don't.

But this report was wrong. Five years earlier Cliff Gould,

Lee's alert public defender in San Francisco, had hired a private criminalist to test the evidence. He had discovered no match whatsoever. Bullets fired from the murder weapon twisted in one direcion; the slug Lee accidentally fired into a wall twisted in the opposite direction. Bullets fired from the murder weapon had a different number of lands and grooves than the slug removed from the wall. These differences were so elementary it was incredible the police criminalist had missed them. Yet miss them he apparently had.

The mistaken match had never been presented at trial; it had played no part in Lee's eventual conviction. But it had led to his arrest in June 1973. And now, in October 1978, it was producing a subtle change in my olfactory sense as I pulled into a parking lot off Columbus Avenue. Len was right: the case stank.

Chinatown lies on the side of a hill that sweeps up from the docks near the Ferry Building to the heights of Grace Cathedral, the Pacific Union Club, and the Fairmont Hotel. The up-and-down streets—Pacific, Jackson, Washington, Clay—get steeper as they climb the hill. The cross streets—Powell, Stockton, Grant, and a host of small alleys—intersect the others in a series of terraces.

My ribs hurt for the first time in days as I walked up Pacific Avenue carrying an accordion file of documents. As Pacific Avenue got steeper, the sidewalk became more crowded. Just beyond Brandy Ho's Hunan Food was Lee Kun Kee's produce store, where boxes of Bok Choy, long beans, and broccoli were piled on the sidewalk, shaved ice glistening under the broccoli. Above, on the third floor, laundry hung in the window. I looked in the doorway of the New China Bookstore, its window filled with photos of stiffly heroic Red Chinese troops. My eyes met the hard gaze of a young woman in black skirt and white blouse. I looked away and kept walking.

Up ahead, Len was talking with someone at the corner. It must be Ramirez. Mustached, dressed in jeans, sport coat, and blue button-down shirt with no tie, he looked a bit like Geraldo Rivera. They were standing at the corner of Grant and Pacific, with their backs to the Ping Yuen Bakery, whose window contained row upon row of giant fortune cookies, each at least six inches across.

Introductions were made, and Ramirez continued his narrative of the killing. "Two of the three witnesses," he said, pointing cater-corner across the intersection, "were over there. They'd driven up from LA and were looking for a place to have dinner in Chinatown. They heard a shot and looked over here in time to see the killer finishing the victim with a shot into the back of his head. He fell right there in the crosswalk.''

The light changed, and pedestrians streamed across Pacific Avenue. Atop the stoplight facing us, an ornate light fixture suddenly came to life. Its glow sparkled on the bells hanging from its pagoda roof. Two dragons held up its underside.

"What time of night did all this happen?" I asked. "It was June 'seventy-three, right?"

"Yeah," said Ramirez. "June third, a Sunday. The police report said the first radio call went out at seven twenty-five.''

"Seven twenty-five in the evening in early June," I said, thinking out loud, "would be lighter than it is now. Were the streets as crowded as they are now?"

"Hard to tell," said Ramirez. "Probably about the same. Lots of people would be out on the streets at that time on a nice summer Sunday. Anyway, the killer turned and ran down Pacific to Columbus, where he disappeared around the corner. He threw away the gun in that alley—it's called Beckett Alley—and then passed a couple of sailors who were coming up Pacific.''

We walked a hundred feet to Beckett Alley. It was only wide enough for one car. Ramirez pointed to where the snub-nosed .38 had been found lying in the gutter. Then we retraced our steps and walked along Grant Avenue.

Ramirez was direct but also kind—not just in words, but in the gentleness of his movements as he threaded his way through the crowds. Len was quiet, listening to Ramirez's account of the origin of the Wah Ching in the generational battles between older and newer waves of immigrants, both crowding into the few blocks through which we strolled.

Turning uphill on Jackson, we paused for a moment at the windows of a combination butcher and fish shop before entering a small restaurant Ramirez knew. Roast ducks, their skin dark brown and parchmentlike, hung suspended from hooks lodged in their necks. In the other window, hundreds of fish milled around in a three-by-six-foot tank.

Three cups and a pot of steaming tea were put on the table as we sat down.

"At Lee's trial," said Len, "the prosecution took the line Lee was an outside killer hired by the Wah Ching to make the hit on Yip Yee Tak. That make any sense to you, Raul?"

"Not really. The Wah Ching have always taken care of their own business. If the word on the street is only half accurate, the hit on Tak was an important one. Tak was a kind of *consigliere* to the Wah Ching, and supposedly was taking care of the money that'd been collected to pay for Anton Wong's lawyer."

"Who's Wong?" I asked.

"He was the leader of the Wah Ching in the spring of nineteen seventy-three."

" 'Was'?"

"He was killed on the street about a block from here ten days before Tak's murder."

"Oh."

"The word is that Tak said he'd been robbed of a couple thousand that'd been collected for Wong's legal defense on an assault beef. No one believed him, and he'd pretty much dropped out of sight until Danny Choi spotted him that Sunday night."

"You talk as if it's a sure thing Choi did Tak?"

Ramirez didn't answer. He looked around the restaurant, not to see if we were being overheard but because my question had come across as a challenge and he wasn't looking for an argument.

"The police rounded up six Caucasian witnesses on the night of Tak's murder," he said quietly. "Probably a hundred Asians saw either the killing or the killer's escape. Not one of them came forward or gave any information to the police. But some recognized Choi; it was all over Chinatown the next morning. Choi himself wasn't real quiet about it. This was his first hit, and he bragged about it. Before this, he went by the nickname Trout; afterward, people started calling him Killer. I've even heard a detailed story about how he hid in the men's room of a service station. The Chevron down on Columbus. He dropped his wallet there, supposedly, and had to send a friend back to collect it later that night."

"So what's this case all about, anyhow, Raul?" asked Len.

"The usual. It's about being odd man out, being unlucky and poor and getting caught in the gears of the justice system. The irony is that you guys wouldn't be here if it weren't for the prison killing. That's when a Korean reporter in Sacramento got interested in the case and started calling it the Alice in Chinatown Case. Because of his articles, the Korean community organized and started to hold church suppers and all the rest. So we're talking today and I'm telling you about Choi and what really happened five years ago. But it's crazy, isn't it? You get put away for life for a killing you didn't do, and the only time anybody pays any attention to you is when you kill someone in prison and the State of California starts cranking up the little green room.''

Len and Ramirez were talking now, but I wasn't paying close attention. I was thinking of the ''little green room.'' I'd seen it once, on a visit to San Quentin years earlier. It wasn't really green, but a sickly-pale shade of cyan. The prisoner—I thought of him as ''the victim''—is strapped into a metal chair painted the same color as the room. He can look out through the windows of his space capsule at the witnesses in the adjoining room as the final arrangements are made. The warden of San Quentin then gives a nod, the executioner pulls a lever, and the hockey puck of cyanide drops into the acid. There hadn't been an execution in California since 1967, but a recent court decision had prompted the San Quentin authorities to refurbish the chamber. Apparently they'd tested it by strapping a pig into the chair and timing how long it squealed after the pellet hit the acid. Somewhere in the back of my mind I knew how cyanide worked: it blocked cells' capacity to absorb oxygen. You died after convulsions.

The waiter arrived with Dim Sum, and I tuned back in to the conversation. Ramirez no longer reminded me of Geraldo Rivera, but rather of a Latin American worker priest. I almost expected him to begin talking liberation theology.

''What chance you think you have, Lenny?'' Ramirez was asking.

''Realistically, not much. I read somewhere that less than one in five hundred of these *habeas* petitions are granted. We got the hearing on the basis of some documents not turned over to the defense at the time of the first trial. They don't look like much on the surface, but who knows? I'm hoping over the next week Tink can turn up something in the way of new evidence for the hearing. Hardly any investigation was done for the first trial, so there ought to be *something* out there—if five years hasn't buried it.''

The conversation became desultory, and soon Ramirez left to meet a deadline at the *Examiner*.

''You think something really is out there, Len?''

''Don't you?'' he asked in reply, tapping the folder I'd deposited on an empty chair.

"I didn't find much in the file. Lee claims he called his girlfriend about the time of the killing, and she was never talked to. Apparently there's a woman who knew Lee and claims to have seen the killing from a window. On the surface, that's it. With an innocent defendant, the more you dig, the more good stuff you get. But it takes time, and we don't have much. You're right, the case stinks. That 'mistake' on the firearms ID was outrageous. You're not holding anything up your sleeve, are you?"

"Only one lead," he said, pulling a business card from his wallet and writing a name and phone number on it. "This woman has been with the case since 'seventy-three. I'm told she's smart and gutsy. Evidently she's got a witness who saw either the killing or the getaway. For good reason, the witness is scared to testify and shy of lawyers and investigators. So tread carefully."

He glanced at his watch and said, "I've got to get back to Stockton."

Outside, we paused in front of the fish tank. Several hundred eyes stared through the glass, mouths puckered as they jostled for breathing room. A mistlike rain bathed the street and sidewalk.

FRIDAY, OCTOBER 27

There was no signal, no brake light or turn signal flashing on. Suddenly the van was there, its rear mud-spattered and dimpled, its wheels throwing plumes of spray in front of me. I braked and heard two heavy thuds. The monitor and VCR had hit the back of the front seat. I pulled onto the berm to check for damage.

Although it was quickly fading, there was enough light left to see that neither piece of equipment was harmed. They had simply hit the padded backs of the seats and then gotten wedged in the space behind. I put them back on the seat and edged into the heavy traffic streaming west toward San Francisco on Interstate 80. Davis had just receded in the rearview mirror; the pylon with the orange ball at Dixon would be coming up soon.

I'd lugged the VCR and monitor all the way to Sacramento that morning. All for nothing: they hadn't been used. But when you get right down to it, I hadn't expected anything else. How could a judge admit into evidence a videotape of a witness in a ski mask, known only as Mr. X, answering questions from Len

Weinglass? The prosecutor had called it a joke, but that was wrong. It wasn't a joke.

I'd first interviewed "X" the previous Monday night at Ranko's apartment out in the Sunset. Ranko was the "smart and gutsy woman" Len had mentioned, an attractive Japanese law student who was extremely protective of her witness. Only after I'd promised not to put a tail on "X" or serve him with a subpoena had she agreed to set up an interview.

"X" turned out to be a young Chinese in his late twenties who had been living in Chinatown in 1973. On the night of the killing, he'd been in Beckett Alley with some friends and had seen the killer run away. There was little doubt he'd recognized the killer as Choi, but he wouldn't say that. He would say only that he'd seen the killer earlier that night and then later, after Chol Soo Lee was in custody, had seen him again in Chinatown. He'd bumped into Lee a few times prior to that and was certain Lee was not the killer. But he wouldn't testify in open court. The best he would do for us was to be questioned under oath by Weinglass. If we wanted to videotape that questioning, that would be OK. But in that case, he'd insist on wearing a mask.

During the videotaping the next night, Lenny had asked "X" about the mask. He had passed a polygraph by then, patiently sitting there while the examiner adjusted his equipment and asked a battery of questions. Ranko had brought the ski mask in her purse and handed it to him after we got settled. "I'm afraid of these gangs," he told Len. "I've lived in Chinatown all my life. I've seen guys who were in these gangs, who are no longer there, who're dead. Have you ever seen someone who just got shot? You know, whose head has just been blown away, where you can't see his face anymore? It's too frightening for me to risk my family's life. Or my own. With this particular shooting here, there's more involved than either you or I know about."

So the prosecutor was wrong. It was no joke. The polygraph said "X" was telling the truth, and "X" wasn't being paranoid to hide his face or not tell us his name. On the other hand, the prosecutor was probably right that whatever "X" said shouldn't be admitted into evidence. How do you cross-examine a witness who appears only as a masked figure on videotape? The lawyers would continue to wrangle over it, and their wrangling had already bought us time. But unless "X" changed his mind and agreed to testify, it was a dead end.

There had been other dead ends.

I'd wasted a couple of days trying to trace Chol Soo Lee's girlfriend at the time. One lead had taken me to San Francisco State, and a professor there had provided the address of her family. The family said she was out of state but agreed to relay a message to her. It seemed doubtful that they would, and if they did, there was no telling whether she could provide any useful information.

There was the young Chinese woman who had seen the killing from a window on Pacific Avenue and claimed the killer could not have been Chol Soo Lee. She'd seemed promising until I went to the window where she said she'd been standing, a block away from the murder site. It was impossible to recognize a person on the the street from that distance.

Off to the left now, I could just make out the giant orange ball on the two-hundred-foot pillar at Dixon. I'd started working on this case nearly ten days before, and all I had to show for it was a videotape of a nameless young man in a ski mask.

The wipers were slip-slapping in the drizzle.

It was discouraging, following these leads that led nowhere. Maybe that was why we called them leads, what the Oxford English Dictionary describes as "guiding indications"—clues to the direction in which a path lies. We were tracing out a number of leads in hopes one would take us where we wanted to go. But where was that? Not all cases know where they're going; sometimes you have to spend hours or days in what looks like aimless wandering before you can figure that out. The only detectives who know from the start where their cases are going do their work on prime time.

Looking over at the great orange ball, I thought of the Sky-horse—Mohawk case. That was the way it had been in that case. For a long time we hadn't known where it was going, or where it ought to go. Those two days I'd spent up here going through the Sioux sweat ceremony hadn't produced any dramatic break-through. That had all been part of finding out where the case ought to go. Maybe the same thing was happening now? Maybe we had to bushwhack for awhile in order to find the trail? I hadn't learned that from Hammett or Fechheimer, but it was something they'd probably agree with.

This wasn't like a British drawing-room whodunit, where you wanted to be led to the solution of the mystery. In part, there *was* no mystery here. In all likelihood Choi had done the killing for which Lee had been convicted. We were searching for evidence to overturn that conviction, and it might be of two sorts. It could be new evidence—a witness, for example—or it might be proof that Lee had been deprived of a fair trial the first time around. Over the past ten days, the search for new evidence had produced only the videotape of "X." Of necessity we were being forced back on the documents that had opened the door for the *habeas* hearing in the first place, documents we hoped might show Lee hadn't gotten a fair trial in 1974.

Our possession of the documents was a fluke, the product of a clerk's mistake. When Lee told his current public defender he was innocent of the 1973 murder, the lawyer did two things: he made arrangements for Lee to take a polygraph, and he requested the original case file from the San Francisco District Attorney's Office. When the file arrived, it contained two documents that had not been turned over to Lee's defense in 1974.

The first was a police APB broadcast on the day after the murder. After describing the suspect, it ended with the advisory: *"Minutes prior to the shooting witness observed possibly same subject exit a tan colored El Dorado or Coupe de Ville that was parked on Kearny near Pacific Avenue."* Who was this"witness"? One of the two homicide inspectors who had handled the investigation had been on the stand just that afternoon. Looking a little like Starsky of *Starsky and Hutch*, with curly black hair and a belt buckle emblazoned with 187 (the penal-code number for murder), Frank Falzon had a reputation for being a tenacious detective. Len Weinglass had asked him on the stand about the Cadillac report, and he'd said it came from "either an anonymous phone call or a patrolman at the scene of the crime." Without something more concrete from police witnesses, we couldn't claim that ignorance of this document had hobbled Lee's original defense. It looked like another dead end.

Not so the other document withheld from the defense, a memo written by Falzon and his partner, Jack Cleary, to the chief of inspectors. Typed in capital letters and dated three days after the murder, it outlined what they had learned: "WE HAVE RECEIVED INFORMATION FROM A CONFIDENTIAL INFORMANT THAT ON SUNDAY NIGHT, MINUTES PRIOR TO THE SHOOTING THAT THE DECEDANT [*sic*] AND SUSPECT WERE HAVING COFFEE TOGETHER IN A GRANT AVENUE CAFE. THEY WERE SEEN SHAKING

HANDS AND AN APPARENT AGREEMENT MADE.
THEY LEFT TOGETHER WHEREIN A VERBAL ARGU-
MENT ENSUED AND MINUTES LATER [TAK] WAS
SHOT."

The mere existence of the memo was curious: it wasn't customary for inspectors working a street murder to send progress
memos to their chief. As we'd learned from testimony, the memo
had been written in response to an inquiry from no less a per-
sonage than Mayor Joseph Alioto himself concerning police
progress in solving the crime, the thirteenth unsolved Chinatown gang murder since October 1970. Who was the "confidential informant" who had either witnessed or heard about the
meeting between Tak and his killer? Testimony this afternoon
had shown him to be Deputy DA Leonard Louie, who had probably gotten the information from his uncle, Park Louie, owner
of Louie's of Grant Avenue. If Park Louie had witnessed the
encounter between victim and killer or could lead us to the
person who had, then the memo in defense hands four years
earlier could have produced the same result. Assuming whoever
it was who had witnessed the meeting could testify that Chol
Soo Lee was not the person he'd seen with Tak, we'd have what
we needed: evidence that the prosecutor in 1974 had made it
impossible for Lee to get a fair trial.

As the drizzle turned to sheets of rain, I started wondering
how I was going to find Park Louie. Two Asian law students
would be meeting me at Grant and Pacific that evening at seven.
If he wasn't at his restaurant, they could help me find him; if he
was, they could smooth over the rough edges of language.
Weinglass would meet us later at the singles bar below the office
on Union Street.

By seven the rain had stopped and Chinatown was bathed in
mist. Climbing the long flight of steps to Louie's of Grant Avenue, I hung back, letting Happi and Kim run interference. They
spoke animatedly with the manager and then reported Park Louie
was not expected at the restaurant until Sunday. The manager
thought he was out of town.

By eight-thirty we'd been to four other restaurants and three
small apartments, but were no closer to finding Louie. We'd
also learned a large political meeting was taking place at a restaurant on Pacific, a block up from the murder site. Louie was
a well-known businessman in Chinatown and could be expected
to be there.

We trooped into the restaurant, scribbled our names on name tags picked up from a table by the men's room, and began to mingle with the guests. In deference to the English-speaking politicos, name tags were written in English, and I started scanning them for the name *Louie*. Kim knew Park Louie by sight, so we all separated and worked different parts of the room. Unexpectedly I found myself in a line moving toward the speaker's table. I shook several hands, then looked up to see the familiar face of Governor Jerry Brown, hand extended. I mumbled something about the importance of the governor supporting the aspirations of Asian-Americans. He looked at me strangely and then shook the hand of the Chinese Episcopal minister to my left. I spotted three *Louie* name tags—none, alas, belonging to Park Louie.

After half an hour, we regrouped outside. Happi had brought along a young Chinese woman wearing a windbreaker.

"Now what?" I said, mostly to myself. "I sure would like to know if he's really out of town. His family ought to know. Any way we could call them?"

"I went to high school with his nephew," said Happi's friend. "Maybe I could get him to find out."

The three of them went off in search of the nephew and I headed for Union Street.

The Friday-night singles crowd was just assembling at the Tarr and Feathers when I walked in. Lenny hadn't arrived yet. That was par for the course. Our breakfast the week before was the first time Lenny had been on time for an appointment in the year and a half I'd known him. I ordered a St. Pauli Girl and told the bartender my name and that I was expecting a call. When he brought the beer, I put a five-dollar bill on the bar and told him to keep the change. He took it unsmilingly, but I figured I'd get the call. This early in the evening, the crowd was largely unaffected by controlled substances. There were the usual knots of cruising secretaries and a smattering of solitary middle-aged men hunched over their drinks, trying to look interesting.

By the time Lenny arrived half an hour later, the tempo had picked up. The bar was crowded, and a folk singer had started singing sixties songs from the little stage in the back. Lenny wasn't overjoyed with my lack of news.

We were talking about the recent massacre in the Golden Dragon restaurant in Chinatown—again gang-related—when I heard the bartender asking loudly, "Is there a Pink Johnson here?" I walked to the phone at the end of the bar.

It was Kim. They'd gotten the same information from Louie's family and from a business associate: he was in Boston and might be back Sunday.

"Could you get the phone number where he's staying?"

"No. He's at a hotel, but I don't think anyone knows which one."

"Thanks, nice work," I said.

"In a way," Lenny said after I told him what Kim had come up with, "that's good news. It means no one else can have gotten to him first. Let's go back to your office and try to track him down."

Half an hour later I had the phone numbers of twenty-five Boston hotels. I'd told the supervisor for directory assistance in Boston I was trying to find a witness in a murder case. This caught her interest, and she went over a list of hotels, picking out the ones Park Louie might be staying in.

We split the list in half and sat down at different phones. On Len's eighth try we got lucky. Park Louie was registered at the Cradford Hotel in Boston. Len gave the night clerk the same story I'd given the supervisor. The clerk said Louie had ordered a wake-up call for 7:45 the next morning.

Our first contact with Louie would be critical. If I didn't tape the call, it would be only my word against his as to what was said. Taping a phone call without both parties' consent was illegal in California. So we couldn't use a tape as evidence. The best thing would be to have Len on the extension, taking notes. Since the call would have to be made just before five in the morning our time, Len offered to spend the night on the couch in the office.

We were both groggy when I placed the call at 4:50 A.M. A very ungroggy Asian voice answered the phone. I told Park Louie I was the defense investigator in the Chol Soo Lee case and that Lee's defense attorney was also on the line. Louie remembered the Lee case but thought it had ended long ago. So far, so good. I asked him if he remembered talking with police inspectors about the case back in 1973, and he said no. Then I told him we had information he'd told his nephew about an argument between Tak and another man just before the killing. He didn't say anything. I asked him if he remembered passing on any information to his nephew about the case. He said he didn't. Then Lenny asked him if he'd said anything to anyone about two men being in his restaurant that night, or about an argument between them, or anything. He said he remembered nothing like that: "Something must be wrong. Maybe somebody else, another merchant." I thanked him for talking with us. He confirmed that he would be back in San Francisco on Sunday.

I put the receiver down and stared at it. I was cold even with a sweater on under my jacket. Lenny came in from the other room and stood in the doorway.

"We did everything right," I said, looking down at the phone, "and still lost. What now?"

"We'll subpoena 'em all and see what happens. Somewhere out there is a break with our name on it."

THURSDAY, NOVEMBER 2

It was the stuck drawer that made the coffee spill.

The desk had belonged to Professor William Lunt of the History Department. He died long before I got to Haverford and even longer before we moved into the house on College Lane where he'd lived for nearly forty years. The weight and size of the desk accounted for its still being in an upstairs bedroom. It wasn't handsome, not a rolltop, just garden-variety oak of a design current around the turn of the century. For all I knew, it might have been standard issue for faculty offices at the time. It had taken four of us to carry it downstairs to the moving van that July morning the summer before. I didn't understand clearly why I'd taken it, since we'd given away more valuable furniture. But I'd done a lot of writing at that desk; I wanted it for that reason and also, I suppose, because it was a Haverford heirloom, a concrete memento of a tradition I was leaving. And so we'd stowed it in the Ryder truck and driven it across the country and then, only the month before, carried it up the narrow stairs of 2148 Union Street and deposited it in the back room. Jack and Sandra had more conventional office space nearer the street, but I enjoyed being tucked in behind the kitchen in what had once been a pantry.

I'd been sitting at the desk earlier, rereading the polygraph and the transcript of "X" 's videotaped testimony. I'd wanted to underline the space where "X" said Tak's killer had been "at least five-seven"; it meshed nicely with the bulletin's description of the suspect as "5 feet 6 inches to 5 feet 8 inches." (Chol Soo Lee was five foot two.) Needing a pen, I'd tried to get the center drawer open, but, either due to warpage from the California climate or because it had been sprung by all the moving, it stuck fast. Forgetting the coffee mug sitting between the files, I'd gotten up and yanked on it. It hadn't moved, but the desk had, sending coffee cascading over "X" 's transcript.

I was holding the sodden file, shaking coffee onto the linoleum tile, when the phone buzzed. It was our receptionist-secretary, Eva.

"Tink, one of your clients is here."

"Terrific. Which one?"

"No," she went on, "you don't understand. He didn't ask to see you. He wanted to talk with Jack. He's in there now. I thought you might like to join them. It's Glenn Morgan."

"Thanks, Eva," I said, "but no thanks. I've got other things to do. I'm giving 'X's' transcript a coffee bath to see if it reads any better."

"What?"

"Never mind."

A terrific beginning for Thursday. Morgan was Green's lawyer. What did he want? I hadn't seen him since the Saturday surveillance. The retainer Green had given me just about covered the bill, so he couldn't have come all the way over here about that. And why ask to see Jack and not me? Who knew? Who cared? More important was the continuing question of what the hell we were going to do about the Chol Soo Lee case. As far as I could see, we were stymied.

The judge had given us a two-week continuance after the hearing a week previous. That was its only positive result. I'd worked through the weekend serving subpoenas. Unglamorous work, but necessary. Deputy DA Leonard Louie and his uncle were easy: after Len and I interviewed them, I left subpoenas on the way out. Jack Cleary was another matter. He'd been Frank Falzon's partner five years before, but had left the police force to become a district attorney's investigator. A friend had given me a list of the home addresses of San Francisco police officers, and it was old enough to contain Cleary's address out in the avenues. I spent most of Saturday afternoon sitting on his house, and then went back that night. When I finally served the subpoena on

Cleary at eleven-thirty, I figured he might be irritated. But he turned out to be a hearty Irishman who appreciated what it was like to sit in a car for most of a Saturday with nothing to show for it. With a reversal in circumstances, he could have been the one in the car. He took the subpoena in good spirits and even offered a beer.

All three showed up for the hearing in Sacramento. For all the good it did us, they could have stayed home.

After five years, Cleary couldn't even confirm Flazon's dim recollection that the Cadillac information had come either from an anonymous phone call or from a patrolman at the crime scene. When Leonard and Park Louie finished testifying, the account of the supposed meeting between Tak and his killer was left in even greater obscurity. Leonard Louie said his uncle told him some street talk about the murder, and he'd passed it on to the inspectors. Park Louie was unable to remember the incident at all. By the end of the afternoon, the informant story had vanished into thin air, and with it any chance of winning a reversal on the basis of it.

For the past two days Len and I'd been trying without success to find some other weakness in the prosecution's case. Now, on Len's instruction, I was about to start a search for Tak's widow, largely because neither side had ever talked to her. There might be something there; on the other hand, it was difficult to believe the widow of the victim, even after five years, would want to talk to—let alone help—the defenders of her husband's supposed killer. I could whistle loudly in the dark about how with an innocent defendant, the more you dig, the more chance you have of finding something, but the fact remained we were running out of places to look.

I heard Jack's office door open and voices in the hall. After a few minutes, Jack came into the kitchen next to my office. I put the drenched file on the desk and went in.

As he poured a stream of coffee into a heavy mug with a cracked rim, he was chuckling.

"What are you laughing about?"

"You, Thompson, have been reported to higher authority."

"Higher authority . . . you? You must be kidding."

"I'm not. Your client Glenn I. Morgan, attorney at law, has just now left my office, having duly reported you for not following orders. He's pissed you went into the travel agency when that wasn't part of the original plan."

"It also wasn't part of the original fucking plan," I exploded, "to send the doctor in there with only a bug and no tape recorder. You must be kidding—"

"Len Tauman's on line two, Tink," interrupted Eva from the doorway.

I looked at Jack, who was still chuckling, and went to my phone.

"We just got a new piece of paper on the mysterious Cadillac," Tauman reported. "Trouble is, it's handwritten, and the photocopy's so bad you can hardly make it out. But there's a name and address attached to it. Looks like it was a phone-in. The guy who took the report is named Gus, and he put a time and date on it: twelve twenty-five hours on six/four/seventy-three."

"That's the day after the killing."

"Brilliant deduction, Holmes," said Tauman. "I knew it was clever of us to get a Ph.D. for a detective."

"What else does it say?"

Tauman read me Gus's two-page report over the phone. A witness had described seeing two OMAs (Oriental Male Adults, in police lingo) get out of an El Dorado or Coupe de Ville shortly before the killing. The Caddy and the witness's car tapped bumpers. The witness was having dinner in Chinatown with others; when they got back to their car, the Cadillac was gone. One of the OMAs matched the description of the killer in the paper, so the witness called in.

"Not much there," I said. "Probably a lot of OMAs were getting into cars around Chinatown that night. Even if we find the witness, we don't have much."

"His name's Steve," said Tauman. "That much I can make out. But absolutely nothing on the last name. I can't read a single letter of it. The town is Point Richmond, and the street looks like Santa Fe, but I can't be sure. One fifty-three or One eighty-three Sante Fe. And then there's a phone number. The first number of the exchange is two, but I can't make out the other two digits. The phone number itself is seven, nine—those two I'm sure of—and then it looks like eight, four. Or it could be three, four."

"You sure you can't make out anything on the last name?" I asked.

Tauman said he couldn't.

"I'll get on it now."

"Good hunting. I'll mail you a photocopy of our photocopy."

On my way out, I looked into Jack's office to add a few words about Morgan's "report," but Jack was on the phone. What a chickenshit trick; you expect attorneys to bitch and moan when they lose, but not when they win.

Eva looked up from her typing as I passed. "Remember," she said, "you've got a two-o'clock appointment with that Chase woman." I nodded and picked a jellybean from the bowl on her desk. "Once again," I said, "down these mean steps a man must stumble." She smiled, and I went down the steps, stumbling loudly at the bottom.

My first stop was Hal Lipset's office.

The antique grillwork outside the Victorian had been freshly painted, black with gold accents. Inside, the first floor seemed different too. The electronic equipment in the room just off the entry hall had been replaced with bookcases, and the hall was also newly painted. Even Hal, talking on the phone at his antique desk with a cigar burning in the porcelain ashtray, seemed somehow spruced up. Each time I'd seen Hal over the previous two years he'd seemed more congenial and more nattily dressed. Today he was in shirt sleeves, "working the phones," as he put it, his shirt monogrammed, with French cuffs. He greeted me warmly, and I got quickly to the point: I wanted to use his Haines crisscross directory for Point Richmond.

"I guess you really weren't an agent," he said, a smile curling his lips.

"What?"

"Back in 'seventy-six, David thought you might be working for somebody. That's why we sent you off to Oakland."

"What d'you mean?"

"Back then we'd just come off the San Quentin Six case and were still working for Huey Newton. David thought some spook agency might have sent you over. I mean, it didn't make a lot of sense. Here you are, some forty-year-old philosophy professor wanting to be a gumshoe."

"Why didn't you just not hire me?"

"You were cheap. It's tough hiring Ph.D's for five bucks an hour," he said, smiling slyly. "You couldn't hurt us in Oakland."

"*Paranoia investigatorus*, eh?"

"That's professor language. Anyhow, you've been doing it

too long now to have been an agent. The Haines is in the other room. When are you hotshots gonna make enough money to buy your own?''

Hal was called away to the phone, and I went into the anteroom across the hall. The only exchange for Point Richmond was 236. I looked up 7984; it traced to a Floyd Morris, with an address that wasn't on Santa Fe. I did the same thing for 236-7934. Again the number was assigned, but not to anyone on Santa Fe. It would have been simpler to look up the Santa Fe address in the 1973 edition and see who had the number, but each year the Haines people collected the old book when they delivered the new one. The only thing to do was to drive over to Point Richmond and see what I could find out in the 100 block of Santa Fe.

It was a short, tree-lined block, the street curving northeastward down a hill. It had a nineteenth-century flavor like similar streets in Connecticut or Pennsylvania mill towns. There were three apartments at 153, but no one answered the bell for any of them. Next door was a building with flats above a store. A sign over the door had the words *Wood Art* carved into it. The shop sold tools and woodworking equipment.

"Steve hasn't lived here for a couple of years," said a brown-haired woman of about thirty. She wore no makeup, and her cobalt-blue eyes looked directly at me. There were freckles across her nose. "I don't know where he moved to. I think it may have been Berkeley or Albany."

"You remember Steve's last name?"

"Sure. Morris."

"Did he have a brother or any relative named Floyd?"

"I wouldn't know. I scarcely knew him. We used to say hello if we bumped into each other. That's all. You say he's a witness—what to? A traffic accident or something?''

"Yeah, something like that. You don't remember what year it was he moved?"

"Not really. Let's see. It's been at least three years, though—I'm sure of that."

The sun broke through as I drove to the Richmond Public Library. The day had started out dismally, but the hunt was fun. It didn't matter if this was a goose chase; it was satisfying to be getting somewhere. Steve Morris. Floyd Morris. The coincidence was too great. I'd have him in half an hour.

The reference librarian pointed to the old telephone books,

and quickly my eyes ran down the page of Morrises in the 1973 directory. Bingo! Steven Morris at 153 Santa Fe, phone number 236-7984, the same number Floyd Morris now had. Piece of cake. I checked the 1974 directory. Steve Morris was no longer listed. He'd moved sometime before May 1974, when the new directory had come out. What was the address for Floyd Morris I'd jotted down at Lipset's? I looked at the yellow pad: 276 Chanslor Avenue, about twenty blocks away.

It was a little after one-thirty when I got back on the freeway and headed for San Francisco. Sylvia Maradona was living at 276 Chanslor and had never heard of Floyd Morris. Just a temporary glitch. We'd have our witness soon. I already knew his name was Steven Morris and that he'd moved from 153 Santa Fe sometime before May 1974. Not bad for a couple hours' work, but now I had to get back to the office. I thought of the woman in the Wood Art shop. She'd been pretty and wholesome-looking. I wondered if she came from a mill town in Pennsylvania or New England.

TUESDAY, NOVEMBER 7

"Think we got the right Morris?" I asked Paul Palladino.

We were standing in the nicest room of the office, the one with the fireplace and Sandra's small desk by the window that looked over the Bay to Alcatraz. The light was fading now, and headlights were twinkling on the Golden Gate Bridge as the commuter rush began.

"You know everything I know," he said. "What do you think?"

I'd learned to trust Paul's opinion. He worked under the shadow of his elder brother, but he was far and away the best operative we had. Doing even the most routine tasks, he was always thinking ahead, figuring out the next move. For the last few days he'd been point man in the search for Morris.

"It's the best lead we've got," I said, not really replying to his question. "Datasearch is spitting Steven E. Morrises out of the computer faster than we can check 'em, and Jerry Goldstein's having the same grief with credit-card lists. The name's so damn common. How'd you get this Pine Street address?"

"One of the tenants at One fifty-one Santa Fe was pretty sure Morris had moved to San Francisco. Datasearch gave us a bunch of Steven Morrises for San Francisco but only two Steven E. Morrises, one at Four fifty-four State Street and the other at Nineteen fifty-six Pine. We know we're looking for a Steven E. Morris 'cause that's the name connected with the Santa Fe address on the 'seventy-three voter's list. You checked out State Street last night, right?"

I nodded, thinking of the three hours I'd spent sitting on the State Street house, waiting for the wrong Steven Morris to come home from a double feature at the Castro Theater. I could have checked the address over a number of days, but I was antsy and wanted to get the Morris search done. On the surface, it shouldn't have been high-priority; after all, what would we have when we found him? But it was the only active lead we had, and I felt bad I hadn't produced more for Lenny.

"I went over to the Pine Street address this morning," Paul continued, "but no one there ever heard of Steve Morris. I got the landlord's number and reached his answering service around noon, and then put in a request for Morris's forwarding address with the post office. Here's the landlord's number if you want to try it again. I'm going home."

I walked through the kitchen to my desk and dialed the number. The landlord's answering service picked it up on the second ring.

Working for Fechheimer, I'd learned to trade on the private eye's identity and on the dull routine that was the reality of most people's jobs. If you tell them a bit about what you're doing, people will often hop aboard and help with anything that has the scent of the unusual or the dramatic.

I gave the woman on the other end a heavy pitch about how important Morris was, saying he was a "critical witness in a death-penalty murder case." She got interested and wanted to know more. Her name was Cheryl, and most of what I told her in the next five minutes was true. She said she'd call the landlord's unlisted home number every hour until he answered.

I didn't look forward to spending another night in the city. I'd been running for several days now, and it would be nice to get back to Bolinas for dinner with Nancy and the kids. Ev would be riding high because his soccer team had pulverized Lagunitas the day before. But I had two reports on other cases to write, and I ought to go over what we had on Tak's wife, for whom we were still searching. It was already after six. I wrote the reports and then walked down Fillmore to the Edwardian cafeteria.

This early in the evening, it was almost empty. Over a pastrami sandwich and a beer, I read the paper.

Congressman Leo Ryan would be making a trip to Guyana to check on stories he'd heard about the People's Temple settlement. While working for Fechheimer, I'd done some work for the Temple. The previous July, our contact in the Temple had told me that dissidents were circulating ugly rumors about the Reverend Jim Jones and the Guyana settlement, one of the craziest being that the settlement doctor had stockpiled cyanide to use in a mass suicide. Evidently some of this rubbish had reached the ears of Congressman Ryan.

I'd been back in my office only about twenty minutes when the phone rang.

"I found your witness Morris," Cheryl said. "He's in Los Angeles. He said he almost got shot himself. He was only about ten feet away."

"What?" I said, bewildered, the significance of what she was saying not registering.

"I found Morris," she repeated. "I reached the landlord about an hour ago. He said he thought Morris had moved to Los Angeles, but he wasn't sure. I called your number, but no one answered."

"Yeah. I went out to eat."

"Anyway, when I couldn't reach you—" Cheryl hesitated. Another call had come in. She'd call me right back.

Morris was in Los Angeles, and she'd talked to him? Was that it? But how could he possibly have seen anything? The police report said he'd been blocks away and had only seen someone in a car, a Caddy.

I leapt when the phone rang.

"So anyway," Cheryl continued, "things were quiet here so I got LA information and asked for Steve Morris. They'd only give me three numbers at a time, but I got lucky. Nobody answered the first number, but the second number was him. There's no doubt about it. He was in Chinatown looking at a fortune cookie when it happened. That's what he said, anyway."

I thought of the giant fortune cookies in the window of the Ping Yuen Bakery.

Cheryl went on: "He couldn't believe anyone would want to talk to him after all these years. I told him you'd be calling. You want the number?"

"You kidding?"

She gave me the number, and I told her I'd call her back after I reached Morris. I sat and looked at the phone for half a minute and then dialed.

The voice on the other end was young and white. Somewhere in the tonalities of voice and choice of words, I picked up the fact Morris was gay. He'd worked as a waiter for a while, and now he was bartending in Westwood. He was surprised to be called about this case after five years, since the police hadn't shown much interest in him earlier. He hadn't heard that anyone had been convicted.

His account of that Sunday night was simple. He'd driven into Chinatown for dinner with a couple—Ray and Shelley—and two gay men. They walked around a bit, looking for a restaurant. He and Shelley were looking at some giant fortune cookies in a store window when a "commotion" broke out behind them. He turned around to see one Asian man shoot another on the crosswalk. He thought there'd been two men chasing the victim, but only one had a gun. The gunman wheeled around and then ran down the hill.

"When did you report this to the police?" I asked.

"At first I didn't want to get involved, but the next day I called them up and told them what I'd seen and about earlier seeing the guy in the Cadillac with two of his friends."

"Did you ever go to a lineup?"

"No. Some policeman got in touch with me a couple of times, but he never said anything about a lineup."

"Remember that officer's name?"

"It's been five years. Some Italian name, I think."

"Was it Inspector Falzon? Frank Falzon?"

"That sounds right."

"It wasn't Jack Cleary, was it? Inspector Jack Cleary was the other homicide inspector on the case."

"No, it was Falzon. The name clicked when you mentioned it."

We agreed to meet in Los Angeles the next night. He didn't

have to be at work until nine. I would pick him up at six, and we'd get something to eat at a nearby diner.

I called Len Weinglass. He was already in Los Angeles and would meet us at the diner. Then I called Len Tauman in Stockton.

Finally, I called Cheryl back. She agreed to meet me at a café across the street from the answering service when she got off at eleven. We had coffee and pie, and she wouldn't take the twenty bucks I tried to put in her purse.

SEVEN

"SPLENDIDLY, JUST SPLENDIDLY"

WEDNESDAY, NOVEMBER 8, 1978

Coming out of the Criminal Courts Building, my jacket hung loosely over the sweaty crook of my arm. It was hot in Los Angeles; one of those odd fall days that carry along the rag end of summer. I switched on the air-conditioner in the rented Escort while still in the underground garage. Up to this point the day had been a washout. Two sweat-stained hours in various court and public records offices had produced nothing about the background or whereabouts of Yip Yee Tak's widow. Morris could make the search for her irrelevant, but I wasn't taking any bets. Before leaving San Francisco, I'd read over the notes the police inspector had jotted down when he took Morris's call. There was no mention of Morris having witnessed a shooting. Toward the end of the two pages, the policeman had written, *"He didn't hear any shots tho. They asked people what happened."* How could Morris have seen the killing from close up and not heard any shots? If Morris and Shelley had been right there, why had "they asked people what happened"?

Morris lived in an unremarkable frame house on an unremarkable street. The grass pressing through cracks in the broken sidewalk looked tired, and so did the flaking paint on the white clapboard walls. Morris led me through the living room to the kitchen, where he took a can of V-8 from the refrigerator. We sat at the Formica kitchen table, sipping the juice from small glasses etched with flowers, my eyes wandering over the freshly painted walls of the room.

The wall directly opposite held several unusual photos of Marilyn Monroe. It turned out she was a particular fascination of his; he collected memorabilia and books about her. We talked of the Kennedys and of the rumors surrounding her death while I tried to take his measure.

He worked at Lillian's, a bar/restaurant on Santa Monica Boulevard, where he'd started as a waiter and worked up to bartender. For a time he'd also worked as a model, but hadn't been able to make a living at it. Not strikingly handsome, as I'd imagined male models to be, he was in his midtwenties and about five foot ten, with a slim build and long fingers. There was nothing of the kook about him, and no sense he was hustling us for anything. He seemed amused a private eye would show up on his doorstep after all these years, but not terribly interested. All in all, he seemed as unremarkable as his house.

As we pulled into the diner's parking lot, I scanned the windows to see if Len had arrived. For the second time in three weeks, I saw him through the glass of a restaurant window, reading in a booth. After introductions were made, we chatted amiably about things of no consequence while scanning the menu. After the waitress took our orders, we got down to business.

Morris began his story.

He had driven over to San Francisco that night with friends. They parked on Kearny Street near Jackson. Two parking spaces were free. Just as they pulled into one, the Cadillac backed into the spot just ahead. Its back bumper tapped their front bumper, and for a moment Morris feared there would be trouble. Three "Chinese guys" got out of the Cadillac, looked at their car, and then walked away.

"Could you tell they were Chinese, and not Japanese or Korean?" I asked.

"No," said Morris. "I should have said they were Orientals, I guess."

Morris and his friends ambled up Jackson and turned left onto Grant Avenue, looking for a restaurant. Morris and Shelley got separated from the others and were looking in a window at some giant fortune cookies. Morris heard someone running behind him and turned around.

"There were two of them, I think. But only one of 'em had a gun. That was the guy I'd seen getting out of the backseat of the

Caddy. He shot the other guy right in the crosswalk. The guy was holding his hands up, and he just shot him."

"Did he shoot him in the back or the front?" asked Lenny.

"Looked to me like he shot him in the chest. You know, from the front. And then I think he shot him again as he was going down. But I'm not real sure of that. I was trying to get away, pushing Shelley ahead of me into some kind of doorway. Then the guy ran away down the hill."

Our orders came, and Morris excused himself to go to the men's room. Lenny looked discouraged.

"What're you thinking?" I asked.

"I think the guy's a turkey. The other witnesses have Tak shot in the back. And no one else saw two assailants. How the hell can we use a witness who saw it happening a way it couldn't have happened?"

"Uh-huh," I mumbled, trying to remember what I'd read in the file. "I don't think I ever read the autopsy closely. Let's bracket the whole thing until we get a chance to go over it."

Morris came back. Over the meal, we talked of other cases. I told them about a lecture I'd heard on hypnosis, where the speaker, a doctor, told of its usefulness in retrieving information thought to be forgotten. Morris admitted that five years had taken their toll on his memories of that night. Over coffee, we prompted him to pick up his narrative.

He remembered a crowd forming a circle around the body in the crosswalk. He and Shelley took a closer look and then walked away. They rejoined their friends before the police arrived. Louie's of Grant Avenue was the first restaurant they came to, so they went in. They had a strange meal, dazed as they were by what they'd seen. When they got back to Kearny Street, the Cadillac was gone. The next day Morris read about the killing in the paper. He didn't want to get involved, but around noon finally called the police. Later that week and again later on, a police inspector called, and Morris went over what he had seen much as he'd done for us tonight.

"And the killer," I asked, "what did he look like?"

"He had long black hair, at least shoulder-length. He had on black stovepipe pants. And he was wearing one of those black quilted jackets you see around Chinatown."

"How tall was he?"

"He seemed tall for an Oriental. It's hard to judge exactly. But he didn't seem short. I'd say he was at least as tall as you are, maybe taller. I mean he was thinner than you are, but at least as tall."

"I'm five-eight," I said, thinking that Danny Choi's height was given in a booking record as five-nine. I looked at Len. He must have been thinking the same thing, for his jawline had softened.

Len and I went to the men's room. We agreed Morris was worth a run for it. I would try to get him to San Francisco as soon as possible, and we'd take it from there. Even if this story had problems, he was still the first break we'd gotten in the case. And there were ways we could corroborate what he was saying. There was Shelley, who had been standing right beside him and might herself remember something significant about the killer. And there were the other people in the car, who could at least confirm Morris's presence at the scene that night.

Len pulled out of the parking lot first, a fifty-pound bag of Purina Dog Chow propped up in the passenger seat of his VW hatchback. We cruised leisurely to Morris's house through the soft air of the Los Angeles night. With the windows down and the air conditioner off, the mercury-vapor-lit avenues of West Hollywood seemed almost tropical. Lazily, we talked of trivial things, and then, abruptly, I asked if he'd come to San Francisco, preferably that night. Morris didn't answer right away. He asked if I'd ever talked with Chol Soo Lee.

"Not really. A couple of times we've been in court together at Sacramento. But talk? No, I guess not."

"I was just wondering," he went on, "if he'd ever told you what was going through his head sitting in jail those five years. I mean, what's it like to draw a life sentence for something you didn't do?"

"Must be rough," I said noncommittally, not knowing what Morris was getting at.

"I was just thinking of all that. I mean, what am I doing here that's so tremendously important? I can get a fill-in for tonight at Lillian's. You can call United from my place if you want."

While Morris made some phone calls and packed, I thought of his question about Lee. Even if I'd talked extensively with Lee, I probably wouldn't have asked him Morris's question. In the criminal world, the question of just punishment never arises. Like Nietzsche says in the *Genealogy*, punishment is undergone as "a sickness or a misfortune or death . . . with a fatalism without revolt." Neither deserved nor undeserved, it's a natural evil to be suffered. Most people in that world have done so many things for which they were never punished, it comes as no surprise to be punished for something they didn't do. They see punishment as a random misfortune, an unlucky roll of the dice.

But what would it be like to be put away for life for a murder you didn't commit? How could you ever see that as simply "bad luck"? I was still asking myself that question when Morris and I left for the airport.

Back in San Francisco four hours later, the night was cold and overcast. After dropping Morris off at a hotel on Sutter Street, I hurried back to Union Street.

I found the file folder and pulled out three eight-by-ten photos. They showed the person first forgotten in a murder case: the victim, in this instance one Yip Yee Tak, stretched out on a table in the San Francisco Coroner's Office. His head rested on a firm, black-rubber support just this side of which stood a wedge-shaped stand containing the autopsy report number and, under it, the designation *"John Doe 67."* Upside-down under the "John Doe" designation was the obscure legend *"Calculator for the Henderson—Hasselbalch Equation."* Beyond the wedge-shaped stand was something in no way obscure—Tak's body, with a large-caliber bullet hole in the chest, about three inches above the right nipple. I took a magnifying glass out of the recalcitrant middle drawer. Cleanly cut, with a small collar of bruising, the hole looked like an entry.

What did the autopsy say?

I flipped through the official document. Here it was: *"The thorax reveals a gunshot wound of entry of the upper right anterior thorax near the axillary fold, about 8 cm. superior to the right nipple and 11 cm. lateral to the midline of the sternum."* The chest wound *was* an entry. What Morris had seen was what had really happened. The killer had shot Tak in the chest, as Morris remembered. He'd also shot him in the back of the head—probably as a *coup de grace*—and that was what the other witnesses remembered.

I wanted to check one final piece to this puzzle. I pulled out the file folder that contained contemporaneous press clippings. Morris could have read the *Chronicle* article before calling the police that Monday. It was dated June 4, 1973, and described the killing of Yip Yee Tak:

As [Tak] reached Pacific Avenue, officers said, the youth fired, hitting [Tak] twice in the back. [Tak] crumpled to the ground in the middle of the intersection, then attempted to get up. As [Tak] struggled to get to his feet, witnesses told police, the killer ran up behind him, took hold of his collar with one hand, and pumped two more slugs into the back of his head.

Later the same day, the *Examiner* printed a short article on the killing that was already becoming stale news. *"Three shots hit Tak,"* it reported, *"in the left arm, left chest and right chest, all entering from the rear. The second two shots were fired as he fell from the impact of the first, according to Homicide Inspector Frank Falzon."*

What only a few hours earlier we'd taken to be a weakness in Morris's story was really a strength. He'd seen Tak take a chest shot the other witnesses had missed. More important, if he hadn't been there watching a tall Asian youth pump bullets into Tak, how could he have known Tak was shot from the front? And we owed all of this to Cheryl of Executone Answering Service. On such slender reeds, I thought, do human destinies depend. Then I flicked off the light and tried to sleep.

FRIDAY, NOVEMBER 10

The office was on Market Street, not more than a block or two from the Flood Building, where, during the years of Hammett's employment, Pinkerton's National Detective Agency had an office. Built in the early years of the new century, both buildings had similar tile corridors with oak-framed office doors, the name of each occupant painted in block letters on the glass. In either building you could find the usual roster of doctors, dentists, lawyers, and accountants. But there were also diamond merchants, watch repairmen, software firms, and, here and there, names like Halcyon Ventures, Ltd. or Swift Industries, Inc. With no clear idea what awaited us, Morris and I strode purposefully through the lobby and rode the elevator to the sixth floor. The legend on the door read *"George Karalis, M.D."*

The first step in recovering the past was filling out a form. Not an insurance form, but a personal-history form. While Morris worked on the four pages, I went into the back office to explain privately what we wanted and to give the doctor a check.

In his midthirties, Karalis was dressed in a tweed jacket over a crewneck sweater and shirt—no tie. I mentioned that I had heard him lecture on the usefulness of hypnosis in criminal investigation, and he quickly pointed out that for Morris he had in mind not hypnosis but "deep relaxation therapy." The distinction was elusive, but I got the idea he wouldn't be using any watches or crystals to put Morris in a trance. After hearing a five-minute summary of the case and Morris's role as a witness, he took notes on what we wanted: a better description of the Caddy and more details about the killer. He asked about tape equipment, and I told him I'd be setting up two recorders. He cautioned me not to make any noise after the session began, but to pass him a note if I thought of anything. He stressed that the "evidentiary value" of the session depended on him not leading Morris in any way; hence in certain respects his hands were tied. I asked if he'd learned words like *evidentiary* in medical school, and he laughed, saying he'd been going to law school at night for the past few years.

Morris took his place in a dark-green vinyl lounge chair with an adjustment lever on the side. While I set up and tested the two recorders (I had a backup in case the primary recorder failed), he and Karalis chatted about what the session would be like. Morris fiddled with the lever until he was comfortable, and the doctor handed him a black satin eyeshield. Morris looked at it and grimaced; it was the sort of thing a hung-over suburban matron might wear. He slid the band around the back of his head and dropped the eyeshield in place. After a few seconds of moving around, he settled in the lounger, and the doctor began to speak from a chair behind his head.

"Now, relax completely," Karalis began. "All other sounds fade into the distance; pay attention only to the sound of my voice and everything I suggest to you. You will listen very intently."

These beginning words were pronounced much like an invocation, as if, in a clearing flourish, "all other sounds" were being banished to the distance. The voice was rich and subtle. A priest's voice, I thought, or an actor's—a voice that knows the power of words.

"Today," the voice continued, "we're going to perform a procedure called relaxation therapy. This simply means we're going to relax you very deeply, and we're going to talk to you while you're deeply relaxed. It's very easy. Just listen to my voice. If your mind wanders, just go back to my voice.''

The last words were uttered more matter-of-factly, more in the reassuring tone of the physician.

''Imagine you're in the most comfortable place you've ever been in your life. Or you may imagine you're in a place you've never been to. In other words, be in the most comfortable place imaginable, whether it's real, past, future, present, or imaginary. Perhaps it's in someone's home, near a fireplace on a rainy evening. Wherever it is, you're there,'' the voice said with authority. ''Now I'm going to give you a period of silence to settle into this very, very comfortable place. That period of silence begins right now.''

On the coffee table, both tape recorders were running. The office seemed so normal it made what we were doing seem normal. As the seconds of silence turned into minutes, I wondered who had occupied the office before Karalis. The carpets were clean but a little worn; they'd probably been there when he moved in. On the oak windowsill I could see the burn-mark from a cigar and imagine a CPA having his desk by the window, close enough that his cigar would fall out of the ashtray as he bent over a column of figures. Then the doctor's voice brought me back.

''Now tell me where this place is.''

''A waterbed,'' murmured Morris. ''I'm lying on a waterbed.''

''Good. You're lying on a nice warm waterbed. Now you're surprised and amazed to find you *really are* on the waterbed. Right there, and you can actually feel your body float on the waterbed. Now feel it. You move a little and you can feel the water move, and your body sways a little to the right and the left, to the right and the left.''

His voice had a singsong rhythm. I was beginning to feel a sense of *déjà vu*. I'd heard all this before somewhere.

''Now take a few moments to let yourself sink into the waterbed. You float on down into the waterbed, deeper and deeper relaxed, deeper and deeper and deeper relaxed . . .''

The words were becoming a chant.

''Deeper and deeper [pause] and deeper relaxed, deeper and deeper [pause] and deeper relaxed, deeper and deeper . . .''

The voice trailed off. Morris seemed impassive under the mask. I shut my eyes as the voice began again.

''Now let your mind drift a little bit. Your mind drifts and drifts to a scene I direct. The scene I direct is a movie theater. Your mind drifts to a movie theater.''

With the words *movie theater* something clicked in my head. It had been in a movie theater, back in the 1940's, in the Ceramic Theater on Fourth Street in my hometown, and I'd been only nine or ten. The magician—was it Blackstone the Magnificent?—had gone through most of his act before asking for three volunteers to be hypnotized. Two women and a teenage boy had made their way down the crimson carpet and up the stairs to the stage. Squinting at the audience over the footlights, they'd looked self-conscious and wary. Then the magician had spoken to them. I couldn't remember his words, but his speech rhythms were the same as those of the voice I was hearing now. I listened to it with my eyes closed. I could smell, like a faint afterimage, the scent of the theater, the popcorn, the stale aroma of the red carpet.

''You are inside a movie theater with a blank screen in front of you. You are sitting in a seat, and you are the only audience. You are tranquil, peaceful, and quiet. You can't see me in the theater because I am the projectionist. Some images will project onto the screen, and you will see them very, very clearly. You will be surprised at how clearly you see them. These images will be products of your subconscious mind. They will be a specific kind of image.''

The voice paused and then started again in the same authoritative tone. Morris's muscles seemed to relax.

''As I count back, you leave today's date, November tenth, nineteen seventy-eight, and go back in time. Far back in time. When I reach the count of one, you will find yourself on June third, nineteen seventy-three, a date when you're in the Bay Area. You'll see yourself on the screen from your seat in the audience. Fifteen, fourteen . . . going back in time . . . thirteen, twelve . . . very relaxed . . . eleven, ten, nine, eight . . . back in time . . . seven, six, five, four . . . almost there . . . three, two, one.''

''Now, what is on the screen?''

''Give me a light!'' Morris asked. But it wasn't from us he wanted a light. It was from someone in a car. It was from someone named Ray. Ray was driving a car over the Oakland Bay Bridge, and Morris was a passenger. I looked at Karalis, who indicated with his eyes what I already suspected: we were on track.

"What do you see?"

"There's a sign off to the right. We're curving by it now."

"What does it say?"

"It's green with white letters, and I can read them easily. The first line goes W-A-S-H-I-N-G . . ."

I knew where Morris was. He was sweeping north on the Embarcadero Freeway, and the sign was the Washington Street Exit sign. He wasn't remembering this; he was experiencing it. He was reading the sign's letters as they swept by him in present time. Soon he'd be off the freeway, and it'd be only a couple of blocks to the parking spot on Kearny.

At the outset, Morris had been speaking to way. Now he was reporting back to Dr. Karalis. Karalis would ask him what he was seeing, and Morris would describe it. Most of the time Karalis would simply repeat what Morris said. But sometimes he'd ask Morris to "freeze that frame" or "imagine that the image before you is coming into focus." It was as if we were enacting some bizarre science-fiction plot, with Dr. Karalis as the mad scientist using Morris to travel backward in time and me the faithful amanuensis, taking notes. They were getting out of the car on Kearny Street, when, unexpectedly, Morris drew a blank.

"Take the last image," said Karalis. "Develop it. Feel yourself in the car. Feel the seat under you. Feel where your hands are. Feel what it's like to be in the car."

There was a forty-second pause, and then Morris said, "I see a lion. It's big and dark purple, and above it are some birds. I can hardly make them out."

Morris paused, but I knew what he was describing. Half a block north from Kearny and Jackson is a giant mural covering the side of a building, an ad for Marine World-Africa USA. In its center is the figure of a lion.

Karalis was moving Morris along, asking what was going on in the car.

"There seems to be another car there." Morris's voice sounded as if it were coming from a well. "It's a tight squeeze. I think he nudged us. I felt something."

"Tell about this nudge," said Karalis. "How did it happen?"

"The other car must have nudged us. Just a little. No big deal. Now Shelley's getting out."

"Freeze the image of the other car as you're getting out. What do you see?"

"It's a two-tone hardtop, a Caddy and pretty new. It's sort of a light tan on the bottom and darker on top, and I see him looking at me, looking right at me, out the back window. He looks ugly and mean."

I wrote *LICENSE PLATE?* on a slip of paper and handed it to Karalis.

"Now I want you to look around in the image of the car," said Karalis. "I want you to let the image get sharper and sharper. You're doing fine. Just fine. Now make the image very sharp, and look at the rear. Is there a license plate?"

"It's not there," said Morris. "I can see where it's supposed to be, but nothing's there. There's a name on the holder but no license plate."

"Can you read the name on the holder?"

"It's a man's name. It says 'Ellis Brooks,' and then there are some letters in the same writing."

"What are the letters?"

"C-H-E-V."

"Fine, you're doing just fine. Now look over the rear of the car and tell me what you see. Are there any stickers or labels?"

"He's looking at me, and I don't like it."

"Hold the image for just a little longer. Do you see any other letters on the rear of the car?"

"There's something white over on the side. On the bumper. Something white taped to the bumper."

"What does it say? Now zoom in real close. It should be getting clear."

"I can scarcely make it out," Morris went on. "It's like it's stenciled on. There's a number—I think it's a three—and then some letters. After the three there's an *F* and then a *T*. I can't make out anything else. I can see them, but I can't make them out."

Morris was sweating from the exertion, and his hands were clenched. Karalis led him easily through a description of the Asian males who were getting out of the car, first the two in the front seat and then the third, "ugly and mean," glaring out the back window. Morris was becoming agitated. So as not to exhaust his subject, Karalis deftly shifted the focus to Jackson Street and their stroll up it before dinner.

Morris began to describe the shops and how hungry he was. Ray, Shelley, and he had driven over from Point Richmond with a gay couple who lived down the street; he believed one of the men was named Jim, but otherwise drew a blank. I was watching Morris's mouth and the position of his hands. Both relaxed as he got further from the encounter with the men in the Caddy. Soon they reached Grant Avenue, and he found himself walking with Shelley, window-shopping. There was a drug store, he remembered, and a shoe store. They crossed the street to look in the window of the bakery. Gradually his voice became tighter, and small droplets of sweat appeared on his upper lip and jaw. His hands tightened into fists, the flesh drawn white over his knuckles. His breathing sped up. I knew what was coming.

"You and Shelley are looking in the window at the fortune cookies," said Karalis. "What do the cookies look like?"

"They're big. And they're wrapped in something. Shelley is wondering how much they cost, and then I hear it. The bang. I don't know what it is. And then there are feet running. I look around and see him. The one with the gun is in front of him, and he puts up his hands and turns his face away but it doesn't do any good. There's the noise and I can see the flame from the gun and there's a funny smell."

The words were gushing out of Morris's mouth in a mixture of surprise and terror.

"Everyone is pushing, running to get out of the way. Shelley's ahead of me, and we're in some doorway. There are more bangs, and people are screaming. He's looking right over at us now, swinging the gun in front of him. He swings it in a circle, and no one says anything or does anything. He's looking at me with those dark, mean eyes, and I'm scared. There's nothing I can do, and he's looking right at me. I can't move, and I hear Shelley breathing. I look away because I think he'll shoot. But he doesn't. I look back and he's gone. He and the other one aren't there anymore."

Morris paused to get his breath, and Karalis led him back to the split second when the killer looked at him.

"What does he look like?" asked Karalis.

The description was very much what we'd had before. The gunman had no mustache or glasses, was tall for an Asian (at least the same height—five foot nine—as the victim), and had dark hair to his shoulders. His clothes were as Morris had described them earlier. Then Morris added an extraordinary detail.

"His eyes are dark, maybe brown or black, I don't know. And he has this mole under his eye."

"Which eye?"

"Right eye. He's facing me, and it's . . . Yeah, it's under *his* right eye, sort of close to his nose."

Karalis looked over and asked with his eyes if there was anything else. I shook my head. He began guiding Morris back from the movie theater and June 3, 1973. When the countdown was completed and Morris awoke, he didn't look as if he felt "wonderful" or had just had "eight hours of refreshing sleep." The sweat was drying on his upper lip, and he said he felt stiff and thirsty. His fingernails had gouged deep indentations in the palms of his hands.

"How did I do?" he asked.

"Splendidly," I said, "just splendidly."

THURSDAY, NOVEMBER 16

Heading east over Altamont Pass, the freeway was almost deserted. On the sweeping hills to either side, two varieties of giant windmills sprouted. One variety, nearly thirty feet tall and turning slowly in the light morning breeze, looked like a Mixmaster blade stuck upright in the turf. The other variety had a three-bladed propeller set horizontally on its tower. They were planted in rows on the upper reaches of the pass to take advantage of the constant wind that flowed eastward from San Francisco Bay into the San Joaquin Valley. I'd read a Sunday-supplement piece about these "wind-farms," an outgrowth of the energy crisis and the baroque tax breaks it produced. They were mainly experimental, the few kilowatts produced and sold to PG&E offsetting no more than a fraction of their construction costs. Passing over the crest, I could see them stretch half a mile or so in either direction, another monument to the surprise the California landscape always promises and sometimes delivers.

Dropping down the eastern slope, I was thinking not of kilowatts or tax breaks for limited partnerships but of Heidegger. I'd taught *Being and Time* five years before, but I'd never been able to take it seriously. As with so many other works of philosophy I'd been unable to take seriously, what remained in my mind was a metaphor—in this case, a metaphor for life as lived in the trenches of World War I and its aftermath. Where would it be clearer that life was being-toward-death, and where would a philosophy of transcendence be more necessary? But as Interstate 580 descended to the valley floor in a series of sweeping curves, I was thinking of something closer to detectivery. I was wondering what Heidegger would have said about the nature of "the lead."

In a slim volume (the title long forgotten) I'd read some of his reflections on truth. It'd been spring, I remembered, and I'd been sitting on Merion Field. In the intervening years the point of Heidegger's account had leaked from memory. I could recall only sitting by the pond and thinking of the walks Heidegger used to take in the Black Forest, thinking those walks must have been in his head when he likened truth to a clearing in the forest, to an absence of "the thicket." Truth was where "the lightening" occurred; it was unconcealment, a kind of "standing-in-the-light." That much I could remember. Built upon that memory, and teasing the back of my mind, was the thought that the successful lead brought you to such a clearing, a standing-in-the-light. It wasn't that the lead delivered you to the truth; the truth wasn't just lying there like a treasure waiting to be discovered. Rather, the lead took you to a "clearing" where you could look around and where, among other things, you could see other leads. The lead wasn't about finding; it was about seeing.

At the beginning, seeing had been our problem. We hadn't been able to see, and for a time had wandered in the underbrush, playing the odds or our hunches, probing, hoping. And then the name *Steve* on a lousy photocopy had materialized into the Steven Morris whose memory bloomed on Dr. Karalis's couch. Morris, whom I'd be picking up an hour later at the Stockton Airport, had become our "clearing." Through him we could see a number of new leads. For example, the car.

The "something white taped to the bumper" had probably been a temporary license plate. The empty license-plate holder had come from Ellis Brooks Chevrolet, one of the biggest dealers in the Bay Area. We didn't know when the car had come from that dealer, but we knew that on June 3, 1973, it had had a temporary plate with a *3* followed by an *F* and a *T*. Paul Palladino was working today with the Brooks bookkeeper, trying to determine whether the tan Caddy had been sold by them.

Meanwhile, Jack Palladino was working another angle. Earlier, he'd done some digging on the background of Danny Choi, who, according to court records, had been involved in the torture murder of another Chinese youth in May 1974. Two cars had been used in the abduction of the victim from a streetcorner in Chinatown. If Jack could identify the cars used in the 1974 kidnapping and murder, we might be able to work backward to the car Steve Morris had seen a year earlier.

In addition, there was Shelley and Ray.

All Morris had been able to give me was the name of Shelley's aunt in Belvedere. The aunt had been more than a little suspicious to hear a private eye wanted to talk to her niece. She wouldn't give out Shelley's address but was willing to pass on a message. Two days later Shelley had called from Los Angeles. She'd agreed to come to San Francisco, talk with us, and undergo a session with Dr. Karalis.

After she arrived, we'd walked around Chinatown before going to Karalis's office for a session that proved less than successful. Shelley remembered the trip to Chinatown and the fact another car had nudged theirs as they were parking; she even remembered looking at the giant fortune cookies with Morris. But her memory of the killing itself was wrapped in vagueness. There had been "confusion, a lot of noise, people running to another person," and she remembered feeling "scared." At one point in the session she exclaimed, "I'm too short; I can't really see. I hear people saying somebody's shot." She remembered someone later, at the restaurant, expressing "disbelief" that there'd been a shooting. Apparently she either hadn't seen the killing itself or had repressed it. No matter. She could place Morris on the streetcorner when it happened. She also led us to Ray.

The day before, I'd walked around Chinatown with him. He recalled driving the car that night and another car "tapping bumpers" with them as he parked. He couldn't remember whether the people in the other car had been men or women. He remembered being very hungry and irritated that the others wanted to do some window-shopping before eating. He didn't recall seeing any killing or hearing anyone talk about it. His memory didn't seem good enough to justify a session with Dr. Karalis, so I'd taken his statement and left it at that.

From a dim photocopy of the "Steve" notes written down by Gus (the police inspector) a little after noon on the day after the killing, we now had Morris and two witnesses who could place Morris in Chinatown that night, one of whom who could put him at the corner when the shooting happened.

Unfortunately the notes did more than that. In addition to giving us Morris and, ultimately, all the corroboration we'd put together for his story, they gave the prosecution a basis for impeaching that story.

There were a few minor discrepancies between Gus's notes and what we had learned from Morris and his friends. According to the notes, Morris had been in the company of five others—not four, as he, Shelley, and Ray recalled. The notes indicated the "suspect" had been alone in the car, while our witnesses said he'd been with two other people. These discrepancies could be chalked up to miscommunication. They weren't bothersome.

What *was* bothersome were the two lines of notes I'd read the night before interviewing Morris in Los Angeles. If Morris had told Gus he'd witnessed the murder, how could Gus have written down that Morris "didn't hear any shots . . . they asked people what happened"? I'd gone over the notes with Gus, last name Coreris, now a retired homicide inspector. After five years, he had no recollection of the phone call itself but was certain that the writing on the notes was his and that they were accurate. "One call can open up a Pandora's Box," he'd told me. "Every call in a murder case is important."

Just as troubling was Morris's description of the "suspect," scribbled out by Coreris:

Suspect: OMA, Black hr., shoulder length, 5'10", wear. dark green pants, tan jacket, short waisted lapel, front like a cowboy style "V" design sewn on front, lite print shirt.

Other witnesses had given generally similar descriptions of the shooter. All, for example, had said he was wearing a "tan" or "yellow" or "light-colored" jacket. And they had all agreed Tak was attacked by one person with a gun. Morris, on the other hand, recalled two attackers. One, apparently unarmed and wearing a tan jacket, had blocked Tak's way; the other, dressed in a black quilted jacket, had shot him with a revolver.

This whole tangled package had come from a dim Xerox of Gus Coreris's hastily scribbled notes. You could call it a Heideggerian "clearing" if you wanted to. But it was a clearing filled with its own brambles, its own questions and mysteries. That was the nature of leads: they brought some things into the light only to produce new obscurities. No matter. On this sunswept Thursday morning, the dice were to be thrown. If Steven Morris had even a glimmer of suspicion the man across the courtroom from him in the orange prison jumpsuit might be the youth with "the mean look" who had shot Yip Yee Tak, all the patient work of the last two weeks would be for naught.

Two hours later, in the courtroom, Lee wasn't wearing an orange jumpsuit. His hands manacled to a waist chain, he was wearing standard state-prison garb—denim shirt and jeans a bit too large for him and shower flip-flops. He looked tiny.

Morris was sitting alone, six rows in front of me, dressed like a college student: jeans, checked shirt with button-down collar, V-neck sweater. The prosecutor, Meleyco, noticed me toward the back of the courtroom but didn't pay any attention to Morris. He probably thought I was there to meet Len Tauman, and if he thought of Morris at all, took him to be a local college kid attending a court session as a class assignment. So far, so good. The night before, on the phone, I'd asked Tauman to get Lee to stand up as much as possible and turn around to let Morris see him from various angles. Kiddingly, I'd also told him to make sure Lee didn't wear elevator shoes, which might account for the rubber thongs. Up close and sitting down, Lee didn't appear so little. He had done a lot of weight lifting during his years in prison and had developed his chest and shoulders. His hair had been cut, and he was no longer wearing a mustache. He looked extremely handsome and clean-cut. He knew the importance of what we were doing today; what was he thinking?

The session was brief. Afterward, Lee lingered at counsel's table, standing and turning but never searching the courtroom with his eyes, his hands cuffed closely to his waist chain, until the deputy sheriff insisted he leave. Outside, in the hall, I clicked on the recorder: "This is Josiah Thompson in the case of Chol Soo Lee versus R. M. Rees (Habeas Corpus). The date is November sixteenth, and the time is eleven fifty-two, and I'm outside Department Twelve of the San Joaquin County Superior Court. I'm talking with Steven Morris." Morris was right beside me, and I motioned to a vinyl bench by the courtroom door.

"Steve," I said, the turning tape making me feel like a reporter, "we've just come out of court, where, for the last twelve minutes by my watch, you've been observing Chol Soo Lee. Did you see enough to make a determination whether he was the man you saw shoot someone in Chinatown on June third, nineteen seventy-three?"

"Yes."

"Was he the man?"

"Not possibly. Lee's tiny. The man I saw was about average

height, maybe five-nine or so. And the face is completely different. Lee's good-looking. The man I saw was mean, you might even say ugly. And Lee's hair is a lot shorter.''

"Recognize,'' I interrupted, speaking a bit formally for the tape, "that Lee's hair has been cut many times since nineteen seventy-three. You should disregard any temporary features of appearance like that in making your judgment.

"The hair is minor,'' he said. "It's just not the same person. I'm sure of it. And one other thing. I think the killer had a mole under his right eye, and Lee doesn't have any mole.''

This was the first mention Morris had made of the mole outside of Karalis's office. I'd been scrupulous in not telling him anything he'd remembered during the session. What had been dredged up the previous Friday must be filtering into his conscious memory of the event.

"Is there anything else you'd like to add?''

Morris said no. We made out way downstairs and out of the building. As we left the gray marble foyer, I held the door open for him.

"Lee's beautiful,'' he said mischievously. "I think I'm in love.''

"Great. Just what I need. You say that on the stand next Monday, Lenny'll kill me. And that's not the end of it. The state'll go ahead and put your beloved on death row.''

"Yes, boss.''

We joshed a bit more on the way to the airport. It seemed a relief to Morris that Lee could not have been the shooter. He mentioned he hadn't been hired back by Lillian's after his trip to San Francisco with me. At first I thought it was a roundabout way of asking us to pay him something (say, for "lost wages'') now that he'd established his bona fides as a critical witness. But that wasn't it. He just wanted to know when this would "all be over.'' I told him I thought Monday ought to do it. Morris was simply riding with it, following through on the decision he'd made that balmy night in Los Angeles. I didn't know if Morris was a rare kind of selfless individual; what I liked about him was that once he'd climbed on board there was no whining. I left him in the coffee shop reading *Gentlemen's Quarterly* and headed back to San Francisco.

Back on Union Street, several things had happened—or rather, not happened. Paul had gone through three months' worth of invoices with the bookkeeper at Ellis Brooks Chevrolet and found only three used Cadillacs, none of which could have been our car. Jack had left a note saying the only way to find out about the cars used in the 1974 abduction was to talk to the abductors, one of whom was in state prison at Tehachapi. These reports seemed to draw the curtain on the car as a lead. Was there any way to use the three digits we had to get a fix on the temporary plate from 1973? Paul said he would try, but he thought DMV records went back only three years.

The subpoenas I'd wanted were typed and ready. And Glenn Morgan, Esquire, had called.

At first I decided to ignore Morgan, but then relented. I called him and was laughing when I hung up two minutes later. The tape from the transmitter was virtually unintelligible. He would need me as backup for the good doctor at Wylie's preliminary hearing on fraud charges.

I flipped through the subpoenas: a *duces tecum* for James A. Lassart, Lee's original prosecutor, who was assisting on the *habeas*, and an ordinary appearance subpoena for Frank Falzon. We were asking Lassart for numerous items, but there, toward the bottom, was the hot one: *"a photo or mug shot of Danny Choi as nearly contemporaneous to June 1973 as possible, or, in the alternative, a photo lineup which contains a photo of Danny Choi as nearly contemporaneous to June 1973 as possible."* These subpoenas were returnable in Sacramento on Monday, and it was already Thursday. We wanted Falzon on the stand to nail down his knowledge or ignorance of Morris before we put Morris himself on. And if Lassart produced a photo of Danny Choi showing a mole under his right eye? In that case, Monday might be extremely interesting. But first I had to get these subpoenas over to the Hall of Justice.

From any angle, outside or in, the San Francisco City Hall of Justice conveys a sense of flat brutality. Although jail cells occupy only its sixth and seventh floors, leaving the first five floors for courtrooms, offices of the DA and the Public Defender, and SFPD Headquarters, the building signals "jail" throughout. I found Deputy DA Lassart doing what he'd gained a considerable reputation for doing: prosecuting homicides. I sat in a back row of the courtroom and listened while he finished questioning a witness. Like many prosecutors, Lassart was an ex-Marine, and his carriage suggested the military. He was wearing a striped tie and well-cut tan suit, and his hair was brushed back. He looked sleek; if you bumped into him in Washington you'd take him for

a staff officer in civvies. Abruptly, he ended his questioning and
the court session was adjourned. I waited until he was in the
hall before giving him the subpoena. Not recognizing me, he
took the subpoena and began scanning it.

"For Monday morning?" he asked.

"Yes, sir," I said unthinkingly, for a moment transported
back to the Navy, delivering something to a superior.

"I hate to disappoint you," he said, "but I'm in the middle
of a murder case. Monday morning I'm before Judge Daniel
Hanlon in Department Twenty-three. That takes precedence over
any subpoena from Sacramento."

"I'll tell Weinglass. Is there any way I could pick up these
items from your office tomorrow or Monday early?"

"No," he said easily. "But tell Weinglass we're hoping he'll
be able to come up with something better than a mysterious
Asian in a mask."

"I will," I said, holding back the *sir* that was just behind my
lips.

Inspector Frank Falzon had a desk in the squad room of the
Homicide Division. When I asked for him at the counter, another inspector with handcuffs and a large automatic on his belt
yelled into the room behind, "Frank. Somebody for you."

Falzon came out in shirt sleeves and tie, a coffee cup in his
hand. His face showed recognition: the hippie investigator
working for Weinglass and that ragtag defense committee in
Sacramento. He took the subpoena and glumly asked the same
question Lassart had asked.

"Monday, eh?"

"Yeah," I said. "Monday morning. Usual time."

"Will you tell those attorneys to get their act together?" he
said testily. "I was on the stand for over an hour last time up
there. Can't they get it together enough between them to figure
out what questions to ask me?"

"I'll tell 'em that, Inspector Falzon," I said without even
starting to smile. "I'll tell the attorneys you said to get their act
together."

MONDAY, NOVEMBER 20

Shelley had flown in the day before. She and Steve Morris were
on the floor below, waiting their turn to testify. It was customary

to put witnesses in the hall outside the courtroom where they were to testify; in this case, however, we didn't want the prosecution to know what cards we held. Len and I didn't mention even to reporters or defense-committee people the surprise testimony we were about to present.

We moved quickly into the courtroom, all business, and Weinglass took his place at the defense table, where Len Tauman and Bob Ball, Lee's public defenders, were already seated. I took a chair a few paces back from the defense table, appropriate for an investigator who was not an attorney but who might have comments or papers to pass to Lee's attorneys.

Inspector Falzon sat at the prosecution table with Deputy DA Kenneth Meleyco. They seemed confident, perhaps even a little bored. A few seconds before Judge Karlton took the bench, Lee was brought in, manacled as before. He smiled weakly on seeing the forty or so Korean spectators in the courtroom.

There was the usual wrangling over motions. Judge Karlton asked for final arguments on the question of "Mr. X" and said he would decide within ten days whether to admit the videotape as evidence.

Inspector Falzon took the stand as the first witness of the day. He had on a brown sport coat and white shirt, tasteful, low-key, the sort of thing a more mature, less frazzled Starsky might wear to court. He betrayed no sign of irritation at being led over familiar ground. Steve Morris? He connected the name with the Cadillac report, but it was all very hazy. And that report—where had it originated?

"The way it was written up," said Falzon, "it was probably written up by a police officer, by Gus Coreris."

"But didn't you say earlier," Weinglass asked, "that you didn't recall Inspector Coreris having anything to do with this case?"

There was no contradiction here. Coreris never had had anything to do with the case; he'd just been there—"brown-bagging" it at lunchtime—when Morris's call came in. Len ruffled through his papers as Falzon explained Coreris's role. Meleyco chose not to cross-examine, and Falzon stepped from the witness chair.

Weinglass called Steve Morris.

I felt the quizzical eyes of reporters and friends from the defense committee on me as I hurried from the courtroom. Morris was sitting on a vinyl bench, chatting with Shelley. His eyes asked the obvious question.

"You're on," I said.

As Morris got up, I noticed that his wrists and forearms were bare. On the drive up, he had mentioned that he'd forgotten to bring cufflinks. I thought he would just leave his shirt cuffs open under the sleeves of his sport jacket, but he had elected to roll up both. Taking the stairs two at a time, I kidded him about being a fashion plate from *Gentlemen's Quarterly*. I held the courtroom door open, and he entered a couple of paces ahead. Passing up the aisle, I looked over his shoulder at Falzon. What had I been expecting? Some expression in his eyes, some grudging acknowledgment from San Francisco's premier police detective that the hippie private eye had scored one? Nothing but puzzlement escaped Falzon's eyes as he watched Morris stride up the aisle with his sleeves rolled up.

Morris's testimony went better than expected. He was nervous at first, but then settled into a matter-of-fact telling of what he'd seen on June 3, 1973. Len's questions became almost superfluous as Morris quietly covered the familiar ground of the drive to San Francisco, the encounter with the other car, the stroll down Grant Avenue before dinner, and finally the shooting.

"The bullet hit the man in the middle of the upper chest and I saw blood pouring out, more blood than I had ever seen before. The two men took off, and I started moving slowly toward the body. I got sick to my stomach and started crying."

The room became utterly still as Weinglass pointed to Lee, sitting perhaps twenty-five feet from Morris, and asked, "Is this the man you saw do the shooting?"

"He is not," said Morris. "I'm positive."

Chol Soo Lee visibly relaxed, and Weinglass moved on to cover Morris's call to the police ("I spoke to an older gentleman in his late forties or early fifties") and Falzon's two calls to him.

Prudently, Deputy DA Meleyco chose not to attack the substance of Morris's testimony but used his cross-examination to gather information about Morris and his friends. It was a sensible strategy. At the end of his time on the stand, Morris was excused, subject to recall. Over the following week or so, the police would go over his background and testimony with a fine-tooth comb. His real cross-examination would take place later.

Trailing Morris out of the courtroom, I made my second trip to the floor below. Shelley had never testified before, but she performed like a veteran. Careful not to overreach herself, she testified simply and convincingly as to what she remembered.

During the lunch break, I huddled with K. W. Lee, the Korean reporter whose articles in the *Sacramento Union* had led to the formation of Chol Soo Lee's defense committee. He could hardly contain himself. This was a vindication of everything he had worked for, and he'd been working on this case long before either Weinglass or I ever heard of it. He was particularly delighted to be reminded that the press reports had Tak shot only from the rear; Morris, closer to the killing than any other witness, had seen the chest shot everyone else had missed. K. W. Lee emphasized this fact in a front-page story filed later in the day.

By day's close, it was clear Morris's testimony had made an impact on Judge Karlton. Meleyco complained of the "surprise-a-week" tactics of the defense. "I wonder where it's all going to end," he asked rhetorically. Judge Karlton responded that it was "reasonably related, to say the least," to the issues raised in the *habeas*, and that it was "not insubstantial evidence." When the prosecutor persisted, Karlton pointed out that since it had taken five years and some assiduous detective work to bring Morris to light, it was "not for the people [the prosecution] to be hypercritical." Leaving the courtroom, I was relieved.

Outside, newspaper headlines blazed the latest on Jonestown. "FOUR HUNDRED STOOD IN LINE TO DIE," trumpeted the *Chronicle*. There was a chill in the air as our little group crossed Eighth Street to the parking garage. Steve and Shelley seemed like athletes after a game. I felt oddly subdued. Was it Jonestown? Evidently the "ugly rumor" about the settlement doctor stockpiling cyanide had been true. I wondered if my contact at the Temple had known in July that it was true. More important, I wondered if she was still alive. The day before, I'd tried unsuccessfully to reach her at the Temple in San Francisco. The flat skies promised rain. I hoped we wouldn't hit fog on the drive home.

TUESDAY, MARCH 20, 1979

Moving faster than the few cars heading east on the freeway, the wind-driven clouds scudded low over Altamont Pass. At the summit, dirty wisps of cloud brushed the rotors of the highest windmills. Along a line perpendicular to the highway, they had expanded their numbers like rows of giant fruit trees. Where four months earlier there had been ten or twelve in a line, now there were twenty. Much had changed in those four months, but once again I was driving to the Stockton Airport to pick up Steve Morris.

On the Monday following Morris's testimony, I'd been on the phone with Len Weinglass when the radio delivered its first reports of the murders at City Hall. Supervisor Dan White had shot to death Mayor George Moscone and Supervisor Harvey Milk. Before getting into politics, White had been a San Francisco policeman. In 1972, he'd been MVP of the Police All-Stars softball team. Together with player/manager Frank Falzon, he'd led the team to a league championship that year. Falzon, that Monday morning, was unlucky enough to be the homicide inspector on duty. He'd been in the office of Deputy DA Lassart—perhaps discussing the Chol Soo Lee case—when the phone rang and he was told to head for the crime scene at City Hall. When, later that day, White turned himself in, Falzon drew the assignment of interrogating his erstwhile teammate.

Three days later, both Lassart and Falzon were in Sacramento to assist Deputy DA Meleyco in probing Morris's story. Their presence mattered little. As we'd expected, the police investigation had gone over Morris's story carefully, finding, for example, that Morris had not been employed where he said he was when he took the second of Falzon's calls. But the substance of his story held firm, buttressed as it was by Shelley's testimony. Judge Karlton ruled, as expected, that there was no legal basis for considering the videotape of "Mr. X," and he took the *habeas* petition under advisement.

Meanwhile, preparations moved forward for Lee's death-penalty trial on the prison killing. Jury selection in that case began in Judge Pappas's Stockton courtroom on January 18. In a decision two weeks later, Judge Karlton cited Morris's testimony as grounds for concluding that Lee had not received a fair trial in 1974. He granted the *habeas* petition and ordered Lee's immediate release.

I went to Sacramento on the evening of Judge Karlton's ruling to celebrate our victory. Both Len Weinglass and Len Tauman were there. Ranko drove up from San Francisco, and K. W. Lee arrived just after filing his story on the ruling. The head of the defense committee, Jay Yoo, proposed a number of champagne toasts, and we all left feeling very pleased with ourselves.

Now, six weeks later, descending the far side of the Altamont Pass in a light rain, I didn't feel at all pleased. Our "victory" had proved Pyrrhic. I felt angry, depressed, and apprehensive about what the day might hold.

The state had immediately appealed Karlton's ruling, and Lee never left his cell. With the appeal in place, the system ground on as if there'd been no ruling. Lee's Stockton trial moved into high gear, and the previous week the jury had returned a verdict of guilty of murder with "special circumstances." This meant that Lee's trial would shift into a penalty phase. Both sides would present testimony and argument. The jury would then retire for a second time to deliberate whether to sentence Chol Soo Lee to death or to life in prison without parole. Meleyco had put the defense on notice he would be presenting testimony to show the heinous nature of Lee's murder of Yip Yee Tak. As an antidote, the defense intended to put Steve Morris on the stand. That was why Morris was making his second trip to Stockton.

Both Len Weinglass and Len Tauman were waiting for us outside Judge Pappas's courtroom, the same courtroom where four months earlier Morris had judged Lee was not the man who had killed Tak. The conversation was brief and subdued. Len Tauman suggested it was far from certain Judge Pappas would permit Morris to testify. The fair thing, he said, would be for the judge to disallow testimony from either side on the China-town murder. The two lawyers disappeared into the courtroom to argue their case out of hearing of the jury.

When they came back ten minutes later, the ruling was written on their faces. Weinglass was angry, color rising in his face, while Tauman looked ashen, as if he had just stepped from another scene in a continuing nightmare.

"I'm really sorry," said Weinglass to Morris. "You've given us more than anyone had a right to ask in terms of time and inconvenience. Now it looks like we've wasted another day for you. The judge ruled the issue of guilt was decided in the first trial, even though Karlton reversed the conviction. I'm sorry. We've got to go back in. They're bringing in the jury."

"Can we watch?" I asked.

"Sure."

When he was brought from the holding cell, Chol Soo Lee looked stonily ahead, hardly glancing at us. Quickly, one of the witnesses from the first trial, a skier in his thirties who had flown in the night before from Colorado, took the stand. The usual questions were asked, and then, to a flurry of objections, Deputy DA Meleyco took a revolver from his briefcase and approached the witness. The gun from Beckett Alley had been destroyed long ago; this was a replica. The defense's objections were swiftly overruled.

At Meleyco's urging, the witness left his place on the witness stand. He took the gun and moved in front of the jury box. Holding out one outstretched hand, he demonstrated how the killer had held Tak by the collar before firing into the back of his head as the already wounded man slipped to the pavement.

"And the person who did that, the man who cold-bloodedly killed Mr. Tak, do you see him in the courtroom today?

"Yes."

"Please point him out to the jury."

The witness turned and pointed an outstretched finger at Chol Soo Lee.

I don't remember what happened after that. Morris and I left without talking further with Weinglass and Tauman.

Two days later, the jury retired to deliberate. The death verdict came quickly. On May 24, Judge Pappas confirmed that verdict and sentenced Chol Soo Lee to die in the gas chamber. Lee was immediately transferred to death row at San Quentin.

PART THREE

EIGHT

"THE LUCKIEST GUMSHOE"?

MONDAY, JANUARY 7, 1980

A little after two o'clock, the ferry slipped its bow line and headed out the channel. Off to the right lay the *Queen Mary*, her old transatlantic self gutted and prettified to become one of Long Beach's major tourist attractions. On the left, three oil derricks pretended to be tropical islands, each with its own palm trees and painted concrete "grass." The sea was flat and the day was flat—a January Monday on San Pedro Bay.

On the stern, Nancy and I sat back in our chairs, watching the breakwater edge into view and then fade again as the ferry picked up speed. The air on shore had been dead calm and a little yellow; it was nice to feel a breeze and to watch the wake churned by the twin screws. Soon the coast became a hazy line, broken by an occasional plume of refinery smoke drifting skyward. A southwesterly wind kicked up a chop, and we could see sailboats tacking into it as they made their way westward.

I was reading a magazine article on Jerusalem "sappers"— the Israeli equivalent of what the U.S. military calls an explosive ordnance disposal team or what any big-city police department calls the bomb squad. In Jerusalem, over seven hundred reports of likely bombs came in every year. According to the article, the more experienced men in the squad had a kind of sixth sense that told them when a call was not a false alarm. One of the "old-timers," a twenty-six-year-old sergeant named Aryeh, claimed he could feel a tingle in his left ear when a "live one"

211

came in. I chuckled. The only "live one" in this story was the journalist.

I put the magazine down, took Nancy's hand, and shut my eyes. She mumbled something, and we lay back feeling the sun and listening to the drone of the engines. This vacation had turned out perfectly. We'd started the Wednesday before, wandering down the coast from San Francisco—Santa Cruz, Monterey, Big Sur, Morro Bay, and Santa Barbara—with no fixed itinerary. Nightly calls to Bolinas showed the kids were happy to have us gone, enjoying the novelty of functioning on their own. We'd spent the previous night with old friends in Redlands, and they'd suggested the trip to Santa Catalina Island.

The last year had been bruising. About the same time Chol Soo Lee was condemned, the partnership of Palladino, Sutherland & Thompson came apart. That same month—May—I'd gotten my California investigator's license and hung out my shingle on the same block on Union Street, renting a two-room flat with little floorspace but a view stretching from Alcatraz to the Golden Gate. For the last seven months I'd worked as a lone wolf, using an answering service for a secretary. Without enough business to hire operatives, I'd had to do everything myself. Even the holidays had given no respite from the tyranny of things to be done. That's what this minivacation was about: *not* having to do anything.

There was a rustle as passengers started moving toward the bow of the vessel. The natural amphitheater of Avalon came into view. It looked like a hundred similar villages in Greece or Italy—a semicircle of beach with arid hills beyond, narrow streets forming terraces that echoed the crescent of beach. On the right stood the Avalon Ballroom, where big bands had performed in the forties.

The ferry slid into its pier, and we joined a knot of twenty or thirty people strolling north along the beachfront. The town was like an amusement park in winter, a place where time had absconded into the past or the future.

We turned up a side street to find a place to stay. Here and there lay patches of concrete, but the street was mainly cobblestones. Cobblestones! We turned into a small flagstoned patio, but a Closed sign was propped in the hotel window. On the next street over was a small guesthouse with individual units scattered diagonally across a terraced hillside.

We registered, and I called my answering service to give them a contact number for the next two days. They gave me two messages: the antique chair was ready for pickup, and Mr. Grove still hadn't gotten the money from the court. I didn't know any Mr. Grove, but I had sent a deadbeat attorney named Gough a dunning letter at the end of December. Back in San Francisco, Cathy agreed she might have misread the name on the message. Iris had taken the message on Friday, and everyone had trouble with Iris's handwriting. Cathy was probably the best operator on the switchboard, so I didn't grouse at her. We laughed about the time Iris had given me the message that Fechheimer "hadn't wanted to murder him." Translated, this meant he "hadn't gotten the murder" we were both supposed to work on.

We left our suitcase in the room, pulled on sweaters, and went for a walk before the light faded. The sky was overcast, but the wind had dropped and the air was still. We felt washed-out and flat. Like all tourist places in the off-season, Avalon seemed bereft—half the hotels and restaurants closed, their owners and employees gone. Drained of energy and depressed, we bought a couple of magazines and headed back to the room.

There was a knock on the door before I'd gotten halfway through *Newsweek*. A Chicano handyman pantomimed that "Señor Thompson" was wanted on the phone. I followed him down the flagstone path to the front desk. On the glass-topped counter sat a black, circular dial phone, its receiver off the hook. I gave the handyman a buck and picked up the phone.

"Hello, Tink, it's David Chadwick."

I hesitated, trying to identify the name.

"You know," he went on, "from the Zen Center."

Now I had it. "Oh. Hi, David. How are you?"

We had met through mutual acquaintances, and he'd invited me to dinner at the Zen Center. We'd talked philosophy and politics with some of his friends during dinner, then gone back to one of their rooms for beer and more talk. The Center itself was serviceable but not luxurious, with its own small library and dining hall. The students and teachers [it would be misleading to call them monks] lived in the Center and in apartments scattered nearby. Among other things, I'd asked them about Green Gulch Farm. Nestled in a valley above Muir Beach, it lay along one of the main routes between Bolinas and San Francisco; it was an organic farm, and also a retreat and conference center. In addition, the Zen Center had a monastery at Tassajara Hot Springs as well as a bakery and a restaurant, Greens, on the water at Fort Mason. The evening had been pleasant, and I'd liked Chadwick. But why was he calling now?

"Sorry to bother you in the middle of your vacation," he said. "Your office gave me your number when I said it was urgent. And it *is* urgent. Our team is supposed to leave for India on Wednesday. Baker-roshi suggested I call and . . ."

"Whoa! I'm lost. Baker who?"

"Baker-roshi. He's the head of the Zen Center. Technically I suppose he's the abbot, the successor to Suzuki-roshi. We talked about him that night. I thought you'd remember. I told you his other name is Richard Baker and that he's Harvard 'fifty-eight. Remember? I asked if you'd run into him in the East in the fifties?"

"Vaguely. What's this all about, anyway?"

Concisely, Chadwick laid out the problem. A young Zen Center member—apparently a nice Jewish girl from Brooklyn—had married an Indian architect she'd met in California. They had a daughter, who was now about six. The marriage had been rocky, and from time to time the young woman would flee to the Zen Center. Finally the marriage had blown up, and the architect had split for India with the child. Daddy and daughter were now living in a medium-size city in northern India. After much soul-searching, Baker-roshi had been willing to lead a Zen Center team to India. The team would explore alternatives and, if all else failed, try to snatch back the little girl. They were to leave for India in two days. Before they left, Baker-roshi wanted to speak with me to pick up whatever technical hints I could provide.

"I thought you people were nice, sober, middle-class Zen Buddhists," I said to Chadwick. "I didn't know you were certifiable crazies. You're going to cause an international incident. I can see the *Chronicle* headline: 'Cult Members Arrested In Attempted Kidnapping.' I wouldn't touch this with a twenty-three-foot pole. None of you has the foggiest idea how tough it is to bring off a successful snatch in this country, let alone in India."

"Most of the people on the team speak Hindi," offered Chadwick brightly.

"Terrific. They'll be able to talk to the other prisoners."

"Won't you talk to Baker-roshi about it?" asked Chadwick. "I mean, tell him what you just told me?"

"Sure. But I'm not going to give any advice. And how're we gonna do this? I'm on vacation."

"I'll get in touch with him and have him call you right back."

"OK," I said testily. "You've got ten minutes. Then I go back on vacation."

The phone rang after four and a half minutes. Baker-roshi and I talked for nearly half an hour. By the end of the conversation, we'd made an appointment to meet for lunch on Friday at Greens, the Zen Center restaurant at Fort Mason. In the meantime, the "snatch team" would postpone its departure.

I walked outside to the terraced garden. During our conversation I'd been reading the pamphlets taped to the underside of the glass counter. One advertised a tour of areas where wild boar might be seen. The boar were dangerous to hikers, said the pamphlet, but posed no threat to tour vans. I looked above the diagonal line of cottages to the fog-shrouded hills beyond. Wild boar up there, and Buddhists on the loose in San Francisco. A child snatch in India? Not bloody likely. I hadn't felt so much as a quiver in my left ear—certainly not a tingle—when that call came in.

FRIDAY, JANUARY 11

I sat across from her, with the trunk that served as a coffee table between us. Behind her, one of the Red & White fleet's boats made its turn under the Golden Gate Bridge before heading back to Fisherman's Wharf. The light was clear but not intense: winter light. The steepness of shadows on the roofs showed it was after five. She was tentatively, almost shyly, telling about her time at Bennington in 1970.

I hadn't noticed it earlier at Greens, but now there was no mistaking it: the woman was beautiful. Darkly, exotically beautiful. She had long black hair, the front and sides pulled back and clipped, high cheekbones, and a softly sensual body. Dressed in a sari and with a black mark on her forehead, she could pass for Indian. But she didn't use her beauty or, strangely, even seem to be aware of it. That was why, at the restaurant, she hadn't made much of an impression when Baker-roshi introduced us.

After my long, delicious lunch with Baker-roshi, she had simply appeared. Had she been sitting in some back room of the restaurant, awaiting his signal to come forth? I didn't know. All I knew was that he and I had hardly talked about her problems. Instead we'd talked about Buddhism and Kierkegaard and the Ivy League in the 1950s—about anything that came to mind. There came a point in the lunch when I virtually forgot what our meeting was about. We were talking of the beat poets and their vision, and I remember liking Baker-roshi enormously and thinking it was a pleasant way to spend a Friday afternoon.

She had appeared then, as if by magic, and Baker-roshi had introduced us. There was a flatness to her, a lack of vitality in her eyes and movements that deflected attention. She was like an actress auditioning for a part she knew she wouldn't get; the world had hurt her and hurt her again, and she was getting tired of even pretending it wouldn't keep on hurting her. Having already accepted our eventual failure, she was only going through the motions.

When we first arrived at the office, she was so reticent that I had to play social worker and take down—questionnaire-style— the elementary facts of her life. Born Neva Alicia Sarsfeld in Brooklyn, New York, on September 21, 1950. Father an orthodontist, died in 1969. Mother living alone in Brooklyn. Older brother and sister. She was the baby of the family by seven years. No diseases, no allergies, no psychiatric treatment. Blood type? She smiled when I asked, almost making a joke of it, and then drew back, saying simply that she didn't know. Never arrested. Went to Erasmus Hall High School in Brooklyn and then to Bennington for two years—1968 to 1970. Did graphic design and painting. Spent the rest of '70 at the Zen Center in San Francisco, '71 in Israel, and '72 at Berkeley, where she met her husband, Krishan Chalam Sahni.

I asked if she had a photograph of him, and she pulled out a color snapshot of the happy family.

Krishan was small and wiry, with graying hair and sharp features. The dates of birth she'd given me made him forty-six to her twenty-nine. I looked more closely at the figure staring out of the photo. There was an intensity to the eyes and a lift to the chin that suggested something like arrogance. He was wearing a light chambray shirt and jeans with work boots. The three of them were standing in front of some half-completed structure with summer-tanned hills rising behind. He seemed pleased both with the structure and with the little family standing before it.

I could feel myself starting to take his measure as adversary.

Was he an American citizen? Yes, she replied, he'd been naturalized in 1972, the year before he got his architectural degree. And when was the picture taken? In 1977.

And the child?

Asha Naomi Sahni was born in August 1973. She had a normal medical history, with the usual childhood vaccinations. May have had typhoid during the past year. Blood type unknown. No allergies. A passport in her own name was in her mother's possession. Recent photo?

The photo Neva pulled from her wallet had been taken on Christmas 1978, about a month before Asha disappeared. It showed a stunning child with piercing black eyes, sitting on a sofa with a small Mickey Mouse doll. Long black hair tumbled to her shoulders. She held the doll in the crook of her elbow and looked impishly into the camera.

After Asha's birth, Neva and Krishan had lived together for four years before marrying in December 1977. They traveled to India in January 1978 and stayed with Krishan's family for two months. The town bore the unpronounceable name of Gorakhpur (accent on *akh*). His family had servants and lived in a compound with two houses, a garden and enclosed courtyard, a pump, and a latrine. The matriarch of the family, Krishan's mother, was nearly blind but still ruled the family with an iron hand; she treated Neva more as a servant than a daughter-in-law. To make matters worse, Neva didn't know Hindi, and she struggled with dysentery for most of her time there.

The beatings had started shortly after Asha's birth in 1973.

"Yet you stayed together and got married in 'seventy-seven?"

"Yes," she replied wearily, "but I always thought things would get better or thought it was my fault or something."

Things didn't get better when they returned from India. They lived in a house Krishan was building in Woodside. There was something about a dog being kicked out by Krishan and maybe killed—I couldn't follow it. Finally, one day in the late summer of 1978 when Krishan was out shopping, Neva took Asha in her arms and literally ran away. Friends cared for her, and within a week's time she and Asha were settled at the Zen Center. Hostilities began in earnest with the hiring of attorneys. Neva obtained Asha's U.S. passport from Krishan by court order in November 1978.

"Don't tell me," I said. "Krishan then added Asha to his passport and used that to get them both to India."

Neva didn't know what papers they had used to get to India.

"How much did you pay your attorney for all this great work?"

"We paid her just over seven thousand dollars, but—" Neva hesitated for a moment, looking even more weary. "But I think we owe her twenty thousand above that. She said she could wait until the property was settled."

"Terrific."

Neva told the rest of the story. Like an accident victim talking to the last in a series of insurance adjustors, she had done it so often there was little emotion in the telling.

Krishan had taken Asha for a weekend visitation in mid-January 1979. He was to bring the child back at noon on Sunday, but he never showed up. No phone call. No note delivered by a third party. Nothing. That night Neva called her attorney, and court actions began. Neva was awarded custody and a bench warrant issued for Krishan's arrest. All this was to no avail, since no one knew where they were. A private investigator was hired (paid two thousand dollars, owed four thousand) but wasn't able to find them. Later it turned out father and daughter had stayed in the Napa Valley from January until April. In late April, they flew to India and settled with Krishan's family in Gorakhpur. The U.S. consul's inquiries in October 1979 served only to alert Krishan and perhaps drive him underground. A cable from the consul confirmed that Krishan and Asha had arrived in India in May 1979 but weren't living at home that October. Krishan's family claimed not to know their whereabouts. Krishan was still seeking an English-language school for Asha; it was possible the child had been treated for typhoid in September.

Neva related all this wearily but without any noticeable affect. She started rummaging through her purse. Her mouth tightened, and for the first time, as she pulled out three rumpled sheets of paper, her voice became tense.

"Could you tell me what you think of this?" she asked, handing over a sheet of cheap notebook paper with writing on both sides.

It was dated October 27, 1979, and was addressed to "*Respected Auntij*." It was signed "*Ashok Sahni*," and to the side of the signature was printed: "*c/o Rakesh Angkor, Behind Pant Block, University of Gorakhpur, Gorakhpur, India*."

She explained that Ashok was Krishan's nephew, and that

the letter was addressed to her. I could feel her eyes on me as I read.

For the first time I am writing you because the circumstances prevailed us to write you. I think you would not mind, but I thought to report you.

Probably you are in search of Asha even today. As per the American and Indian Embassy officers came here recently. But he [Uncle K.C. Sahni] ran away along with Asha from school and were under ground for a week.

One thing to tell you, he is giving unbearable tortures to your pretty doll Asha. These tortures really a baby this age can't bear. She has strange bearing capacity. He convince her against you all the time. He beats her in such a way that she sometimes loses her sense and lives on bed for a week or a fortnight. You know well about his habit of loosing the temper and so one day she may be dead.

The same behaviour he has with us now-a-day, and he separated himself from us. Now he has the plan to escape from Gorakhpur along with Asha. He may go in Nepal or any other place.

If you are interested we will give you all the reports and support where he lives. We are ready to go up any Court with you.

Aunti, we need, one his certificate of citizenship of U.S.A. He has to sell all the Properties on his name on behalf of India and Nepali citizenship.

Now please if you need to reply me the letter should be registered so that no one Post Office is checking my letters.

Rest everything is moving well. The letter should be on the address given below.

"Have you written back?" I asked.

"No. I didn't know what to do. I wasn't sure this wasn't just another of Krishan's schemes. Then I got this second letter three weeks ago."

I skimmed it. It repeated the first letter, saying at the outset, "*perhaps you did not receive my first letter.*" Once again it asked for information on Krishan's U.S. citizenship, adding that he "*bears Nepali citizenship and Indian as well.*" It also explained the use of the "in care of" return address: "*Uncle checks all the letters in post office delivered in favour of my own address.*" The very end of the letter contained a warning:

If you think to come over here please do inform me first by letter because Ambassy members were talking so. But beware, Uncle can take any step against you as he himself announced one day. He has the plan even to murder you whenever you are in front of his eyes. But if you will inform me previously nothing so will happen here. We are enough for all his resources.

"It was when I got this second letter that Baker-roshi decided to help. I didn't know where to turn or what to do."

For a moment I thought she was going to break down. Instead she simply looked down at her lap and brushed a loose wisp of hair from her forehead.

"You asked me what I thought," I said, hesitating. She looked up. "These letters are manipulative. They ring all the changes on a mother's emotions. I thought they'd be asking for money, but they don't do that. The first letter asks for Krishan's citizenship papers. You'd don't have them, do you?"

"I've never even seen them."

"OK. We're not going to be able to figure this out today. We can't trust the letters or the letter writer, and we could waste days speculating on what they mean. Maybe later on we can figure out how to use the contact to our advantage. In any case, you don't have to write back right away. What you *do* have to do right away is get yourself a new attorney."

"Baker-roshi was saying the same thing," she said pausing to rustle again in her purse. She pulled out a slip of paper. "He suggested a man named Dick Werthimer. Do you know him?"

"Only by reputation. He's got a good name around town. Used to do criminal defense, political cases, things like that. Now does a little bit of everything, including being virtual house counsel for the Zen Center. I hear he's a real mensch. I'd recommend that you make an appointment with him as soon as possible. If you like what you see, you might have him go over the legal bills you have. Twenty-seven thousand seems pretty high to me. But he could tell you better than I. Ask him to give me a call after he's seen you."

She had her checkbook out and was fishing in her purse for a pen.

"Baker-roshi said you'd expect a retainer. How much should I make it out for?"

"How about five hundred dollars? Given what you've told me,

I want to do some checking with the passport office to see where Krishan stands. Five hundred will get us started."

After she left, I moved to my desk in the other room and began a file. I wrote *Sahni vs. Sahni* in the case log, assigned it a case number, but left the name and address of the attorney blank. I typed a label for the case file and attached my notes to the right side and a billing sheet to the left. All this was so pedestrian—typing, labeling, filing. The most bizarre of human adventures become banal when pressed between the covers of a file. And this case was bizarre. Would it end with some heroic rescue of the child from India? Probably not. It would cost a lot of money, and very likely Neva didn't have any.

It struck me no one had asked Neva whether she wanted to hire a detective. Or, if so, whether she wanted to hire *me*. In all that had transpired that afternoon, Neva had seemed almost irrelevant. Willingly, she'd played "patient" to our "doctor." She would go along with the charade until it fell apart. But she wouldn't believe in it, because if she believed in it she'd be hurt when it failed. And she'd already been hurt quite enough, thank you.

Where did that leave the case?

I looked out the window. Clouds were building up to the west of the Golden Gate. The light had faded, and headlights on the bridge had become pinpricks of light against the dark Marin hills.

Simplify it, I told myself, simplify it. If we're going to get the child back, we'll have to know where she is. Where's that? Probably the Indian city with the unpronounceable name. But that's not certain. The visit from the American consul may have spooked Krishan into leaving. So now the first task is to find them. To do that we'll have to hire someone reliable to carry out a reconnaissance. That will be the first move.

There might be an outside chance of retrieving Asha through Indian courts and law enforcement. We'd have to look into it, but the risks of going that route are great. In any custody action, Krishan would simply need to gain a hearing and then flee again with Asha before the court date. But if we could somehow bring about Krishan's arrest, the situation would be different. That was why I wanted to check Krishan's status with the passport office. Next week, I thought, you can do that next week. You'll want to know the answer to that question before seeing Werthimer. Fechheimer is back; you could do worse than run all this by him.

MONDAY, JANUARY 14

Fechheimer had returned to San Francisco about a year before. The previous spring I'd visited him a couple of times at the little flat he'd rented in North Beach. It was just up Telegraph Hill from Grant Avenue, and he'd seemed happy to be living in a neighborhood where he could hang out with his cronies in the cafés and coffee houses along Columbus Avenue. At that point he wasn't working as a detective, and he seemed different in ways I couldn't quite describe. He'd stayed in New Zealand only a few months, and when we'd talked about it he'd been as vague about his reasons for returning as earlier he'd been about his reasons for going.

He was now back in business, living at the corner of Hyde and Lombard, in a spectacular house built for Robert Louis Stevenson around the turn of the century. It was late afternoon when I got there, and the corner under his kitchen window was filled with tourists. Lombard Street curved down from here in a series of torturous hairpins, while, at right angles to it, Hyde Street descended to Aquatic Park in a straight line interrupted only by the terraces formed by cross streets. I stopped to watch a cable car complete the haul up the hill, tourists hanging from its sides.

The view from his living room stretched from bridge to bridge, but—as on Laguna Street—we quickly ended up in the kitchen. David handed me a beer from the refrigerator.

"So. How goes it, Professor?"

"Not bad. Things are a bit slow. I guess they always are around the first of the year. I got a possible child snatch I want to talk about."

"I meant to call you. Bill Nolan's doing a biography of Hammett, and he called me last week. I'd sent him a bunch of stuff, including your interview of Effie's daughter. He said he was going to use some of that in his first chapter. I told him you professors begin to doubt your own existence if you don't get mentioned in a footnote now and then, and he said he'd take care of it."

"Thanks. How do you like working as a lone wolf?"

"I like working alone. I go out and do the record searches and the dumb interviews and all the shitwork I had you doing. I haven't done it for years, and I rather like it. Even the civil cases seem interesting now."

"But they're just about the price of onions, aren't they? Just money, who gets how much from whom?"

"Like Willie Mays said, one hit's like any other."

He looked fine, better than I'd ever seen him. His eyes were clear, and there was a calmness to him. We were both actually sitting down. Back on Laguna Street, he would have alighted only for an instant before getting up to pace around. He had on a cardigan over an open white shirt. There was no belt on his jeans, and he wore tasseled loafers.

"Heard anything from your ex-partners?" he asked.

"No," I said. "They have their business, and I have mine. I get a check now and then when somebody pays."

"I told you not to do it."

"True. But you also didn't tell me you'd be back after a month or so. I thought taking on Laguna Street would be a one-way ticket to bankruptcy."

"So tell me about this case you've got."

I sketched the details of the India case while Fechheimer sipped Calistoga water, now and then taking a drag on a Raleigh. I remembered his collecting the coupons that came inside the cellophane. It was nice being with him again. Ever since his return he'd treated me as an equal, not as his ex-operative. When I finished telling him about Neva, he ground out the cigarette in the Villa d'Este ashtray.

"You know what they call these jobs in the trade?" he asked.

"Snatches? Child snatches?"

"Yeah, that, but they're also called seam jobs. That's because they usually turn on finding the seam where the child goes from one person to another. The whole trick is in snatching the kid without stirring up a hornet's nest. Sometimes you can buy off one of the kid's caretakers. That's risky because the person you buy may not stay bought, and may expose the whole thing. Sometimes you can slip one of your own people into the chain of custody: 'Little Jimmy can play here in the park with Matt while you make your phone call. I'll watch 'em.' "

"Best is to find the particular seam in the daily routine when the kid isn't being watched. Last fall, for instance, I found it just inside the door of a parochial school. It was in Belgium,

and we'd been looking at this eight-year-old for a week. There
was no chance near his home, and he got delivered to the school
and picked up by limousine. But from the time he left the limousine until he was in a classroom no one was watching him.
He, his mother, and I pulled away from the school in a rental
car thirty seconds after the limousine left the curb."

"Elegant."

"From what you say," he continued, "you'll probably need
a private plane to get out. That city you mentioned is probably
a ways from an international airport. I may be able to help you.
I know some people who do a lot of flying in that part of the
world and have some influence with customs officials. If it looks
like it's going to go, I can make inquiries."

"Thanks."

"The first thing you're going to need is a detective in India.
Hal will tell you that Henry Bawa in Bombay is your man, and
he's probably right. Trouble is that Bombay is a bitch of a ways
from that place in northern India. What did you call it?"

"Gorakhpur."

"Never heard of it. You're a member of W.A.D. [World Association of Detectives] now, aren't you?"

"Yeah, I joined last October. Thanks for letting me use your
name."

"Sure. Henry Bawa is listed in the directory. He once told
me Hal was his 'guru,' so why not ask Hal to write you a letter
of introduction? Make some inquiries of Henry and when you
get some money send him a retainer. It'll take a while for the
case to gel."

"*If* it gels," I said. "The first problem is getting the money,
and I'm not real optimistic about that. But down the line a bit I
was thinking of getting the father popped so we could take the
kid while he's locked up. Tomorrow, I'm gonna check with the
passport office to see if we can hang anything federal on him. I
figure when Neva's lawyer got the kid's passport by court order,
the father just added her to his own."

"Yeah, maybe. It's too early to tell. You'll just have to ride
with it. You're a lucky sonafabitch, so you'll probably come out
smelling like a rose."

"What do you mean by that?"

"Just what I said. You're not a natural in this business. I don't
know why. Maybe you think too much about what you're doing.
I don't know. Your ex-partner Sandra is a natural. I knew it from

the first time she walked in the door at the Lipset Service. I can't describe what a natural is, but I don't think you're one. That's not to say you're not good. You are. There's no way on earth I could've done the job you did with the taxi meter in Skyhorse-Mohawk."

"That was just an analytical problem," I said. "Figuring out the route from three variables on the meter. You mean, as a detective I'm not a bad philosophy professor?"

"Don't get defensive. You're not a natural, but you're lucky. That's one of the crazy things about you. You get into these scrapes and get out with nobody laying a glove on you. You're the luckiest gumshoe I ever met. I just hope you stay lucky on this one."

I looked at him but didn't say anything. Being lucky, I guessed, wasn't the worst thing in the world. And not being a natural? Was this just conversational jujitsu, or was he telling me something important? If the latter, I guessed I could handle it. Most of detectivery was just working hard and not giving up. A natural might get there quicker than I would, but I'd get there just the same.

On the way out, my eye picked up familiar items from Laguna Street. The parsons table was now in the dining room with the George III samovar in its center. The New Zealand landscape hung in the hall along with some serigraphs of Dashiell Hammett.

"Thanks, David," I said, just before opening the front door, "I appreciate the ideas. And about my being lucky but not a natural, I was wondering about Spade. Which one was he?"

"There you go again, Professor," David said quickly. "You just won't let it go. You keep trying to figure it out. You keep looking around for someone or something to show you how to do it, when the whole point is to give all that up.

"That goes for Spade too. Like Hammett said, he's just a 'dream man.' When this case is over, maybe you'll understand what I mean. That is, if your luck holds. Come to think of it, though, you might learn it faster if it didn't."

"Thanks again," I said, pushing the door open. "You always give a guy such great things to look forward to."

TUESDAY, JANUARY 15

I'd been right. Krishan had simply added Asha to his own passport. But had he done it by applying for a new passport or by amending his old one?

"I'm sorry, I can't tell you that," said Mike Dravo, passport examiner. "I'm not even sure I should have told you the computer lists 'em on the same passport. If you were law enforcement, there'd be no problem. But you're private, and I don't know how far I can go."

"OK, I understand perfectly," I said. "But tell me something about question Four on these forms. Both the basic application and the application for amendment of passport have the same question."

I passed them across the gray metal desk.

"You mean the question that asks if anyone included in the application has ever been issued a passport?"

"Yeah. How about if someone lied in answering that question?"

"Well, his answer would have to be *knowingly* false. If it was, that would be a violation of Eighteen USC one-oh-oh-one and/or Eighteen USC one-five-four-two."

"Great," I said. "But how can I find out if Daddy lied about this?"

"I'd really like to help you," he said. "You seem legit, and that little girl's a real sweetie. But it's against Passport Office regs. You can get the application with a subpoena served on the Department of State in Washington. Or maybe easier: if you got some friends in law enforcement, they can request it, and nobody will say boo."

"I just wonder if going to all that trouble would be a waste of time?"

"I doubt if it would be a waste of time," he said, looking at me straight on. "But that's up to you."

Forty-five minutes later I was in Dick Werthimer's office on Grove Street, a four-block walk from the federal building. It was a serviceable office at street level, with middle-aged Selectric typewriters (no word processors) being used by middle-aged secretaries, slightly worn carpets, and fluorescent fixtures that were beginning to yellow. I was taken down a short hallway, past a small conference room and two other offices, to the corner office in back. Werthimer did not get up when we shook hands, and immediately I saw why. Leaning against a bookcase in the corner was a pair of aluminum crutches. His paralysis, I learned later, had come from a fluke case of polio he'd contracted as a young adult. It had made it impossible for him to work any longer as a stevedore, so he'd gone to school and become a lawyer.

I liked him immediately. Fiftyish, he dressed well, and his tanned face exuded health and expressiveness. He treated me as an equal. Maybe it was the polio; maybe it was his earlier work on the docks. Whatever it was, it had left him with little ego in a field where egos bloom like wildflowers in the spring. We wasted no time on pleasantries. He wanted to know what I'd found out. I told him about the visit to the passport office.

"You think Krishan lied on the application?" he asked.

"Yes," I answered. "I think that's what Dravo was telling me between the lines. The 'knowing false' part ought to be easy to prove; he turned over Asha's earlier passport under court order, for God's sake. Can we subpoena it right away?"

"Sure. But where does that get us? Then I'd have to persuade some U.S. attorney to indict him, and by that time he may have ripped up the passport and be a full-fledged Indian citizen."

"I'm just looking for some piece of paper I can wave under an Indian police inspector's nose to justify arresting him. The consul's visit spooked him, and we may have to get him popped to get the child out of his control. This whole case is a longshot. We ought to go after any legal advantage we can get."

"I hear you. The subpoena can be served by registered mail so we don't have to pay someone to serve it. I'll get that done this week. But what did you find out about custody in India?"

"It's pretty confusing," I admitted, looking at my yellow pad of notes. "Yesterday I called on the Honorable Prem Bhatnagar, Indian vice consul. He gave me several nice tourist brochures and told me what kind of weather to expect in Gorakhpur. But as to hard legal information, not much. He said he 'doubted' a U.S. custody order could be made legally binding in India. He said he knew of one case where an Indian national had returned to India with his child and successfully petitioned an Indian court for custody. It's not even clear whether the custody petition would have to be filed in Gorakhpur or even in Uttar Pradesh Province. If Krishan wanted to hire a Delhi attorney, it could be filed there, or anywhere for that matter. We may be going after a child whose legal custody has already been awarded to

Krishan, with no way of our finding that out. Except, of course, getting caught and learning we're charged with kidnapping, conspiracy to kidnap, et cetera.''

"We'll have to check it with someone who knows Indian law.''

"Bhatnagar gave me a couple of names," I volunteered. "One in San Jose, and another in Los Angeles."

"I've got some contacts. I'll look into it. But that can wait. Right now the problem is to get the money to do this. It's going to cost a lot; expenses alone should be a bundle."

"You read my mind."

"I have an idea for an *ex parte* motion. The filings show they're fighting over a house in El Cerrito that must be worth close to a quarter million with a hundred thousand owed on it. That's what her last attorney was counting on for payment. I don't see why we couldn't use some of that money—or some other money; I haven't finished reading the file—to fund your little trip to India.'' He folded his hands tentlike over his middle, tapping the fingers together, and smiled. "You know as well as I do the law isn't going to get this little girl back. All the law can do is back you up and provide the money to get the job done. Finally, it's your show. Honestly, what do you think?''

"I think it's going to be outrageously difficult, probably impossible. But I also think we have to try. Baker-roshi was willing to try with his team of amateurs, and I talked him out of it. With good reason. But somebody has to try. At the very least, Neva has to know she can't get Asha back in order to get on with her life. And who knows? A break here, a break there—we might get lucky and pull it off.''

"What do you have in mind?''

"I see doing it in stages. First we have to find out what's really going on in India. I'll have to hire someone to make a reconnaissance. That reconnaissance should also tell us something about how to proceed. If we can use law enforcement on our side, it'd be safer and simpler. The dream snatch is one that's perfectly legal: we fly in, get Krishan arrested, Neva takes Asha as next of kin, and we fly out before Krishan has gotten himself out of jail. It's too early to begin thinking of tactics, but that's what I have in mind.''

"And if you have to do it without help from law enforcement?''

"We'll see when the time comes. But the first thing is money. Right now I don't have any money to hire anyone with."

"Neva gave me fifteen hundred dollars. I'll write you a check for five hundred."

"That's more than enough for now. I'll nose around and try to line up someone in India. Looking ahead, we're also going to need some way to get out. We've got Asha's passport, but since she didn't use it going in, there's no entry stamp on it. That, plus Gorakhpur's distance from an international airport, means we're probably going to want to get out by private plane. I'll look into that too."

"Fine. Make your inquiries and let me know what turns up. If everything moves along with my *ex parte* motion, I'll need a tentative budget in about a month."

"See you then," I said.

FEBRUARY

In February, I wrote letters. First there was a letter to Neva telling her of my meeting with Dick Werthimer and the possibility that Krishan may have committed passport fraud in adding Asha to his passport. Next I wrote to Werthimer to let him know I'd found a pilot who flew in northern India and Pakistan and "whose organization has considerable influence at many Pakistani points of entry." The latter sounded better than it probably was. Fechheimer and I'd talked again about it, but the pilot and his plane were in Burma. The "considerable influence" claim might be valid, or it might be simply bar talk, and what I could learn about flying in northern India wasn't reassuring: there were precious few navigation aids or airports, the weather became more hazardous the closer one got to the Himalayan foothills, and the FAA had virtually no information about the Gorakhpur airport beyond the fact it existed in 1967.

The most important letter was to Henry Bawa in Bombay.

I stopped by the Pacific Avenue mansion first to talk with Hal. As Fechheimer predicted, he was effusive in his praise of Bawa and gave me a letter of introduction that I included with my own. In my letter I explained to Bawa the profiles of the case but didn't mention Krishan's name or identify Gorakhpur as the city in question. I described what I wanted done and asked him to quote a rate and a date when he could begin the reconnaissance. I hesitated when it came to asking Bawa if he'd participate in the snatch itself. I didn't like the idea of proposing in writing we do something illegal. Finally, I put it this way: *"Depending upon the results of your initial investigation, it is likely we would want to take steps to return the child to the mother's custody. I would be interested in knowing if you might assist us in making such a recovery and your ideas on how it might be effected."*

Bawa's reply came ten days later, typed under a letterhead that said *"Littlemore Services Pvt., Ltd., I-A-5 Sea Lord—Cuffe Parade Road, Bombay, India."* The address summoned up images of the British raj, of barracks and military formations wheeling on parade grounds, of teeming crowds and giant cranes on the docks near the Gateway to India.

Bawa was succinct. His rate was two hundred dollars a day plus expenses. Round-trip transportation to northern India would cost about $130. The reconnaissance could start as soon as I sent him a check for a thousand dollars, photographs of Krishan and Asha, and the other identifying information I'd promised. As to the "recovery," Bawa noted: *"I would be keen to know: [i] If the mother has a valid U.S. passport for the daughter? [ii] Will the daughter be willing to walk away with the mother, or have you in mind to go to Court?"*

On the basis of Bawa's letter, I made up a tentative budget for Werthimer. We both knew it was like reading tea leaves, but he needed something concrete for the *ex parte* motion. The total came to $22,000, of which $2,500 was to be released to me for the hiring of Bawa, with the balance to be deposited in my trust account prior to departure. And when would that be? The last line I wrote was: *"The target date for departure is April 1, 1980."*

I blinked when I wrote it. It wasn't that it seemed too soon; any date would have seemed too soon. It was the actual idea of leaving wasn't believable. Something would come up; an obstacle would intervene. Most likely, the court would deny Werthimer's motion. The whole scheme would disappear from the human chessboard like a page on a computer screen when the current goes off. Meanwhile, there were more pedestrian cases to pay the rent and occupy my time.

MARCH

The case moved into a state of suspended animation. Until Werthimer's motion was decided, there was nothing to do. It was an ingenious motion, arguing that since Krishan had caused the problem by violating a court order and stealing Asha, he should have to pay for its solution—namely, the recovery. But I couldn't see a judge approving it. The motion would probably be denied and Neva would be told to use her own funds for Asha's recovery. The catch, of course, was that Neva didn't have any funds.

In late February she got another letter from Krishan's nephew. We huddled over it, drafting an innocuous reply that wouldn't burn any bridges with the nephew and at the same time wouldn't alert Krishan to any imminent activity. For whatever reason, the nephew again asked for a copy of Krishan's citizenship papers. In her letter, Neva promised to look for them and asked the nephew to give Asha a small gift. Between the lines, it conveyed that Neva had given up hope of seeing her daughter again. And she probably had.

Then suddenly, on the last day of the month, against all expectations, the motion was granted. By order of the court, we could use Krishan's money to take his daughter away from him.

APRIL

I never met Miss Kumari Raj. Much later, I would see a photograph of her, sari-clad and smiling, standing in front of a temple. She appeared to be in her midtwenties, with dark hair and eyes, attractive but not particularly distinctive. Maybe that was why she was so good, because she *wasn't* distinctive. Hadn't I read somewhere that the best spies were those whose faces you couldn't remember ten minutes later? Of her background, the only thing I ever learned was that she was a graduate student in biochemistry at Bombay University and did odd jobs for Henry Bawa, who called her Rajni. Later on, I read her report and went over her expense-account receipts; it was like reconstructing an Indian version of *The Perils of Pauline* from fragments of silent-movie film, sprocket holes and all. I couldn't help admiring her enormously. It was because of her, after all, that we decided to do what we did.

A few days after the motion was granted, I sent Bawa a check for a thousand dollars, photos of Asha and Krishan, and all the information we had on their whereabouts, family, friends, and activities. He chewed on this for a week before calling me on the crackly transpacific phone. Then, in the final week of April, he dispatched Rajni to Gorakhpur. She picked an alias, and Henry had some phony business cards made up that identified her as the sales representative of an architectural-supplies firm.

As the crow flies, Gorakhpur lies about 950 miles from Bombay. That's as the crow flies, not as the Indian railway system runs. From her expense-account chits, it would appear Rajni left her home in Bombay at eight o'clock Sunday morning, April 27, and reached the Ambar Hotel in Gorakhpur at six-thirty Tuesday evening, April 29. That's an elapsed time of 58.5 hours. Of course, there were the storms.

Pasted to a blank sheet at the beginning of her expense account were a number of news clippings describing the storms that roared through Uttar Pradesh about the time she arrived. "CYCLONE CLAIMS 23 LIVES IN GORAKHPUR DISTRICT," proclaims one headline; "DUST STORM TOLL RISES TO 64," trumpets another.

There was also the heat wave that followed the storms. *"The heat wave raging in Uttar Pradesh has so far taken a toll of 43 lives,"* the *Times of India* stated. *"Monkeys are also victims of the extreme weather. Over 50 of them are reported to have died in the Chitrakoot area."*

Apparently it was some combination of these natural disasters that led to Rajni's personal misfortune. *"During the storm,"* she wrote in longhand on a sheet attached to her expense account, *"the trains were running late as people were jumping from one train to another. The ladies compartment of these trains gets ultimately full of gents, and there is no law and order at all. About this time, someone eloped with my bag containing the files, a few clothes, thermos and 200 rupees."* I grimaced as I recalled Henry's $137 bill for expenses [including travel] on her seven-day trip to Gorakhpur. He'd sent her not by air to Delhi or Lucknow and then by train, but by third-class train, fifty-eight and a half hours' worth of third-class train.

Lacking money, most of her clothes, and the case file, Rajni registered at the Ambar Hotel in Gorakhpur around dinnertime on Tuesday, April 29. A sheet with a number of architect's cards pasted to it showed the results of her next day's trip around Gorakhpur in a rickshaw. In the lower left corner sat the prize.

"Krishan Sahni, Architect," it said. *"B. Arch., U.S.A., M. Arch., U.S.A."* Printed vertically along the left side was: *"America Qualified & Experienced in LOW COST HOUSING & SKY SCRAPERS."*

The Sahni house was *"small,"* wrote Rajni, *"and very, very shabby."* It was part of a *"walled compound,"* and across the wall lived Krishan's other brothers in a house that was *"painted and better off . . . The Sahni family has split, and the elderly mother, who has eye trouble and is nearly blind, lives with Krishan. The daughter, Asha, and her father, Krishan, are the normal inmates along with an old bitch called 'Ducy,' a black, sick dog. The name of the servant, a young strongman, is Bahadur."*

And Asha?

"She is a thin, fair child," wrote Rajni, *"who rarely speaks but is friendly. One feels sorry for her. She's not allowed to go anywhere. So she just goes from the school to home, has limited friends. Her social life is not all very full."*

And Krishan? What was he like?

"He is not very erudite. He speaks English like an Indian. He does not impress one as if he had spent twenty years in America. He had not even read The Fountainhead. *Every architect and designer reads it like the Bible, but not him. His vocabulary is very limited and then he turns to Hindi. He is not fond of music and dance, unless it is strictly Indian, and then only classical. He is still an American and is pro-America. He supported Carter's action in Iran, and even sounded pro-Vietnam War. He has traveled all over the world, but he does not look like he saw anything different in all these places. He sounded like a weary traveller at journey's end."*

Rajni's report was typed on tissue-thin paper on an old manual typewriter. The *m* was lifted above the line, and wear had virtually obliterated the *t*. There were no headings, just two single-spaced pages of thin paper, with here and there a Hindi phrase translated into our alphabet. Apparently it was her report to Henry. I didn't see it until after much had happened, but I marveled at how vividly it brought Krishan to life.

He had a habit of introducing a topic, and just when one warms to it, says: "It's a long story. Let it go." He said he had married a Jew lady, and the child was their daughter. He had won awards, and designed some building for multibillionaires. Now, he said, he has left acres of property—really

all his things—and come to India, because of the child. And
. . . well, it's a long story.

"But won't the child miss her Mama?" I asked.

"No," he replied. "She does not like her Mama. She likes
Daddy. She likes India. She does not like America. Even the
child psychologist has testified to the child's preference for
her Daddy. Why even a court case is going on for custody of
the child. But it's a long story."

"Show me her pictures," I asked. "Photos when she was
in America."

"Someone has stolen all her photos," the father said. "And
a few other things. In fact, my brother across the wall has
done it."

"Why should he steal all her photos?"

At this point, he took a longer pause.

"They even want to take her," he said. "But now I am
very careful."

"Why would they want to take her?" I asked.

"Because of the court case. But it's a long story."

She also learned that Krishan daily wove the two braids of
Asha's hair and, accompanied by the huge family retainer, Bahadur, took her to and from school on his bicycle.

The next day, Thursday, Rajni visited the school and drew a
map of its location. It was around the corner from the headquarters of the district commissioner of police. *"The watchman
is one Mr. Barfilal,"* she wrote, *"who chews* pan *and has gaps
in his teeth. He is very alert and questions closely any outsider
what work they have in the school. I got the following information out of him by saying I wanted to get my sister enrolled in
Class II. Summer hours are 7:30 to 12:30. It was closed and
will reopen on July 8th."*

After visiting the school, she returned to the Sahni compound
to play with Asha and have lunch. She gave Asha a pack of cards
and took her picture *"with Granny and with Bahadur."* Then
Krishan arrived home.

"Why did you take my daughter's photos without asking
me?" he asked.

I did not know what to say

"Please remove the rolls and give them to me. We do not

allow anyone to take photos of our daughter," he said firmly, and snatched the camera from my hand.

He then removed the roll. The Granny, Bahadur, Buwa [a cook], and I—we were all stunned. We dismissed the incident, however, and had lunch. Then I left the place, telling him that I would write to him.

Half a world away in San Francisco, we knew nothing of all this. Henry Bawa, more than nine hundred miles away in Bombay, also knew nothing. The storms had downed telephone and telegraph lines. Before leaving Gorakhpur, Rajni tried to reach Henry to tell him of her success, but failed. Consequently she couldn't report to him until she arrived in Bombay days later.

In early May Henry reported the good news that *"the subject has been traced after a bit of hide and seek, and our investigator is pretty friendly with the subject and the child."* Balancing this was his sobering conclusion that the prospects for a kidnapping in Gorakhpur were dim. *"The subject is quite scared,"* wrote Henry, *"and always escorts the child to school and back. These days the schools are closed and the child is not allowed to go anywhere alone."*

For the forseeable future there was no seam to exploit—at least not in Gorakhpur. Henry saw this and, in the same letter, proposed that Krishan and Asha be lured out of Gorakhpur and to a large city, perhaps Bombay. But then what? *"A suitable plot of cinema style,"* wrote Henry, *"an armed robbery, or a kidnapping can be staged. In three hours, you will be in Katmandu and from there to Bangkok and out. In the meanwhile, we can detain the subject forcibly. The moment we get your call from California, the subject can find his way home."*

I called Henry the next day.

It was around eight o'clock and not quite dusk when I got through to him. I stood in the kitchen, looking east across the lagoon to the Bolinas Ridge beyond, its topmost third still lit by the setting sun. Several coastal deer were browsing in the field this side of the lagoon. From across the deck I could hear Lis practicing her flute.

The line crackled, and I heard Henry's clipped, precise voice on the other end.

"Thompson? Good you called. Did you get my last letter?"
"Yes."

For several minutes Henry described some additional facts

that Rajni had turned up in Gorakhpur. Then he outlined the plan.

"I propose we become his prospective employers and invite him for a big contract for construction, give him free tickets, and make his hotel arrangements. Since the school is closed, he will automatically bring the child."

"Uh-huh."

"And when he's in town, most probably Bombay—"

"When do you hope to bring him there?" I interrupted.

"Either on May thirty-first, which is election day in Bombay—all police and government staff are busy then; nobody would listen to his complaints—or offer him a second date, say the tenth of June. He is busy with some project in his home city now, so perhaps he will not accept the bait this month. Either date will work, but after your General Eisenhower we'll call the thirty-first D-Day. Anyway, when he is in town, suddenly something will happen to him, and, uh, people will ask him for money. He perhaps will go sightseeing till his boss is available to interview him. He is standing on a corner one evening and suddenly something happens and he is taken away. His watch and his pen and his wallet are taken off. He is asked to write a note for money, et cetera, to his family. So it will be made to look like an ordinary little job, a very small job indeed. The child will not know it. And he will be confined for a short time. You will take an airbus to Katmandu with the child."

"How do we separate him from the child?"

"That we take care of, Thompson," said Henry, pronouncing my name as a British brigadier might, with an accent on each syllable. "Leave that to us. And when I hear from you that everything is tip-top, either from Bangkok or California, he will make his way back to his hotel, where he will find his money safe, his pen, and his watch. For a long time he will not know what happened. Let him work out the puzzle with all the raw materials, ha, ha, and design himself a good piece of architecture where all the pieces fit. All of us will just keep quiet."

"In other words," I asked, "instead of kidnapping the child we kidnap the father?"

"That's it exactly. We will only have to hold him for three or four days. A kind of custody."

"Possibly police or official custody?" I asked, recalling my earlier suggestion to Henry we might bring about Krishan's arrest by using the California arrest warrant and money. Anything would be better than trying to grab him off a streetcorner.

"Oh, no," said Henry. "It would be unofficial custody. My boys would do it. And then, when I get your phone call, he will be released. He never knows what happened. He goes back to the hotel, and everything is there."

"Everything," I added, "but the child."

"Yes. Everything but the child. He doesn't know what happened to the child."

I told Henry I would have to go over the new developments with everyone involved. I'd call him back three days hence. Meanwhile he should put into motion whatever schemes he had for luring Krishan and Asha out of Gorakhpur.

THURSDAY, MAY 15

I felt as if it were the midsixties and I was the press officer at the U.S. Embassy in Saigon. Although I couldn't remember the exact words, some phrases stuck: *"reconnaissance completed . . . the operation will have to be moved . . . Bombay or a large Indian city . . . subterfuge offer of employment . . . the subject will have to be detained for a short period of time."*

Unlike the press corps in Saigon, my audience was compliant. There were no awkward questions, no charges that anything was being hidden or euphemistically sugarcoated. Only quiet conversation yielding the consensus that circumstances had "forced a new strategy." The five of us sat there drinking tea from delicate bowls in Baker-roshi's comfortable living room at Green Gulch Farm, all of us, I suspect, wondering what it was we had just agreed to do.

I had driven out from San Francisco earlier that afternoon, leaving the freeway at the Highway 1 exit, following one of the two roads that led across Mount Tamalpais and the Marin headlands to Stinson Beach and Bolinas. I'd passed the grove of eucalyptus and then swung left around the corner that exposed Green Gulch and Muir Beach below. The road crept down the northern side of the ravine in serpentine curves of smooth asphalt, its center line glistening yellow. Two-thirds of the way down, the valley floor flattened and opened into fields that stayed under cultivation year-round. This was Green Gulch Farm. Its entrance was on an awkward curve where I had to glance ahead

for oncoming traffic before swinging left into a gravel lane past
a redwood sign that said *"Zen Center—Green Gulch Farm."*
I'd driven slowly down the lane to the parking lot and let the
Volvo roll to a stop between Dick Werthimer's old Pontiac and
Baker-roshi's BMW 733i.

Neva had been in her room in the large, barnlike structure
across the garden from Baker-roshi's residence. All the spaces
at Green Gulch Farm expressed a Buddhist aesthetic—spare,
serene, giving to each object its space—and Neva's room was
no exception. It was tiny, with a futon piled in one corner, a
small desk and bureau, and, on the desk, a bunch of wildflowers
picked that morning from the fields that stretched down the
gulch to the sea a half mile away.

Neva had received another inconsequential letter from India,
and we'd been talking idly of it, ambling across the garden.
From the right, along another path, came an attractive woman
in her thirties. Neva introduced us. As soon as I heard the name
Ruth Palmer, I knew I was meeting the third member of our
team. I liked what I saw. She was tall and powerfully built, with
clear brown eyes and a direct presence. She had been to India
six times before, and she spoke Hindi.

The sun was slanting through the leaded windows of the living
room as we entered and greeted Werthimer. From a chat I'd had
with him on the phone that morning, I knew he believed the
operation should go forward. Neva would go along with whatever we decided. Since I'd just met Ruth, I didn't know what
she would think of our "detaining" Krishan. But Baker-roshi
was the real mystery. Would he approve the use of violence to
retrieve Asha? In some vague way I assumed Buddhism was
committed to nonviolence, but I didn't know. I was wondering
about that, gazing at the late-afternoon light bathing the garden,
when Baker-roshi walked in.

He'd just come from a service and was wearing his abbot's
full robes. *"A suitable plot of cinema style,"* Henry had written.
With Baker-roshi in his robes and shaved head, Dick Werthimer
dapper in his dark suit, button down shirt, and paisley tie, Ruth
and Neva in their long skirts, and me in denim shirt and cor-
duroys, we were "a suitable *scene* of cinema style." We looked
the part. Just don't say "*forcibly* detained," I told myself.

I described the situation in India as Henry had explained it to
me—Rajni's success (at this time I didn't know her name and
hadn't seen her report), the fact that the schools were now closed

and Asha never left the compound, the huge family retainer who, with Krishan, accompanied Asha to school, the tight security at the school itself, its proximity to the office of the district commissioner of police, Gorakhpur's distance from an international airport, and the attention a private plane might attract. Neva asked about Asha's condition, and I repeated the sketchy details Henry had given me. Then the discussion turned to the obvious question: what to do?

Using sanitized language, I told them what Henry and I recommended. It was not unlike a family conference with a heart specialist in which no one has great difficulty accepting the recommendation that Aunt Ida should go ahead and have a bypass. No one asked about the rope or the gag or the sleeping pills. Or the quick blow that would fix the balance of power.

Werthimer offered the opinion we should either do it this way or not at all. Ruth Palmer asked if I'd ever done anything like it before.

"Of course not," I said. "It's illegal!"

Neva said nothing.

Baker-roshi didn't speak for a long time, and then asked a single question: "Do you trust this detective you call Henry? Has he sent you any proof that things are as he says they are in Gorakhpur?"

I said I'd spoken to Henry over the phone and that a full report was in the mail.

"Yes," I went on. "I trust him. But the real question isn't whether Henry's trustworthy. I'll precede Neva and Ruth to India and be able to see for myself what the situation is. The real question is whether we try it at all. I'm not encouraged by our reconnaissance. The snatch itself is going to be extremely difficult; the only thing we know for sure is that we can't do it in Gorakhpur. Dick and I are agreed: either we try it this way or we fold our tents. Maybe we ought to forget the whole thing?"

As I'd expected, the more I pushed for abandoning the operation, the more the others pushed to go forward. There was no debate. In the background was the overpowering fact that Krishan's money was paying for the whole expedition. If we failed, he would end up funding the failure. And so the discussion drifted off into small talk over the delicate bowls of tea. When it was clear that "detaining" Krishan had been approved, I excused myself and left. Werthimer and Baker-roshi needed a chance to talk privately. At the door, I said to Neva, "Things are moving. It's important you find a hiding place for yourself and Asha after we get back." She nodded.

I had to gun the Volvo getting back on Highway 1, but then settled into an easy rhythm of swinging the wheel from side to side as the highway completed its descent to Muir Beach. By the time I reached the top of the hill beyond and sped along the ridge, the sun was an hour away from setting. The road crossed a shoulder of the ridge and plunged into shadow. Holding altitude, it traced the contours of one of the arroyos that fell from ridge to sea. At the ravine's seaward end, buffeted by the prevailing west winds, vegetation was limited to grass and an occasional coyote bush. Deep in the cleft, where the road made its turn to head seaward again along the opposite bank, manzanita and then oak took over the landscape. I'd always found this sea-swept road a good one for thinking, and right now there was a lot of thinking to be done.

The meeting had gone as expected. No one wanted to face the issue of violence, the fact that our little adventure had taken an unanticipated and unpleasant turn: instead of simply "retrieving" a six-year-old girl, we were now going to "forcibly detain" an adult man in his home country. But as long as I didn't say it so bluntly you couldn't ignore it—by talking about ropes and gags, or how many Indian thugs we were going to use, or how we were going to silence Krishan quickly, or where we were going to hold him, or whether he should be tied up or handcuffed to a chair—as long as I didn't go into any of those details but spoke only of a "zone of operation" or a "subterfuge offer of employment" or "the necessity of detaining the subject," as long as I was willing, like that press officer in Saigon, to use language to sanitize, and thus rationalize, the violence our little group was sponsoring, as long as I didn't emphasize our entry into blood sport, then I knew no one would object. It had been easy.

The details of proper and improper force, of what "restraints" to use, of how to take Krishan—all those details had been quitclaimed to Henry and me. They were our property.

My mind began to dwell on them. I didn't believe that once Krishan and Asha were outside Gorakhpur he'd be willing to let the child out of his sight. That meant we'd have to use force to take her. We'd use guile if we could, but we should be prepared to use force. And the idea of making our move on some street corner was senseless. There would be too many variables lying outside our control. Some spectator might intervene or call the police or, at the very least, recall a license-plate number or a face. Far better to do it inside, in a room somewhere, where we could control what was going on, where Krishan would immediately grasp he had no chance and would yield without a struggle.

Superior force? Weapons? What weapons? I didn't know anything about Indian firearms laws. I imagined Henry could provide guns if we wanted them. But did we want them? And if we didn't want guns, how far down the slippery slope of weaponry were we prepared to go?

Then there was Asha. What if Asha didn't want to go with her mother? What if she was so frightened by the kidnapping of her father that she'd be a risk at exit? Better get a prescription for Valium added to the Lomotil and the Tetracycline and the yellow fever and cholera shots I'd already jotted down in the notebook of things to do. And get dosages for various body weights. How much would Asha weigh now?

The road swung to the right, exposing a jumble of boulders and small gullies. A quarter mile to the northwest, it cut back across a high bluff before descending the last mile and a half to Stinson Beach. My eye caught a speck above the bluff, hanging just seaward of the cliff face, spiraling skyward on what was left of the late-afternoon thermal. Probably a hawk; too small for a turkey vulture.

It's sobering, I told myself, snaking the car through a series of turns, how easily moral boundaries are crossed. Only three months ago Neva was sitting on your couch, listening to your little lecture on how you never do child snatches unless your client—the "custodial parent," as I believe you put it—is willing to accompany you. All of this, you pointed out in your best professorese, was because you had principles, because the child "had no advocate" in this adult game of fetch-and-retrieve, and you, the moral detective, had to "establish some boundaries." If the custodial parent were there at the time of the snatch, you told her, the trauma to the child "would be minimized." And now, a few months later, you're fixing to blow Daddy's head off if he doesn't cooperate. And the kid? Well, if she doesn't like Mommy well enough, we'll just give her a little Valium cocktail to get her out of the country. And all this, of course, is necessary. It is, in fact, what you do for a living.

The tires sizzled on the gravel as I parked on the bluff. Below and to the right lay the extended crescent of Stinson Beach, with Bolinas beyond. It was a hawk I'd seen, a red-tailed hawk whose tail feathers glinted in the light as it sailed upward, gyre upon gyre. Several hundred feet above the bluff, where the thermal faltered and died, the hawk broke out of its spiral, wings stretched, circling. I sat down on a granite boulder and watched.

Underneath everything, it wasn't the moral considerations that bothered me. It was both easy and permissable to play the detective whose willingness to accept dirty hands only emphasized the basic mendacity of others. With jaw firmly set, strong hands on the tiller, he steers through a morally troubled sea. I'd already seen the movie, and I couldn't play the part. The self-doubts and disgust were closer to the mark.

What had I become? By what puzzling route had I moved from lecturing about ethics to determining whether to put a gun to Krishan's head or a knife to his throat? And where would it end? My resentment at the others, my self-doubts and anger about what I was doing and what I'd become—all of it was the tip of an iceberg whose name was not anger but fear. Sitting on that rock, hearing the crash of the sea below and watching the hawk above, I knew it was fear. Stone-cold, clammy fear.

I don't know where you're supposed to feel fear. I always feel it coiled down deep inside, deeper than the heart or the stomach, deeper than the viscera, hidden under layers where I can't get at it. I'd felt it under everything I'd been doing the last few months. I'd be leaving the corner liquor store after buying a pack of cigarettes, and suddenly feel it. Or driving home from a party with Nancy. Or watching Ev and his friends skateboarding. I'd chase it away with a quick denial: "This case is ridiculous. It'll never get off the ground." But it always came back. In a few hours or days it would return, and I'd have to deal with it again. Now, for the first time, I knew I could never again just shoo it away. In the most inchoate yet indisputable way, I knew there would be no heading off the locomotive that even now was rounding the last curve before coming into view. It was going to happen. In a matter of days—weeks at the most—I'd be in India.

What was the fear about?

If we were caught, the U.S. consul would intervene and the women would be released. Henry and I, though, would end up in jail, perhaps for a long time, marking off days on a dank wall while Indian justice followed its Byzantine and incomprehensible course. But even more than that, it was the fear of being in a foreign land, unable to speak the language, in a situation where so much depended on trust and where no one could be trusted, even Henry (especially Henry!). So much was purely and simply unknown.

Child snatches were "seam jobs," but we weren't going to exploit a seam; we were going to force a rupture. It was the force part that bothered me. Not because it was crossing a moral boundary (although it was), not because it was committing a serious crime (although it was), but because it raised the ante and made retreat difficult. Once we moved against Krishan, we couldn't turn back. It wasn't just that he would have to be held until we got out of the country; it was also that after taking that risk we'd be in such jeopardy we'd accept even greater risks to protect ourselves. Finally, there was an appalling irony I'd admitted to no one up to this point: I'd never done a child snatch! Whatever droll divinity it was that arranged things in the human world had determined that my first snatch would occur not in Alameda, or Fresno, or even Salt Lake City, but in India.

The hawk rode steady on the updraft now, beak outthrust, head down, looking for game. This was one of those preternatural evenings that grace the coast of northern California in May or September, a time when the light takes on a singular clarity, when the outlines of things—the oak branch overhanging the road, the lichen-dappled boulder, the beak of a hawk—stand sharp and true.

I thought again of Krishan.

During the previous month, he had taken up residence in my imagination. By a throw of the dice and an exchange of money, we had become adversaries. We were already contemporaries (he forty-six, I forty-five) and fellow fathers. From half a world away, godlike, I was beginning to brush the outer reaches of his world. My aim, to be sure, was not to brush his world but to change it dramatically, irrevocably. I meant to rob him of his child just as, earlier, he'd robbed Neva of her child, their child. In this circuitous way, he had become my quarry, a quarry now pursued by proxy but soon to be confronted.

Many times I had imagined our meeting. He'd be bound and gagged; there'd be fear in his eyes as he learned we were taking Asha. And somewhere in those deep-set brown eyes I'd see a grudging acknowledgement that he had lost.

That filmstrip had run many times in my imagination, but I knew it would be foolhardy to run it in actuality. Letting him see my face would be imprudent and possibly dangerous. Henry, I'd decided, would deal with Krishan; I would remain with Neva and Asha. That wasn't cowardice, Fechheimer explained when I told him of my thoughts, but "good business practice."

The hawk was poised now along a ridge just to the south. It hesitated for an instant and then, talons clenched and beak extended, saffron tail glinting in the light, dropped out of sight behind the ridge.

In that microsecond of delay, had the hawk felt any prompting of doubt, any brief hiatus, any misgiving or uncertainty? Or had the moment been annealed by the same suffusing light that caressed its feathers and the prey it dived upon, so that what seemed like hesitation was only the mechanical repositioning of its wings and muscles for the kill?

Something was going on, and it would not stop. I was outside whatever it was, but I was also inside it, a part of it. Something was happening, and I knew I could not control it. Event would follow event. Some would be expected and might be prepared for. Others would not.

NINE

THE BLUE BALLERINA

TUESDAY, JUNE 3, 1980

There was a click and a hydraulic groan as the landing gear retracted into the belly of the 747. The pilot had used up most of the mile-and-a-quarter north-south runway at San Francisco International before easing back on the stick; the nose had lifted a few degrees, and the huge plane had struggled into the air. The flight was only half full. First class was virtually empty, and business class only a quarter full; most of the passengers were clustered back in tourist. It must have been the weight of fuel needed for the maximum-range, eleven-hour flight to Hong Kong that made the takeoff so labored.

The port wing dipped, and the great craft swung west into the slanting sun, bringing the Golden Gate and the Marin headlands into view. It was 7:15, and below, the evening was beginning bright and clear. A layer of fog hung over the Farallones, but Stinson Beach and Bolinas were clear. Soon, however, there was only sky and sun above, cloud and water below. I ruffled through the *Newsweek* Henry had chosen as our recognition signal in Bombay.

Why hadn't Henry called earlier?

He called the night before with the news Krishan and Asha were in Bombay, lured there by one of his operatives. But he'd also said it was "urgent" we come on the first available flight, since father and daughter had been in Bombay since June 1. Because of the international dateline, it was actually June 3 in

Bombay when he called. Why had he waited two days to tell me of their arrival?

Fortunately I'd been planning to leave the next day anyway. I only had to call Pan Am and get an earlier flight. Neva and Ruth, however, had not been expecting to leave for another week to ten days.

I turned and looked at them, four rows back. Neva had propped up Asha's favorite Disney doll in the back pouch of the seat in front of her. She was talking to Ruth. At the airport she had seemed calm, almost happy. Was she finally beginning to believe we might succeed?

In addition to Mickey Mouse, Neva was carrying Asha's clothes. I had everyone's tickets and passports in the zippered compartment of the Danish book bag at my feet. Made of gray canvas with a shoulder strap, it had two pockets that were the perfect size for a tape recorder and accessories, and its interior was just right for legal-size file folders. For this trip I'd made only one change: a big safety pin inserted through the canvas closed the zippered compartment. I freed the pin and checked the contents.

First the tickets.

Four in all: Ruth's, Neva's, Asha's, and mine. They were identical. Nonstop Pan Am flight 470 to Hong Kong, connecting with Pan Am's venerable round-the-world flight 001 from Hong Kong to Bombay. I laid them out on my tray table.

Asha's outgoing segments had been removed and left in my desk in San Francisco. They could be turned in for credit when we got back. When we got to Bombay, all four tickets would look identical—the two Pan Am flights going out, times and flight numbers left open for the return via Bangkok, Hong Kong, and Honolulu. I hadn't figured out how to get around the missing entry stamp in Asha's passport. In a pinch, we might try bluffing our way out using the tickets as proof of Asha's entry with us.

The visas stamped in our passports should help too. I looked at them.

Asha's photo was two years old, but stamped there on a back page was the official visa entered at the Indian consulate in San Francisco on May 21. The visas were serialized, and Asha's number fell between Neva's and Ruth's. Mine had been issued last.

Everything appeared to be in good order. Only time would tell if it was good enough.

Had I forgotten anything? I went through a mental checklist.

Five thousand dollars in traveler's checks and one thousand in cash. Lomotil for dysentery, Tetracycline for that and anything else that might come along, and, of course, the Valium for whomever and whatever. I'd checked dosages; even if Asha was skinnier than Neva thought she was, I could safely give her two Valium tablets in any four-hour period, but no more than four in any twenty-four-hour period

The three of us had gotten yellow fever and cholera shots on May 21, and I was carrying a document signed by Neva certifying that I could authorize medical treatment for Asha. I also had a brief tape on which Neva told Asha I "was a friend" and that Asha should go with me. Now probably redundant, the last two items had seemed important when it appeared I'd be preceding Neva and Ruth to India.

In the small suitcase under my seat were two pieces of electronic gear Henry had asked me to purchase for him: a telephone scrambler and a long-playing tape recorder.

The transpacific connection had been full of static when I'd talked with Henry the night before. Even listening to it again on tape, I could make out less than a third of what he'd said. A *Newsweek* under the arm was to be our recognition signal, and he would personally meet Pan Am flight 001. Of that I was sure. It had been part of our original plan, which we'd just moved up one day.

I looked at my watch. It was now 7:25. We were due in Bombay in nineteen hours. Because of the dateline, it would be early in the morning of Thursday, June 5, when we arrived, at which time—I looked at my watch again—it would be early afternoon on June 4 in San Francisco. Because of quirks like daylight savings time, Bombay was twelve hours ahead of San Francisco. Better sleep tonight.

But I didn't sleep. Business class wasn't comfortable enough for sleeping, even with an empty seat beside me. Then, too, there were the loose ends. How had Henry managed to lure Krishan and Asha to Bombay? All I knew was that his operative was staying with them at a hotel, and that they'd been there since June 1. Why hadn't Henry called me earlier? Where and when would we make our move? It would be done inside; we'd agreed on that much two weeks earlier. Could we do it without hurting Krishan and without Asha seeing it? There were no answers to such questions. We'd have to act as circumstances dictated, tak-

ing advantage of what breaks came our way. At least now we
were moving.

THURSDAY MORNING, JUNE 5

Sometimes it's like that. The tempo of things changes. You're
going along, marching in time to one cadence, and then everything shifts and you're moving to a different beat. For me, the
change came with the captain's announcement we were over-
flying Bangkok and would land next in Bombay. There was some
trouble on the ground (a hijacking? a military coup?), and Bangkok International Airport was closed. A few moments later he
came back on with the announcement we'd be landing in Bombay at 1:25 A.M. local time. That was ten minutes before our
scheduled arrival time.

We'd arrived in Hong Kong on time, but had to wait two hours
before boarding the flight to Bombay. I'd spent the time prowl-
ing the transit lounge, looking at the Rolexes and Ricoh cameras
and cultured pearl necklaces in the display cases, fretting about
the delay. On the plane, I kept worrying: would Henry still be
there at nearly four in the morning? Would it further screw up
our schedule?

Then came the captain's announcement. We would be landing
in a little more than an hour and a half.

The three of us gathered back by the lavatories, elated by the
news, agreeing it was a good omen. Throughout the trip, I'd
been watching Neva. If anything, she seemed to be getting
stronger and more composed as we neared Bombay. Ruth was
a rock—clear-eyed, funny, good-humored. After our meeting at
Green Gulch Farm, she'd called and asked to talk with me privately. We'd met a couple of days later and talked for an hour
about what the trip entailed and, specifically, what it meant to
"detain" Krishan. She had pressed me hard, probing just how
I interpreted that slippery adverb *forcibly*. The more candid I'd
been about my fears and what was facing us in India, the more
satisfied she'd become.

After a quarter of an hour, Neva went back to her seat and
shut her eyes. She wasn't dozing, I was sure—most likely just
preparing herself for what lay ahead. Ruth and I stayed in the
back, chatting away, enjoying the rush that came with the

knowledge we'd soon be there. Then the seat-belt light winked on.

The next few hours were like a slide down a slick metal tube.

First came a blast of dense, wet air as we left the metal capsule of the plane and entered the international arrivals building. Even at this hour, the temperature was well up in the eighties. We fell into natural lines that snaked single-file to either side of the four passport control posts. The counters were high, each with two officers working side by side like robots, moving the lines along. As each passenger reached the counter, a control officer took the passport and looked at the person's face and then down at the photo in the passport. Sometimes a few words were exchanged, sometimes not; an Australian couple's names were checked against a computer printout. Finally the officer stamped the passports.

When I saw the control officer was actually checking each passenger against his or her photo, I slid Asha's passport back into my bag. Ruth and Neva were ahead of me in the same file. I handed over the three passports and received the officer's impersonal gaze. He stamped them and handed them back to me just as the phone on the counter rang. He spoke into the telephone, mumbled something to his colleague, and left. The entry stamp lay on its side, burning a hole in my eyes. I hesitated for a moment. The passengers behind us were complaining of the delay; the other officer kept up his routine of taking-looking-stamping; the flies were buzzing around the unshielded light fixture; I started to move my hand toward the counter. Then, unobtrusively, like a soccer player withholding his shot, I pulled it back and moved on.

Stupid, I thought, as we continued into the customs area. Stupid even to think of taking a chance like that. For all you know, Henry has already solved the entry-stamp problem.

Leaving the customs zone, I saw Henry, *Newsweek* under his arm, standing behind a barricade. He had on a loose-cut white shirt with a red-and-green-striped cravat. About my size and build, he looked five or even ten years younger. He had no difficulty picking us out of the arrivals crowd, and soon we'd all exchanged pleasantries and were walking toward the exit.

Sleeping forms huddled in corners and along the tile walls. In the parking lot, puddles of water dotted the asphalt. "Yes, my friends," Henry was saying, "you can see the puddles. You have brought with you the beginning of the monsoon. We had our first showers last evening.''

Henry led the way to the car, a late-fifties Austin sedan, and the luggage was stowed in what he called the boot. While helping Henry and the driver put away the bags, I got Henry's confirmation that Asha and Krishan were still in Bombay, thus quieting my worst fear. Neva and Ruth—"the ladies," as Henry unerringly referred to them—climbed into the back seat. I joined them, and Henry slipped into the front passenger seat. The driver started the car but couldn't get the stick shift into reverse. A few words were passed as Henry and the driver switched places. No one in the back seat said anything or even traded glances. Would this be the driver and car used for the snatch? It was a strain to keep up the small talk as Henry drove the half mile to the Intercontinental Hotel Centaur. Our bags were taken, and car and driver disappeared.

We registered at the desk in the opulent lobby, decked out in the burgundies and golds one associates with the India of the British raj, and followed Henry into the lounge for a get-acquainted drink. No one ordered alcohol. I sipped an orange Fanta, and Henry started to explain his numerological theories. The circular black marble table was just large enough to hold our drinks, and the chairs were uncomfortably rigid. I felt ragged and irritable. Neva was trying to find out about Asha, but after a moment or two Henry turned the talk to astrology. I tuned out but was drilled awake by Henry's remark that astrology was the reason he hadn't let us know earlier of Krishan and Asha's arrival in Bombay.

"What do you mean?" I asked, my voice taking on an edge I couldn't control.

"It was regrettable," he replied, "but everything is just fine now. My man, Passi Prem, is taking care of everything. He is good, is he not? I told you he would succeed when we talked on the telephone some time ago. Do you remember it? He succeeded just a bit sooner than expected. I consulted the charts over the last weekend and saw that no operations should be initiated between Saturday and Tuesday. Very bad prospect. Extremely bad. So I disconnected my phone. Pee Pee (that's what I call him), the poor chap, endeavored in vain to reach me when they arrived Sunday morning. Alas, I was not available until Tuesday. So that was regrettable. But now all is smooth.''

Henry smiled beneficently at Neva.

"You are here," he went on, "and we will soon have your charming daughter back in your arms."

Mouth open in bewilderment, I could only ask, "You mean it is now Thursday morning and they've been here since Sunday morning?"

"Yes," said Henry brightly and returned to his talk of numerology.

My face sealed itself into an impassive mask so as not to betray to Neva and Ruth my growing belief that Henry was one hundred percent, off-the-wall, certifiably crazy. As he continued his line of patter, a nightmare was taking shape behind my sinuses. We'd flown eight thousand miles for nothing—worse than nothing. We'd spent thousands of dollars in court-administered funds on a wild-goose chase. Asha and Krishan weren't in Bombay, maybe not even in Gorakhpur. There'd been no trip to Gorakhpur. Rajni didn't exist. Pee Pee was a figment of Henry's imagination. Only the driver was real, and he couldn't drive a car. This would end with me having to make good the funds. My investigator's license would be jerked and my reputation ruined. I'd end up groveling on the floor of a shoe store in Oakland for three hundred dollars a week. That's how I'd always feared it would end, and now, in this sterile lounge of the Centaur Hotel, with Ravi Shankar on the stereo and my knees bumping this silly marble table, it was all coming true.

Blessedly, it was late and the scene in the lounge couldn't continue long. Trailed by a retinue of white-coated, gold-buttoned bellhops, one for each of the three carry-on bags constituting our full complement of luggage, we made our way to the seventh floor. There we were greeted by another white-coated figure, clad like the bellhops except for the addition of a Sam Brown belt that gave him a vaguely military air. On our way down the corridor, Henry explained that the uniformed figure was the floor security guard charged with keeping "undesirables" from annoying the guests. After leaving Neva and Ruth in their room, Henry and I retraced our steps to the elevator.

My room was on the fifth floor. It had two beds and a Western-style bathroom. The ceiling fan was stirring the heavy air. The bellhop switched on the air conditioner, which screeched metallically, groaned, and died. Henry paid him off and closed first the white-louvered outer door, then the solid inner door.

"I brought the expense receipts and our operative's report," he said, pulling a sheaf of papers out from under the *Newsweek* he'd earlier placed in a thin, Samsonite briefcase. "As you will see, everything is in order."

I looked at the jumble of papers. There were two punched railway stubs from Indian Railways for the passage Bombay-Gorakhpur-Bombay, a bunch of small receipts printed on news-printlike paper from the Hotel Ambar in Gorakhpur, K.B. & Sons Refreshment Room (Non-Vegetarian) in Lucknow, and the like. Typed on two pages of tissue-thin paper was Rajni's report, and folded between that and another sheet was the card of "Krishan Sahni, Architect" with its odd spelling of "SKY SCRAPERS." There was also the carbon copy of a letter to Sahni from a Bombay architect. I looked up at Henry.

"Right now they are staying at the Hotel Siddhartha in Bandra," he said. "Earlier tonight they had dinner at Wong's Chinese Restaurant. Pee Pee, of course, is with them, staying in the same hotel in the same or an adjoining room. I have taken the liberty of changing their accommodations daily so no suspicions will be aroused when they disappear. I trust you agree?"

"Of course," I said.

I was flabbergasted by the change in Henry. Now we were talking detective to detective. The showing of expense chits and operative reports was a universal method of demonstrating the work had been done. Not only had it been done, it had been done brilliantly.

I went to my suitcase and withdrew the Panasonic PC 22 long-play recorder and the Superphone 7720 telephone scrambler. "I didn't forget," I said, handing them to Henry.

He smiled, thanked me, and asked what he owed me.

"Nothing," I said. "They're a gift. You're just as good as Hal said you were. You make me look good. This is just a small way of showing my appreciation."

Henry was pleased with the gift. Swiftly, we got down to business. Henry reviewed what Rajni had found out while I glanced over her report. At one point, he asked me to look at a particular paragraph:

The sister of KS [Krishan Sahni] has come to stay with KS. She is a professor of sociology at some college. Her husband is a section officer in the Supreme Court of India, and is on fairly good terms with Indira Gandhi and Sanjay Gandhi. They have two children who now have gone to their other grandmother in Delhi.

"Does this mean what I think it means?"

"Yes," said Henry. "After I received this word from Rajni, I checked the name she had with an associate in Delhi. What she says is correct although it is unclear how close is the connection."

"We're in the process, then, of kidnapping the niece of someone who is personally acquainted with the prime minister?"

"Yes. But people often brag about these things. As I say, it is not clear how closely they are acquainted. Before things had progressed further, I did not wish to alarm you. But you are what they call the boss, and you should know this."

"Out of tens of millions of children in India," I said, "there are only a precious few, I figure, whose families are acquainted with the prime minister. We must count ourselves lucky, must we not, that we've drawn one of those precious few?"

We both laughed. In spite of the lateness of the hour and the brevity of our contact, we were coming to like each other. Henry's new revelation had kicked my nervous system into high gear, and I could feel myself speeding up, energy replacing the exhaustion I still felt from the flight.

"Tell me how you brought them here. It's incredible. How'd you do it?"

"It was simply a question of laying enough bait around. Sooner or later, if your quarry is hungry—and our quarry was quite hungry indeed—he will take the bait.

"The first offer of employment was made by my friend, R. J. Kumar. We play billiards together at my club here in Bombay; had we the time, I would show it to you. Kumar is a well-known architect, he built a big hotel in Delhi and many, many projects here in Bombay. We were playing one night, and I asked Kumar if as a young man he had ever been in love. He replied that of course he had and that it had brought him a vale of tears. 'Exactly,' I said. 'That is exactly what it does.' Then I went on to tell him of this family, clients of mine for the longest time. 'They are from north India, and they are wealthy,' I told Kumar, 'enormously wealthy. Alas,' I told him, 'they have a son who has fallen in love with an American, and they have forbidden him to see her. He sits and sulks and they do not know what to do with him. He is trained as an architect in America, but he has nothing to do in north India. And so he sits, and the family worries.'

"I suggested to Kumar the family would be willing to pay a

good sum to achieve their son's employment and that the payments would be continuing. I implied that a small portion of their monthly payment might stay with me and another portion with him. A final portion would suffice to pay the son's monthly salary. Thus Kumar would acquire the services of a U.S.-trained architect for nothing and also enjoy a small honorarium on the side.

"He responded with alacrity. Did you notice the carbon of his letter to Sahni?"

We ruffled through the papers until we found the letter. It was not hard to find, typed on higher-quality paper with the distinctive crispness of an IBM Selectric. The letterhead included an announcement of Kumar's credentials: *"R.J. Kumar, Chartered Architect, B.Sc. Hons., A.R.I.B.A., F.I.I.A."* After introducing himself, Kumar made his pitch to Sahni:

> I have now an inquiry from a very rich and resourceful client, who wants to put up big industrial projects in Bombay, Poona, Nasik and surrounding areas.
>
> I have been on the lookout for a responsible man who could take up such works on my behalf in order to relieve the workload on me, and your name has been recommended to me by Miss Kumari Raj who has spoken very highly about you and your work. I also gather that you qualified from the States and have 10 years experience behind you.
>
> In case you are interested, I would be happy if you could make a trip to Bombay on 3rd, 4th, 5th and 6th of June, when I could have an opportunity of meeting you and also discuss the terms and prospects of our collaboration. Your to and from traveling expenses plus all your expenses for your stay in Bombay in one of the top hotels shall be reimbursed.
>
> Should you like to bring your family, you are most welcome to do so, which will also give them an opportunity to get away from the heat-wave now gripping U.P. [Uttar Pradesh].
>
> Kindly let me know by return of post whether you are interested and if so, please also bring some samples of your work that you have done.

"The date on the letter is May twentieth," I said. "What happened?"

"At the time," said Henry, "nothing. That was in fact our problem in late May, you may recall. You told me to hurry, that you could not hold together—I believe you called it 'this circus'—much longer. For my part, I told you I required time above all, that I could not remove the heat wave from Gorakhpur or open the schools before July eighth. It was then, as I recall, we were both becoming somewhat testy.

"So I dispatched my number-one man, Pee Pee, to Gorakhpur. Posing as the representative of a wealthy and well-known movie star—the man is known to all of India, but you would not be acquainted with his name—Pee Pee let it be known that he was interested in building movie theaters in north India and a low-cost housing project in Bombay. Soon the quarry took the bait, and Pee Pee brought the father and daughter here. As I said tonight they are staying in Bandra. Naturally Pee Pee has not had the leisure to give me a full report even by phone. I should point out that he has been on the case now full-time for eight days, so that fees for him alone amount to sixteen hundred dollars. I trust that is satisfactory?"

"More than satisfactory. I'll turn over two thousand dollars in signed traveler's checks before you leave tonight. I trust that method of payment is satisfactory?"

"More than satisfactory," said Henry, a smile beginning to show around the corners of his mouth. He looked tired. He'd had more sleep than I over the last two nights, but probably not much more.

"Tell me," I asked, "Was that story about the charts looking bad last weekend true? Did you really pull out your phone and not get Pee Pee's message until Tuesday?"

"Actually I first heard of their arrival when I received a very worried call from Kumar. 'They are here,' he said. 'What shall I do?' I told him to stall them, and it was several hours later that Pee Pee reached me. But yes, I did consult the charts and disconnect the telephone. For the first of this week, the prospects were indeed discouraging. Fortunately they have improved for the next few days. The day after tomorrow should be splendid."

During the time we'd been sitting in the room, I'd slowly come to the conclusion Henry's performance in the lounge had simply been his way of entertaining the women. Now I didn't know. After we had Asha in hand, there'd be ample time to find out what he really believed about numerology, arcane gemology, and astrology.

"I'm not sure we've got till the day after tomorrow," I said.

"I'm not even sure we've got till tomorrow. They've been here almost four days already. How do you propose to do it?"

"There is a motel on the beach some thirty kilometers from here. It is called the Blue Ballerina, and I use it regularly in my divorce cases. The owners, they are friendly. For a small payment they let me set up my cameras. What we plan now is more serious, so we must wait until the owners leave for the evening. Say half past eight, or nine o'clock. Pee Pee will bring them there when I say so. It is very near the site for the low-cost housing, or so Pee Pee has led them to believe. If Sahni is to design the housing, he must inspect the site, no?

"If you wish, we can bring the little girl to the hotel. She would be here by midnight on the day we choose. Afterward, my people will hold Sahni in the room until they receive word from me that you have departed."

"No. I want us all to be at the motel so that the child goes directly to her mother with no time between. Who will you be using to take care of Krishan?"

"Their names would mean nothing to you. There are three of them. Trustworthy men. And also big. Then, too, there is Pee Pee. And myself, for that matter. Do not concern yourself. There will be no problem."

"OK. But we still have the problem of the missing entry stamp in Asha's passport. I almost tried to steal one this morning at the airport, but then I thought you might already have worked out a solution. Have you?"

"Not in detail, but I do not think the problem is insuperable. You are carrying her passport?"

"Yes," I replied, digging the passport out of the zippered pouch and handing it to him.

"Good," he said. "I see you have a visa issued in San Francisco for her."

"And her air ticket is identical with ours," I added. "It looks like we all came in together. The only thing missing is the damned entry stamp."

"I will make inquiries. It may be possible to have it added to the passport. If not, you can fly to Delhi and then take the airbus to Katmandu. I happen to know there is no passport control on that flight. Once you are in Katmandu, it is but a five-hour flight to Bangkok."

He handed Asha's passport back to me. "You are carrying

the court order that grants custody of the child to the nice lady, your client?''

"You bet."

I removed the case file from my bag. Opening it to the custody order, I handed it to Henry.

"Behind that," I said, "is the warrant issued for Krishan's arrest."

"Yes," he said. "I think you mentioned this to me on the telephone. He is a fugitive from justice, then?"

"Technically, I suppose so. But it's not a serious charge."

"He is a bad man," said Henry heatedly. "He is not honorable. He took full reimbursement from Kumar while his expenses were being paid by Pee Pee. He is a cheat."

"Henry," I laughed, "*he*'s paying for the whole thing. The money from Kumar and from Pee Pee is really coming out of his own pocket. I told you that on the phone. He's paying for you and for me and for everything. If he's cheating anyone, it's himself."

"He does not know that," said Henry testily. "He demanded that Kumar pay him four hundred and twenty-five rupees for airfares when he had not paid out a single rupee. That is no way for a professional man to behave. Dishonesty always secures its proper reward. He will receive his."

I couldn't fathom Henry's hostility.

I went to the phone and ordered a couple of Heinekens from room service. The fan was slowly stirring the humid air. Cobwebs of exhaustion were creeping back onto my head. I wanted time to think out the next step. How long could we wait before moving? That was the crucial question.

After the gold-buttoned waiter brought our beers, Henry and I traded details about our personal lives. As a young man, he had lived in England for several years, and his wife still lived there. Apparently they were separated. I showed him photos of my family, and we traded funny stories about Hal Lipset. For reasons that seemed more honorific than real, Henry referred to Lipset as his guru.

Gradually the conversation drifted back to the case at hand. I said I thought Krishan would come after Neva and Asha, and for that reason I had asked her to find a hiding place to go to after we got back. Henry said it was hardly fair that "such a nice lady" must hide like a fugitive simply because she wanted to live with her child. It was Krishan, he pointed out, who was the fugitive. Fair or not, I replied, that was the hand she'd been dealt. "Sometimes," Henry said enigmatically, "it may be proper to change the cards. There are ways to make sure she is not pursued."

I didn't know what he meant, and I was certain I didn't want to know. Light had been filtering through the draped windows for the last half hour. We were both exhausted. It was after six.

"Can we make the snatch today?" I asked.

"I don't know," he replied. "Pee Pee will be calling at nine. The other arrangements are not complicated. I will see. Do you want anything added to the plan?"

"If possible, I'd like to double the personnel. People are cheap, and I want to make sure Krishan doesn't try to resist."

"No problem. If you wish, I can put one group of three in the motel and a second group out on the road. When the times comes, the second group will be moved up to support the first."

"Fine. Thank you. You will be calling me here when you know?"

"Yes."

I made out twenty traveler's checks as Henry finished his beer. When I looked up, his face was filled with exhaustion and something else I couldn't put my finger on. He caught the query in my look.

"It is nothing," he said. "But what we are doing is quite serious. In India, kidnapping—especially a girl-child—is a very serious crime. We have the death penalty here for such things. It is not often imposed, but still . . ."

He put his glass down on the bureau and stood up.

"I shall be calling you between half past eleven and noon. I hope you can get some sleep." He extended his hand. "Cheerio, Thompson."

"Cheerio, Henry," I said and watched him shut the double doors behind him.

THURSDAY AFTERNOON, JUNE 5

Henry wore very dark glasses, dark-blue trousers, and a light-blue shirt, open at the neck. As we drove toward the beach, I noticed that most men in the streets wore their Western-style shirts outside their pants, while of course Henry and I wore ours tucked in. Shortly after leaving the hotel, we passed through an area of ramshackle huts where occasional figures in rags, lay curled up in the dirt. Dead? Dying? I didn't ask. Farther along we passed through a village where black and orange taxis—there were few private cars in sight—mixed with young men on foot bearing great loads on their heads. The storefronts had signs in Marathi, with an occasional sign advertising "*Chemical Stores*," "*Xerox Photocopy*," or "*Gem Electronics*." Above the shops, laundry hung on lines stretched over balconies, and higher up a jumble of phone and electric lines looped from pole to building to pole like the remnants of a great spider web. The sky was overcast with patches of cumulo-nimbus under a canopy of high stratus. It was the start of the monsoon, and the gray-white skies moderated the heat and gave everything a flat, solemn cast.

At 1:45 we arrived at the Blue Ballerina.

Henry got out with us but had the driver retrace his route and park two hundred yards away. The motel owners were reliable, I supposed, but he didn't want to take the chance of someone connecting our car with the motel and the events that were about to take place there. Neva and Ruth moved quietly into our room, number 1 in a series that ran from 1 to 14. When Krishan, Asha, and Pee Pee arrived later on, they would be put in Room 2. Already registered and inside Room 3 was Henry's three-man group, which, in a quaint return to military lingo, I'd designated Assault Team Alfa the night before.

As we faced the motel, our rooms were to the extreme left. The owners' office and the kitchen were to the right. As far as I could tell, we were the only guests. One story high, with yellow stucco walls and columns supporting a light-green corrugated metal roof, it was the only structure within a half mile. The beach, such as it was, lay directly across from the hotel, on the other side of the road and the breakwater that protected the Blue Ballerina from winter storms. It was a fifty-foot wide crescent of brown sand that stretched half a mile to a point of land guarded by a crumbling sixteenth-century fort. Here and there along the erosion-streaked bank separating road from beach grew isolated palm trees. Everywhere the earth seemed dusty and overused, like the diamond in a city playground after too many ball games. As Henry and I walked to the point, an emaciated cow passed, stopping wherever some gray-green vestige of leaf or grass caught its eye.

"It's not quite the Bates Motel," I said, looking back from the fort to the forlorn scene before us, "but it'll do."

Henry laughed and then turned serious.

"Pee Pee said they would take a cab out from Bandra and arrive here shortly after four," he said. "But you must be patient if he has difficulty. It may even turn out they do not arrive at all today."

"I understand," I said. "Just so they don't go back to Gorakhpur. Were you able to get the extra people?"

"Yes. They are sitting by the road very near where my driver parked the car. Since this is the only road that gives entrance to the motel and fort, I have given them the duty of resting by the roadside and alerting us if any police enter the vicinity."

"Let's call them Assault Team Bravo," I heard myself saying, surprised at how serious it sounded. "You'll be moving them up to support Team Alfa when the time comes, I take it?"

"Actually I intended to use them to do it and use what you call Alfa in support."

"Fine. These are your people, and it's your country. When the time comes, you'll be running things. I'll stay in the room with Neva and Ruth. There's only one thing I require. Before anything happens, I must give the go signal. And before I do that, with my own eyes I want to see that Asha is here. Are we agreed?"

"Of course. Pee Pee understands that for security we must wait until the owners have left the establishment. That should be around dusk—say, half past eight or nine o'clock. He will then try to separate the child from her father, perhaps by taking her down to the beach. When we see that has been accomplished, we will take care of Krishan."

"Gently, Henry, gently!"

"Do not concern yourself. Our task will be completed in a thoroughly professional manner. For our own protection and that of Pee Pee, we will have to put on a little show for the father. Put them together tied up, something like that. A bit of theater to send the hounds off in the wrong direction, eh?"

We walked back to the hotel and then beyond it to where the car was parked.

Sitting on their haunches some twenty feet beyond a drainage ditch were the members of the second team. They stood when we appeared. One was shorter than either Henry or I, with a mustache and fine features. His short-sleeved yellow shirt was smudged with dirt. The other two were larger and tougher-looking. One was missing an incisor and had an odd indentation in his left temple. Henry talked to them in Marathi, and they replied with affirmative gestures. I hadn't asked Henry who these men were; I figured they were not his permanent staff, but *goondas* (the American word *goon* comes from it) hired especially for the occasion. I thought of Henry's use of *D-Day* on the phone and of a photo I'd seen of Eisenhower visiting troops of the 502nd Parachute Regiment on the eve of the invasion. Eisenhower's visit had also been made on June 5, exactly thirty-six years earlier. I looked at my troops. They weren't the 101st Airborne, but for a forty-six-year-old, rather slight architect, they should be enough.

Back in the room, Neva and Ruth were sitting on the twin beds. Asha's Mickey was propped up with his back resting against one of the pillows. He was smiling directly at us as we came in the door.

I went into the bathroom and was surprised to find no toilet, only a tiled drainage hole in the floor. Above was a handle that caused the area to be flooded with water. On each side of the hole were two footlike shapes molded into the tile. My toes faced the ceramically indented ones as I urinated in the hole and then turned on the water.

Back in the room, Henry was entertaining the women. He was telling the joke about the rabbi, the priest, and the Buddhist. It went on for a long time, and I missed the punch line thinking of the *goondas* outside and of what Henry had said the night before.

Most of the fear I'd felt back in California was gone, and I thought we might really pull it off. Either they would show up or they wouldn't, and we'd know the answer within the next few hours. If they showed up, we could not fail; there was no way Krisan would walk away with Asha. I'd write out a statement in English for Henry to read to him, and that would be that. We still had no solution to the entry-stamp problem, but that was secondary to getting Asha. We'd solve that problem when we actually got to it—say later that night.

I looked at Neva. She displayed no uncertainty and seemed in good spirits.

In the back of my mind percolated a Fechheimer story. He'd snatched a woman's six-year-old twins in Colorado. Afterward, as they'd lunched together in a nearby town, she'd changed her mind and told David to take them back. Later that afternoon, he had dropped off the kids around the corner from the school where earlier he'd picked them up.

Would Neva change her mind when she heard or saw Krishan and Asha together? Would she want to talk to Krishan after we took Asha? She was an adult and could do whatever she wanted, but a family therapy session under these circumstances wasn't what I had in mind.

I was idly wondering about this when we heard voices outside. Then, unforgettably, a little girl's voice said, "Daddy, can we go to the beach now?"

I looked at Neva. Her eyes widened in shock and then softened. It was Asha. Still looking at Neva, I put my finger to my lips. Henry continued talking. The wooden shutters, I noticed, had already been closed over the front windows. There was a knock on the back door. Startled, I went to it and let in a waiter with our order of soft drinks. I wiped the top of the cola bottle with my sleeve and drank. Across the room, Neva wiped her eye with the back of her hand. She suddenly looked young and vulnerable. We could hear the voices receding across the front patio.

By the time Pee Pee, Asha, and Krishan returned from the beach forty minutes later, Henry and I were sitting at a table on the patio in front of our room, having drinks.

Asha seemed both thinner and taller than I'd expected, and Krishan somehow shrunken. But the deep-set eyes I'd been expecting were there. He seemed jumpy, eyes darting around, his voice sharp and insistent. Pee Pee was thin and angular, taller than either Henry or I and wearing horn-rimmed glasses. They spoke Hindi—it sounded different from the Marathi I'd been hearing—shifting to English when Asha was to be included in the conversation. She sat docilely at her father's feet, looking across the road at the beach. On the horizon, thunderheads were building up over the Arabian Sea.

We came back into the room, and I went over to Neva.

"Asha looks fine, but Krishan seems a bit jumpy. Was his voice always that sharp and raspy?"

"Yes. I've always hated it, and I hate it now. How long will we have to wait?"

"Well," I said, looking at my watch, "it's a little after five now, and the motel owners won't be leaving until after eight. That's a minimum of three hours, maybe longer. Can you handle it?"

"Yes," she said, looking away from me and drawing into herself.

The motel's interior walls were built of something like concrete block, so voices from one room sounded muffled in another. Nevertheless, we agreed that Neva and Ruth should speak *sotto voce*. This put a damper on conversation, and we slipped into our own thoughts. I busied myself with printing out an official-sounding statement I wanted Henry to read to Krishan after we took Asha. *"Your daughter, Asha Naomi Sahni,"* I wrote laboriously between the wide, purple lines of the school tablet Henry had provided, *"is being returned to the jurisdiction of the Marin County Superior Court in accordance with outstanding court orders. . . ."* That seemed about the right tone. At the least, it should persuade Krishan that Asha wasn't being kidnapped by a gang of criminals. Then I thought of how Team Bravo had looked on the road a few hours earlier. When I finished, I took the completed statement across the room to Henry.

"This is the statement we talked about. You can read it to Krishan after everything is secure."

"You won't be visiting with our prize catch, then?" he asked.

"No. When the time comes, I'll be with the women and Asha."

"Very well," said Henry, and he began reading.

At six-thirty, Henry left the room for a few moments to chat with the owners and order curried chicken for our dinner. By the time he returned, Ruth and Neva had started to meditate. Henry suggested that a "spot of meditation" might do us all some good. Agilely, he removed his shoes and assumed the lotus position at the foot of one of the beds. I sat at the head of the other bed, facing Ruth. With some help from her, I forced my legs into an awkward imitation of the correct posture and closed my eyes.

Half an hour later, my thighs had begun to throb when the waiter knocked at the back door and entered with the chicken. Though waiters' faces are supposed to be impassive, his eyes widened as he took in the scene. As a longtime employee of the Blue Ballerina, he must have seen some strange scenes, but this . . . Henry signed the chit, and the waiter left.

I didn't touch the chicken. Since leaving the plane, I'd existed on bottled beer and soft drinks, and I didn't' see any reason why I couldn't keep it up for a few days longer. That morning, I'd even brushed my teeth with bottled water—anything to stay healthy until the job was done and we were on our way home.

After the others finished their chicken and I drank my second cola, the mood lightened and the conversation became expansive. Ruth talked quietly about the Zen Center and her earlier trips to India, and Henry told of his enthusiasm for the Self-Realization Fellowship in Los Angeles.

Suddenly, shortly after eight o'clock, there was a sharp knock at the front door. Henry let in the driver, who looked worried and began to speak to him in Marathi. Henry replied with a few short sentences and dismissed the young man. In lowered tones, he explained what had happened. The owners of the motel had been preparing to leave when they discovered their car had a flat and they had no spare. Krishan and company had arrived in a taxi, which meant our party had the only car. Accordingly, the owner had asked our driver to take his flat to the nearest filling station for repairs, and Henry had just authorized it.

"How long will it take?" I asked.

"Not more than an hour and a half," Henry said. "It is regrettable, but there is no other way. It would be foolhardy to go ahead with the owners still here."

"I agree. But this will push us late, perhaps after dark. Does Pee Pee know?"

"No. But he will not make his move until he receives a signal from me. It is too bad, but, alas, it cannot be helped."

This is the way you knew it would be, I thought. Quirky events are part of it; don't try to force them. Roll with them. It's only a temporary delay. At worst, the snatch will have to be made in the room next door, with Krishan present. Not elegant, but still effective.

The next hour and a quarter passed uneasily. Concern was beginning to show on Neva's face. She and Ruth went back to meditating. Finally we heard the car pull up outside, and a few moments later the driver knocked on our door. He was breathless and red-faced. He said a few words to Henry, and Henry, obviously angry, replied. In seconds, the driver was gone.

"What's up, Henry?"

"Now *our* car has contracted a puncture," he said calmly.

"Do you have a spare?"

"Yes. It should be repaired in twenty minutes or so."

He must have been seething inwardly. It was embarrassing to

have your equipment fail. I liked the fact that the angrier he got, the calmer his voice became. I glanced at my Rolex; it was 9:32.

Over the next half hour, Henry was out of the room much of the time. I imagined he was seeing to the tire change, bringing up Team Bravo, directing what was going to happen. A few minutes before ten I locked the back door, wiped off the glasses, cutlery, and soft drink bottles, and then went into the bathroom and wiped down all the shiny surfaces. Henry came in at five after ten.

"We are ready," he said.

"Have you gotten a signal to Pee Pee?" I asked.

"No, that was impossible. We will have to do it in the room."

"OK," I said. "It's your show."

I wiped down the surfaces of the two bedside tables and both front and rear doorknobs. Then, holding the doorknob with the towel, I cracked the front door half an inch so it would open to the touch. I motioned Neva and Ruth to the other side of the room and stood with my back to the front wall, between the shuttered windows and the door.

For a few minutes we heard only the low drone of conversation from the next room. Then there was a knock on their door. Neva and Ruth heard it and looked my way. The door was opened, and voices spoke in Marathi. The door was shut. Then nothing. What had happened? Had our group just walked away without doing anything?

Suddenly, the front door of our room burst open. The yellow-shirted *goonda* crashed into the room and looked around wild-eyed, Asha in his arms. Asha was crying. Ruth was nearest to Yellow Shirt, and he handed Asha to her, the little girl fighting them both. As soon as the child's feet hit the floor, she was scrambling over the corner of the bed for the open door. I went down on the floor, grabbing Asha and rolling with her in my arms, kicking the door shut behind us. We ended in a pile by the door.

"Asha," I was saying, "your mommy's here!" And then, pleadingly: "Neva. For Christ's sake!"

Neva was there, reaching down to Asha, but it took Asha a second or two to grasp that Neva was not the other woman she'd just escaped from. Then she yelled "Mommy!" and threw her arms around Neva's neck. Neva carried Asha to a chair and sat down with her in her lap. Asha looked in her mother's face and then drew back.

"Daddy said if I ever meet you I should beat you up," she said quizzically.

"Why," asked Neva, smiling, "would you ever want to beat me up?"

Asha looked at her mother and smiled back. They were still smiling at each other when Henry came into the room.

I walked outside with him. In one hand he was holding the tape recorder I'd given him.

"Don't you want to say something to him?" he asked, motioning next door with his chin.

It's your case! his face seemed to be saying.

He'd followed my orders and honored the restrictions I'd imposed. He'd have to remain in India to deal with whatever arose, while I'd be home free. So now it was my turn. Refusing to meet the adversary under these circumstances would mean—according to the rules of the strange blood sport we were engaged in—that it had been a "bad kill." In addition, showing my face to Krishan would demonstrate the plot had originated in America and his hostility should be directed there.

I walked into the room.

A lamp was burning on one of the beside tables. There were shadowy forms in the room, and along the far wall Pee Pee was lying doubled over on the floor, tied hand and foot, a gag in his mouth and his horn-rimmed glasses lying broken in the middle of the room. Krishan was sitting on the bed, facing me. His hands and feet were tied with rope, and there was a two-inch strip of adhesive tape across his mouth. He was barefoot, and he seemed tiny. At first I avoided his eyes, and then I looked straight into them. He wasn't scared; it was more than that. His eyes showed a kind of animal terror that, moving closer, I could almost smell. According to Henry, at this moment he probably believed he'd be killed, and Asha sold as a child prostitute.

I turned to the figures in the back of the room and said, "Take off the gag."

One of them moved forward to comply, and I had a moment to think.

After the adhesive had been ripped off, I heard myself saying to the barefoot, bound figure, "Mr. Sahni, let me assure you of your safety." I hesitated for a moment and then repeated from memory the official statement I'd printed out for Henry.

"I am returning your daughter, Asha Naomi Sahni, to the jurisdiction of the Marin County Superior Court in accordance with outstanding court orders. You will be detained until such time as your daughter reaches the jurisdiction of the court. You will be treated in a dignified and humane manner unless you try to escape. Upon your release, you will be provided sufficient funds to return to your home in Gorakhpur.''

He spat out, "You have no jurisdiction! You have no jurisdiction! This is India!"

As he was saying this, my eye caught a shape lying near the foot of the bed—one of Asha's sandals. I stopped listening to Sahni and picked up the sandal and its mate, lying two feet away. Damn! Until then it hadn't occurred to me we had no shoes for Asha. Was there anything else I'd forgotten?

Sahni was now asking, "Who are you? Who are you?"

I didn't lie to him but said, "As you see, I'm an American. It's not in my interest to tell you who I am."

"You are kidnapping my daughter."

Before I could reply, Henry intervened. "You know what you have done," he said to Sahni, "and it was not a nice thing. Now we have the court order and are doing what is right. You be quiet."

"Your court order," he insisted, "it is no good in India."

I moved between them. "We're taking Asha back to America," I said. "Tell me where her clothes are."

He nodded toward a suitcase near the head of the bed. I went over, pulled out a pitiful handful of little-girl clothes, and looked back at him. His eyes were bereft. He was losing his child, the child for whom he'd sacrificed so much and with whom he'd traveled so far over the last year and a half.

I sat beside him on the bed and put my hand on his shoulder. "Krishan" I said, "you have to understand. It's over now. It really is over. You have to know that." He looked at me but didn't say anything. Then he started to complain. "My hands and my feet, they are tied too tight." I brought the light over and looked at them. The ropes were snug but not tight; his circulation was satisfactory. Then he asked, "How are you going to the U.S.? When will you leave?" I just looked back at him. "Goodbye," I said, and turned away. Going out the door, I could see one of Henry's men stuffing a pill down Krishan's throat. Henry later told me it was a sleeping pill, a "kindness to help him over the worst of it."

In the other room, Neva had gotten out the Mickey Mouse doll, which she'd hidden under the bed when Krishan and Asha arrived. At first Asha was excited at seeing Mickey, but then a worried expression crossed her face. "What if Daddy sees?" she asked. "He will get very angry."

The driver brought the car to the front entrance. I moved our little group from the room, careful to lag back between Asha and the door to her father's room. She made no attempt to break and run, but hesitated before getting into the car. Neva told her that her daddy would be coming later.

Henry took his usual position up front with the driver, leaving the four of us to squeeze into the backseat, Asha sitting on her mother's lap. She kept telling us what she'd seen that night, that "some *goondas* came and grabbed my daddy's shirt and said, 'Do you have any money?' " Then she started chattering away in her Indian-American accent about what she'd seen in India and about a teacher, Miss Mackintosh, who had been "mean" to her. About a mile from the motel, Asha remembered a song she used to sing in America; "If you're happy and you know it, clap your hands." Soon all six of us were singing along with Ruth leading, going through four verses with appropriate sound effects and gestures as the car bumped through a mangrove forest.

There was a rumble of thunder, and just as we reached the main highway to Bombay the monsoon broke over us. It swept across the highway in great sheets, making a steady drumbeat on the roof and windshield of the old Austin. After a mile or so the wiper stopped, and the driver pulled to the side of the highway. I stepped out and freed the blade. It started sweeping back and forth on its own. I looked up at the sky and held out my arms. Warm curtains of rain washed over me.

FRIDAY MORNING, JUNE 6

I was smoking a cigarette. Henry was on the phone, speaking Marathi to some official he'd just woken up at 1:15 in the morning. It wasn't working. I could hear it in the tone of Henry's voice, and could see it in the way his body hunkered low over the phone. The thousand dollars I'd just thrown into the pot wasn't helping either. There were already three cigarette butts in the Centaur Hotel ashtray, and we'd been back only twenty-five minutes. We had dropped "the ladies" (now three) in their room and gone to mine to figure out how we were going to get out.

Our mood of elation evaporated about the time we reached the room. "Buy it, Henry," I'd said after ordering the Heinekens and lighting up a cigarette. "I've got a thousand dollars in that zippered pouch just for that. Buy the fucker, and we'll hop on that nine-fifty A.M. BEA nonstop to London, and later in the morning you can drive out to the beach and send Krishan on his way just after he wakes up." Henry had pulled out his little black book and made three calls. This was the last of them. If no entry stamp turned up through this call, we'd have to try something else.

Henry put down the receiver.

"It is impossible. Not tonight. It would look strange for any of my contacts to visit the airport or their offices at such an hour. Tomorrow, perhaps. It is not certain. I am sorry."

"OK. Scratch buying it. Let's run through the alternatives."

"The best alternative," Henry was saying, "is the airbus from Delhi to Katmandu. . . ."

My mind wandered. The nightmare I had feared was beginning. We had Asha and were holding Krishan. But we had no sure escape route. If the absence of the entry stamp were detected, we'd be detained for investigation. According to the procedures I'd seen at Bombay airport, every person—and that would include Asha—was checked against his or her passport. The absence of an entry stamp couldn't be plausibly explained. But if we were detained while Henry's men were still holding Krishan, we'd be in deep trouble. Asha would be talked to by some official or other, and we couldn't count on her to lie convincingly. She would let something slip about Gorakhpur or start telling the story about seeing the *goondas* grab Daddy and then driving away with Mommy and Mommy's friends.

Why had I let us get into such a spot? I knew why. I'd forced the pace of the case. We could have waited a while longer. Pee Pee could have kept them occupied for another day, and in that day we could have solved the entry-stamp problem. I'd made the wrong call, and now we were stuck with it. I tuned back into what Henry was saying just as he concluded: ". . . at least that's the way it was the March previous."

"I'm sorry, Henry," I apologized. "I was thinking of something else. Could you go over that again?"

He looked at me strangely but sketched it again. The basic

point was that there was no passport control on the Delhi-Katmandu airbus flights. Although Nepal and India were separate states, Nepal operated under India's wing, at least insofar as diplomatic affairs went. Since most passengers on these airbus flights were either Indians or Nepalis (who didn't require passports to travel in either country) or foreign tourists (who would be returning to Delhi), the government had dropped passport formalities. Henry could personally vouch for the fact this system had been in place three months earlier.

"What about getting out by private plane or boat to Sri Lanka?"

"A private plane, as I indicated earlier," said Henry, "would attract unwanted attention. There are few private plane flights in India. Once you arrived in Sri Lanka, none of you would have Indian exit stamps in your passports. That surely would cause new difficulties. Were you still in Sri Lanka when Krishan was released and went to the authorities here, you might be detained there or, indeed, even arrested."

"We could go to the U.S. consulate," I said, thinking out loud. "We could claim Asha's passport had been lost and request a new one be issued. Usually they'll do that in twenty-four hours. That would leave us here another day, maybe two if we got bogged down in red tape. Do you think you can hold Krishan that long in the Blue Ballerina without the owners wising up to what's going on?"

"Most assuredly."

"But there's an enormous hooker in all this," I went on. "The embassy has already made inquiries about Asha and Krishan in Gorakhpur. The name *Sahni* ought to throw up red flags all over the place. The consulate here wouldn't issue a passport without checking with Delhi. The U.S. State Department would not like to end up appearing an accessory to a serious violation of Indian sovereignty. Instead of using the Indian courts, we just went out and kidnapped Krishan. If the State Department got wind of what we've done, they just might turn us over to the Indian authorities: 'Sorry, old chap, to have to do this. But you can't expect us to stand aside and let you cause an international incident, now, can you?' And we can't count on Asha to keep her mouth shut or lie convincingly."

I said all this with my head cradled in my hands, staring at the carpet. Finally running out of steam, I turned toward Henry. He looked exhausted but calm.

"What do you think, Henry?"

"The airbus."

I got up and walked out on the tiny balcony. Half a mile distant stretched the green-lit runways of Bombay International Airport. Beyond those lights was the beach, the waves of the Arabian Sea now crashing along it, and somewhere in that darkness Krishan Sahni was sleeping . . . or thinking. In about eight hours, a British Airways jet would lift off from one of those runways for London. Pity we couldn't be on it.

I turned from the balcony. "The airbus it is. Let's go."

The bowels of Bombay International Airport at two o'clock in the morning probably bear some resemblance to purgatory. That is, if your penance consists in cutting through coils of red tape, shedding hundred-rupee notes in your wake like a molting pigeon, avoiding the stares of beggars who could exist for months on the bribe you've just passed an airline clerk, and stepping around the bodies of sick or sleeping figures in the corridors and tunnels of the lower levels—all the while oppressed by the foreignness of the surroundings, knowing that without Henry's guiding hand you would be both lost and impotent. For a while, crisscrossing incessantly from one office to another, receiving a form here, a stamp there, breathlessly following Henry's deliberate, never-varying stride—for a while, all this seems useless, Sisyphus-like. The obtaining of one piece of paper only leads to the necessity of gaining the endorsement of another, which can be signed only under the authority of Mr. Gupta, who, alas, will not be in until 7:45, thank you. Finally the mystical words announcing our release are uttered by a beautiful, smiling Air India ticket agent who asks "May I have your American Express card, please?"

We leave purgatory with five tickets. Henry will fly with us on the 6:05 A.M. flight to Delhi. We will arrive at 8:17 A.M. Henry will remain in Delhi until he sees our wheels clear the runway; he will then telephone the Blue Ballerina and order the release of Krishan. If there are no delays, that happy moment should occur at 9:25 A.M., the scheduled departure time of the morning airbus to Katmandu.

Since the driver has been dismissed long ago, we take a taxi back to the hotel. It is 4:45 when I knock on "the ladies' " door. Ruth answers quickly—I knew they wouldn't be asleep—and I tell her our schedule. Beyond, I can see Asha lying across the foot of Neva's bed, asleep.

Half an hour later the retinue of gold-buttoned bellhops is reassembled, and with much ceremony and waving we're put in a cab and sent on our way to the airport.

In the departure lounge, Asha sits next to Neva. She is a spectacularly attractive child, and people take an interest in her. She's wearing a new summer dress, green with white lace frills, and her hair is in two long braids. She's been told, back at the hotel, that she'll now be living with her mother. According to Ruth, it seemed not to affect her either way. Now she looks at Neva and asks in a strange, sharp voice, "Who told you to do this?"

Neva must feel Krishan's presence in the sound and content of the question (it displays his presumption she can do nothing on her own), for she visibly recoils and then, slowly gaining control of herself, smiles and answers, "My heart told me to do it, because I loved you and missed you so much. My very good friend Roshi and others told me I must go get you and take care of you." Asha does not give up but instead looks savagely at her mother and says a word none of us understands. Neva asks what the word means. Asha scrutinizes her eye-to-eye and then says evenly, "Every day Daddy used to tell me you were a witch."

On the flight to Delhi, Henry and I sit together. I sign additional traveler's checks (a final reckoning will be made later) and a document stating we have a court order granting Neva custody of Asha. "This won't do you much good," I say, "if the balloon goes up." Henry ignores the point but begins talking about the tablecloth I'm carrying (taking up precious space in my carry-on bag) to his "guru," Hal Lipset. He has chosen an especially "lucky" moonstone ring for me and will be sending it to San Francisco.

I first notice something wrong before we leave the aircraft. As the Boeing 727 pulls to the gate, two uniformed men with automatic weapons approach it on the tarmac. When the engines stop, the men take up stations by either wing, unshouldering their weapons. Inside the terminal are hundreds of armed men, troops or paramilitary units, patrolling in groups of four or guarding access to particular areas. I ask Henry what is going on, and he shakes his head in bewilderment.

"Perhaps a state of emergency has been declared," he says, "or something. There is always something."

To our left in the departure lounge is a long line of passengers behind a roped barricade. Two men with submachine guns stand at the entrance of the roped-off area and make anyone who passes show an air ticket. Henry indicates it is the line for the airbus to Katmandu. Wanting to be sure we get seats, we say our good-byes. I feel a pang of affection for this man who has done so much and whom we are leaving behind to fend for himself.

The line moves with fair speed, and within a few moments we are a hundred or so feet from Henry, who waves at us from behind the roped barrier. I glance toward the head of the line. This should be ticket processing by agents of Air India.

Then I see it.

A distinguished-looking man in a pin-striped suit has reached inside his coat pocket and pulled out not a ticket but a passport, probably British. This is passport control, not ticket processing!

Can we get back out?

I look for Henry, but he's too far away to catch the anguish in my face. We can probably get back through the armed guards with some excuse, but they might call their superiors for per-mission. Any way we do it, we'll draw attention to ourselves, and that's the last thing we want. More important, what do we do when we get to the other side of the barrier? We're now in Delhi. Nepal is fairly close. Could we get out by renting a car and driving across? There's no reason to think passport control would be more lax at a road crossing than here. At least here they're busy, processing hundreds of people each hour. Since there isn't normally any passport control on this flight, it may be more lax here.

I take a long breath and look at Henry, a very distant two hundred feet away. OK, go for it.

Ruth is closest to me, and she, I remember, speaks Hindi—the language in this part of India. No reason to spook Neva. Asha would pick it up in a minute, and we'll want to use Asha.

"If things don't go right," I tell Ruth, "we'll do this good cop, bad cop. If he catches the missing entry stamp, I'll get pissed and you'll sweet-talk him in Hindi, OK?"

She doesn't say anything, looking startled but also very with it.

First I pull out the airplane tickets, arranging them so Asha's ticket is third. Then I do the same with the passports. Finally I sort the Pan Am tickets, opening them to the Hong Kong—Bombay segment and putting Asha's in front. I shove the passports into my back pants pocket and the four sets of plane tickets into my shirt pocket. The official is a Sikh, with white turban and fine mustache.

I hand him the air tickets first. He says politely, "Your passports, please."

I hand him the passports and try to distract him by starting a conversation.

"The weather was just too much for us in Bombay. We want to get up into the mountains for a few days where the air is cooler."

He looks over the first passport—mine—and notices the visa stamp. He grunts acknowledgment to my patter about the weather, then stamps both the passport and the ticket with the exit stamp. Apparently Air India officials will check that stamp later, before they let passengers onto the aircraft.

He checks Ruth's next, going through the same routine.

As he picks up Asha's, I lift her to counter height. She's holding her Mickey Mouse doll and smiling.

He starts leafing through the passport, and I ask him, "Can we see Everest from the plane before we land at Katmandu?" Without looking up, he answers, "Yes, if the weather is fine." His face starts to show consternation as he points to the open passport. "No entry stamp," he indicates.

I point to the visa in her passport and to the visas in the remaining three passports, all the while feigning irritation. Next I pull out the Pan Am tickets to show him that Asha's is identical to our own. He says nothing, silently inspecting the pieces of paper.

Finally, in a voice heavy with significance, he announces, "There is no entry stamp in this passport."

The passengers behind us are fidgeting. A heavyset Iranian woman in a black and white dress shifts from one foot to the other, puffing on a Pall Mall.

"It's not our goddamn fault there's no entry stamp," I explode. "We do everything we're supposed to do. The visas, the cholera shots, the yellow fever shots. We buy currency only from the banks we're supposed to. And then what happens? I'll tell you what happens. Some sleepy officer (I am careful not to say 'clerk') slips up at two in the morning and neglects to stamp her passport. That goddamn airport was so hot—"

I can hear Ruth begin to talk Hindi in a soft, singsong voice, so I grind to a halt, still holding the smiling Asha and her Mickey Mouse doll. "Oh, we are so very sorry to cause you consternation about this matter," Ruth is saying. "We beg your pardon. We can understand the stamp is not there and that it should be there. But the stamp is not ours to use or not use. When we arrived the night before last, the airport was overwhelmed with people. It was so hot. The crowds were so heavy. Evidently a minor error was made under trying circumstances. We beg of you not to punish us for someone else's mistake. After all, the child is only six, and you can see from the visas and the tickets we are all four traveling together. . . ."

Afraid to say anything, I watch his impassive gaze moving back and forth between Asha's face and the photo staring up at him from her passport. Finally he smiles, chucks her under the chin, and stamps ticket and passport.

We're out.

TEN

"THE DEVIL BARKING IN HIM"

FRIDAY AFTERNOON, JUNE 6, 1980

"What?" I said, startled by the question.

"May I help you, sir?" repeated the young woman in the white blouse, irritation sprouting around the edges of her question. The blouse was sticking to her olive skin, and there were perspiration patches under her arms. The air in the offices of Royal Thai Airlines was close and smelled of people, too many people in too small a space. On the wall were the usual posters of Bangkok. When I'd gotten there at two-thirty, fifteen people were already in line. There were beads of perspiration on the ticket agent's upper lip. Was she Thai or Nepali? My eye wasn't educated enough to tell. What was it I wanted here? Oh, yes . . .

"I'd like four seats on your eleven-thirty departure tomorrow to Bangkok."

Booking the space and preparing the new tickets took nearly twenty-five minutes. But after a few questions were answered and an American Express card produced, the work was all hers. My head was pounding, and it was difficult to keep straight what I was supposed to be doing. Once I got the tickets, all I had to do was walk back up the main street of Katmandu to the Hotel de la Annapurna, turn left and go up the stairs, and follow the hallway with the Oriental carpets to the elevators. What was my room number? It was on the key; I could look later. It was right next door to the ladies' room. I chuckled, thinking how Henry's usage had stuck in my mind, and the ticket agent glanced up. I looked away at a poster on the wall. Was there anything else I had to do? Ruth was sending the cable to Dick Werthimer. No, I could go back to the room and lie down on the bed and close my eyes . . .

"Mr. Thompson . . . Sir!"

"Yes," I said, startled again. "I'm sorry."

"That's all right," she said, smiling. "Here are your tickets. Please be at Katmandu International no later than half past ten tomorrow morning. Thank you for flying Royal Thai Airlines."

I walked out into the street. Katmandu International! That was rich. The sun was still high, and the light hurt my eyes. I looked around at the picturesque street scene. I should be exploring this place, enjoying myself. How many times in a lifetime do you get to Katmandu? My eyes hurt, and a drum was banging in my head. The hotel was to the left. Not far. Up the hill.

The lobby of the Annapurna was darker. Once in the elevator, I looked at my key and got off on the fourth floor. I knocked on the door to 415. Ruth opened it, zombielike, and gave me an envelope.

"It's a copy of the cable," she said. "We're wasted." Inside, I could see Neva wearily playing on the floor with Asha. Asha smiling brightly.

"See you all later," I mumbled. "I'll be next door."

I went into Room 413. The light was still too bright. I pulled the drapes and took off my shoes. I lay down for a moment on top of one of the twin beds. . . .

It was eight-thirty when I woke up.

The headache was still there, but less intense. My thoughts were clearer, and I was hungry. That was the reason for the headache. I picked up the phone and dialed room service, at the same time opening Ruth's envelope. Inside was a carbon of the cable. Underneath "*Nepal Telecommunications Corporation*" was printed Werthimer's address and then the message.

MISSION GLORIOUS, SHORT, AND SNAPPY,
MOTHER, DAUGHTER, EVERYONE HAPPY,
DIDN'T MAKE A SINGLE BOO-BOO,
CALL YOU MONDAY FROM HONOLULU.

A chicken sandwich and a beer later, I was feeling a low-grade elation born of the recognition that only time and space— several days, airports, and flights—stood between us and the

United States. If you've got only a few hours to spend in Katmandu, what do you do? You send postcards to your friends, that's what you do. And where do you get postcards this time of night? In the lobby, of course, from that rack just to the left of the registration desk.

Coming back to the room, I knocked on the door of 415. Neva opened the door, looking dazed, her eyes sunken in deep circles. Beyond her I could see Ruth, fast asleep. Asha was on the floor, a coloring book in front of her, bright-eyed and chattering.

"You gotta get some rest," I said to Neva. "You can't keep running on empty."

She nodded vacantly.

"I'll take Asha to my room," I said. "She can color some pictures while I write postcards. How about that Asha?"

Neither Asha nor Neva replied.

"Come on," I said, picking up Asha and her book. "You can ride piggyback over to my room." She giggled when I put her on my shoulders and was still giggling when I opened my door.

Asha sat cross-legged on one of the beds and started to color. Her hair was not in braids now but held back by two pink plastic hair clips, one at each temple. Their color matched her long flannel nightdress.

"Mommy brought it from America," she said cheerfully, fingering one of the clips.

"Are you happy to be going to America?" I asked.

She looked away without answering, shyly, as if she knew we were talking about something important. I started addressing postcards. This child seemed comfortable in all sorts of circumstances, so trusting was she of people and the world. Had the incident with the *goondas* touched that?

She colored quietly on the bed for nearly half an hour. Then she yawned.

"Sleepy, Asha?" I asked, turning around to face her.

She brightened.

"Sometimes he hold my shoulder very hard," she said, putting her right hand up to her shoulder. "Sometimes he grabs me here," she went on, touching her elbow. "Or here," holding her wrist. "It hurt very much."

I moved to the other bed, pulled the recorder from its pocket, and switched it on.

"Why do you think he did that?"

"I don't know," said Asha, pouting and looking as if she was feeling sorry for herself.

"Did you ever have to stay inside for a long time because your daddy beat you?"

"Sometimes he say don't play outside. The others play outside in the evenings, but my daddy, he say don't play outside. He only wants me play inside. In the evening he doesn't take me out, and I am sad. I have so many friends in Gorakhpur you wouldn't believe."

"How about—"

"What is that?" she interrupted, pointing to the recorder, its tiny red bulb pulsing with the sound level.

"That's a tape recorder," I said flipping it off. "Would you like to hear some music on it?"

She smiled, and I put in a cassette Henry had given me on the plane to Delhi. According to the label it was a tape of "devotional chants sung by nuns of the Self-Realization Order," accompanied by a bass sitar. The recorder's undersized speaker gave the music a tinny sound, and the "nuns" had a faint Southern California accent. Henry said it had been recorded in Los Angeles. Perhaps on a small estate in the Hollywood hills, I imagined, the kind with a chapel somewhere on the grounds. It would have been hot the afternoon they trucked in the recording equipment, and the "nuns" would have sprouted mustaches of perspiration as they rehearsed. The chants were simple and would have been committed to memory long before the recording session. The singers would have stood in staggered formation before the stereo mikes. Off to the side the sitar would have begun, and then, a bar or two later, the singers would have joined in. The chant got underway with each line repeated twice in a never-varying singsong:

So do Thou my Lord, so do Thou my Lord,
So do Thou my Lord, so do Thou my Lord,
Thou and I, never apart.

Thou and I, never apart.
Wave of the Sea, dissolve in the sea!
Wave of the Sea, dissolve in the sea!

With the tinny sound bouncing off the walls of the room and the air-conditioner humming in the background, the repetition of the lines became hypnotic. I caught an Indian reflection to the underlying California accent. How would the "nuns" from Redlands and Thousand Oaks and West Covina have dressed that hot afternoon? After the session was over, where would they have gone?

Asha curled up on her bed. I took the crayons and coloring book from under her, pulled down the covers, and tucked her in. The night before, Krishan had probably done the same just before we hit the door.

MONDAY, JUNE 9

The water was clear and the sun bright. Off to the right, a catamaran was moored to a jetty, its striped sail stirring in the afternoon breeze. Behind me, the Hilton Hawaiian Village rose thirty stories into the eighty-degree air. The water lapping at my knees had to be close to the same temperature. The sandy bottom squished as I took a few steps and dove under.

I started to swim. First in a straight crawl with feet kicking rhythmically and arms slicing the surface of the water, then shifting beyond the surf line to a modified sidestroke, a flutter kick with right arm extended and pulled straight down to set up the glide. Without fins, the stroke never worked very well; the feet couldn't produce enough thrust to sustain the glide. We had learned it in UDT training as the most efficient way to get around on the surface. After your legs got strong enough to handle the Navy-issue duck feet, you could go for hours. Glide, pull, glide again. Once we had swum from Vieques to Puerto Rico this way, each of us dragging along a diver's knife and flares on the web belt that always hung too loosely. That eight-mile swim had taken most of a day; now, after less than a minute, I was pooped. I rolled over and started a languid backstroke.

The sun directly overhead was an incandescent mass. The strokes came slower until I floated, eyes shut against the glare. I could feel the muscles in my back and shoulders begin to relax. The water was so warm I could hardly tell what was water and what was me. In the cradle of that amniotic warmth, I felt something starting to grow. It began down deep, below the stomach or the heart, deeper than the viscera, spreading from inside, better than any chemical rush, endorphins permeating every synapse, until finally, eyes shut and heart pounding, ignited by joy, I wheeled and sprinted seaward, arms windmilling and feet churning, cutting the flat surface like a berserk paddlewheel steamer.

I did it! That was the single thought trumpeting through my mind. Not the more modest and truer "we did it." Of course, *we* had done it. Werthimer's legal maneuver, Henry's unbelievable coup, Rajni's travails and Pee Pee's persuasiveness, the *goondas*' quick force, Ruth's soft voice turning the key to Nepal: nothing could have happened without all of them. But now I didn't care. I knew only that against all expectations Asha and Neva were playing together on a beach this side of Diamond Head. We'd done it and gotten out and now, feeling the athletic joy of muscles moving and pulling, of my free body slicing the water, I was going to exult for a moment in victory. For the first time in months, I wasn't afraid.

Even in Katmandu, I'd been afraid, and in Bangkok and Hong Kong, in Narita Airport at Tokyo, and even the day before, entering Hawaii. Haunting me in all those places was the fear that Krishan somehow might manage to telephone ahead and, through his family's powerful connections in Delhi, succeed in getting us detained outside the protective umbrella of U.S. law. I'd pushed our party to exhaustion, of necessity staying overnight in Bangkok but otherwise tarrying not a minute more than necessary, cajoling airline ticket agents to let us on the next flight, getting what sleep we could curled up on planes or in airport waiting lounges.

After only a few hours' sleep in Bangkok, Asha had seemed sick. She hadn't wanted to get up that morning, and later, sitting next to me on the bus to the airport, had been sniffling. She didn't know what was going on and must have sensed our anxiety. Through the window beside her, I'd seen saffron-clad monks crouched by the wayside. I'd reached over and felt Asha's clammy forehead. Should we give her the tetracycline from the vial in my toilet kit? We'd decided against it, and six hours later her fever had subsided on its own.

Then there were the bad dreams: Asha's and my own.

Between Hong Kong and Japan, she'd awakened suddenly full of a dream. Krishan was at the center of it. "He has left me alone in this room," she said, "and I am very, very hungry." She wants him to come, but he doesn't come and doesn't come.

Finally he comes and gives her some food, and she is happy again.

My own was more complicated. Fragments of it had come to me twice as I'd drifted off in airplane seats with the shutter pulled against the sun and the ventilation fan whirring. Then, the night before, as I'd lain curled like a fetus in one of the two queen-size playpens dominating each of the Hilton's rooms, it had come in fuller dress.

Floating now, my eyes sealed against the glare, listening to the slip-slap of the water, I tried to bring it back.

I'm back in Ohio, that much is clear, and I'm inside our family home, the one I lived in as a boy. Oddly, though, I'm not a boy; I'm me, now, grown up. I see some of my relatives. Their faces are familiar, but I cannot recall their names. I feel a sense of danger, and unexpectedly a man begins to swing something at me. Nothing happens; there's no effect to his swinging. He grabs a pool cue and swings again. It breaks harmlessly in his hand. There's a car. The Volvo? Henry's Austin? I am driving. Nancy is in the passenger's seat. We're being pursued by another car off to the right and behind us. It's our family's driveway, and I'm following its curve in from the street while the other car careens brutally through flowerbeds and bushes. I push through a rock garden. Nancy says, "They've just planted flowers there!" I say, "Never mind. The Volvo (it *is* the Volvo!) can get through." We crash through bushes, their branches sweeping the windshield. There is no sound.

Trying to bring back the dream was a strange and not altogether pleasant experience. It was like entering a room where I'd been a prisoner too long; the furniture hadn't been moved, and the aftersmell of stale sweat still hung on the walls. I opened my eyes to let the sun burn away the images behind my retinas. It was too bright, so I jackknifed under the water. The salt water stung my eyes, but the fuzzy underwater light was green and cool. I popped to the surface and then with long, slow strokes headed seaward. As my muscles tired, happiness returned.

By the time I reached the beach, the world had righted itself. At the bar by the swimming pool I ordered a club sandwich. When the barman asked why I was smiling, I didn't tell him, but left a five-dollar tip. White shirt draped over reddening shoulders, I crossed to the lobby and rode the elevator to my room.

There were still loose ends.

After that Thursday meeting at Green Gulch, Neva had nodded OK when I'd asked her to find a hiding place for herself and Asha once we returned. Embarrassed, she'd told me on the plane in mid-Pacific that she'd never believed we would succeed and hence had made no inquiries. They couldn't go back to the Zen Center; Krishan would look there first. Both Werthimer and Baker-roshi knew about the problem and were working on it.

I took a luxurious shower and then called San Francisco. Everyone was happy about our success, but no progress had been made in finding Neva and Asha a hiding place.

I ordered a gin and tonic from room service and took the phone, with its long extension cord, out on the balcony. Even at five o'clock the sun remained high in the western sky. In the artificial lagoon ten stories below, kids were playing along the water's edge as their mothers sunbathed.

I'd been unable to get through to Henry the day before. But now the workday in Bombay was just beginning. When the waiter left, I dialed the transpacific operator. Several relays clicked, and I could hear very faintly a feminine voice saying, "Yes, just a moment for Mr. Bawa."

"Henry?"

"Josiah, how are you?"

"Fine. And you Henry?" He seemed cheerful, but the connection was bad and I could barely make him out. After more pleasantries I asked the time of Krishan's release.

"It was eight P.M. on the sixth of June, Indian Standard Time. That is eleven hours [fade out] lifted off from Delhi."

"Did he sign a receipt for the money we gave him to get back to Gorakhpur?"

"Yes, I have it here. It says, 'Received five hundred rupees for my return journey and all my bills are paid in staying at hotels Siddhartha and Blue Ballerina. I have been treated [fade out] without any grievances. Signed, Krishan Sahni.' But you must also know that he collected twice: once from us and once [fade out] architect."

"It's all his money anyhow."

"Yes. We took them in the car to the Hare Rama Hare Krishna at Juhu. That was in case he needed any moral or [fade out] support. Pee Pee's glasses, alas, were broken in the room. With your permission I will add a charge to the bill."

"Of course."

"We carried the cinema [fade out] a bit further. Presenting

Pee Pee in the [fade out] tied hands. Then we let them off together at Hare Krishna. Pee Pee could then report to us later on his thoughts."

"How did he seem?"

"Oh, he was emotionally upset. But not too bad, nothing to worry about. But there is [fade out] very important. Asha should send a letter to Sahni. Tell him she is all right. Only take precaution her real address is not there. Letter should be posted [fade out] different state, and postcard should show [fade out] scene from a different state."

"Uh-huh. Explain this to me Henry: why?"

"Pardon?"

"Why do this now, Henry?"

"Otherwise, he will go mad."

"I see. What do we know about him now?"

"Presently, not much. Pee Pee left him [fade out] evening. The other operative [fade out]. But he said he was planning to come back. He wants to come back and [fade out] the mother."

"We should take steps then to protect Neva?"

"Yes. But for two months I think you are safe. He will need time to order his affairs and get money. He has started planning his own matters with the ones [fade out] the job."

"You mean his architectural work?"

"No. He wants to start [long fade out] apology from his wife and then start a fish."

"I don't understand. A fish?"

"No. START AFRESH. He wants to come back and start afresh and then run away again [fade out] child. But I shouldn't pay it much heed. It is just the devil barking in him. It will pass."

We talked of how the remaining funds would be sent, and of an affidavit I needed from Pee Pee. The sun was beating down on my shoulders, and I felt a chill from the sunburn. My stomach felt as if it had taken on a load of lead. I told him how happy Neva's mother had sounded when she'd heard Asha's voice, and I conveyed congratulations from Hal Lipset.

"You're a genius, Henry. You really are."

"You were a good leader [fade] team, Josiah."

"I wasn't the leader. I just watched. I'll call you from San Francisco after—" The connection had gone dead. But it didn't matter. Nothing more had to be said.

On the sand below, a mother was gathering up her things and

calling to her child. I felt as I had five days earlier on the balcony of the Centaur Hotel, looking out over the lights of Bombay International, thinking of Krishan. Then I had at least known where he was. Now I didn't.

It hadn't ended. Something was going on, and it wouldn't stop. Everything seemed so normal. Sun and sand and tropical air. A mother retrieving her son from the water. Three sailboats heading out of Ala Moana Harbor. The breeze rippling the flags on top of the Illikai. Whatever it was that was happening was continuing. I was outside it but also—still—inside it, a part of it. And I knew I couldn't control it.

At dinner that night the others were relaxed and easy. They'd spent the afternoon at a small beach near Diamond Head, and their faces were full of color. We dined in the Polynesian room of the hotel amid palms and plants, and Asha laughed when the waiter brought her a giant tropical drink, pineapple slice perched on top. She'd gotten a Mickey Mouse watch that afternoon and was rattling on about it to whoever would listen.

"Still no word from San Francisco," I said. "I told them we'd hang on here until Wednesday. That OK with the rest of you?"

"I'd like to stay here a long, long time," said Asha, "and go swimming with the inner tube again."

"If by Wednesday morning they don't have anything," I went on, "I want you all to come to Bolinas and stay with us. Lis has a horse, Asha, and maybe you could ride it."

"Oh, Mommy, could I?" asked Asha.

Neva smiled. Ruth was looking quizzically across the table at me. She knew there had to be a reason for my offer. A few moments later Asha tripped off for some fruit from the salad bar, and Ruth asked if I'd gotten in touch with Henry.

"Yeah," I said. "Finally got through to him a couple of hours ago, but the connection was bad. They dropped Krishan and Pee Pee at the Hare Krishna ashram about eight on the night we left."

"How come it took so long?" asked Ruth.

"Henry didn't say. I imagine it was because Henry was still teed off about Krishan double-dipping expense money. I suspect Henry just took his own good time getting back to Bombay. You can't say he doesn't have a sense of humor. The Hare Krishna ashram!"

"How was he at the end?" asked Neva.

"He signed a receipt for the money we gave him to get back to Gorakhpur. Henry put on the receipt that we were also paying his bill at the Blue Ballerina, and that he'd been treated well. I'm surprised Henry didn't ask him to sign a thank-you note for tying him up."

Something I didn't understand passed behind Neva's eyes when I said "tying him up."

"Releasing Pee Pee with him was a stroke of genius," I said. "Now we know what he's going to do."

Both Ruth and Neva looked startled.

Looking directly at Neva, I said, "He's planning on coming back, worming his way into your good graces, and then taking off again with Asha."

At the same time, I was trying to recall exactly what Henry had said. Was Krishan going to come back and "harm" Neva, or "kill" her? I didn't know. Neva looked worried enough.

"We've got to be careful, but don't get too concerned. Henry said it would pass."

SATURDAY, JUNE 14

"Organic ant killer?" I asked, checking the four-quart saucepan on the front burner. "You must be kidding."

"All I know," said Nancy, "is that Meg Simonds had lots of problems with ants. They crawled all over her house, and she tried all those little things you get at the hardware store. Allegro, get down!"

Allegro had just leapt onto the redwood counter that stretched along the windows from stove to corner. She liked to sit in the corner and let the sun stream over her, front paws pulled under her chin, eyelids drooping. Three and a half years ago we'd found her—just a three-week-old kitten—huddled under the bushes next door. Now she was a handsome calico who looked at Nancy, jumped to the floor, and padded out onto the deck.

"Anyhow, Meg didn't want to put any poison around, so she started going through catalogs. She said there's a firm that will electrocute termites—"

"Electrocute termites? Come on."

"Nope, honest. She figured if you can electrocute a termite, you can kill ants organically. So she found some catalog that supplies farmers—you know, organic farmers—with all sorts of things to kill pests. She sent away for it, and when it comes we can check it out."

"How're you gonna check it out?" I asked, moving toward the refrigerator.

"If she likes it—I mean, if it kills ants—they'll carry it at the People's Store. Her boyfriend, Mark, works there, and he said they'd stock it if it works. Tink!"

I looked back from the refrigerator. The pan of water was boiling over. I grabbed a potholder and lifted it off the burner.

"Cook on high," said Nancy, smiling, "live on high!"

I mumbled something, turned the burner to simmer, and replaced the still-boiling saucepan on the stove.

The war between the Thompsons had ended shortly after the trip East three years before. I thought I knew why it began, but I never had much of a sense why it ended. Maybe exhaustion. Maybe love. At some point, it had seemed fruitless to continue hostilities. In marriage, you build a world; ultimately you have to decide whether to live in that world or leave it. For some time the answer had been clear to both of us, and that recognition released something that made everything easy that had earlier been hard. It wasn't that we'd looked down the long barrel of divorce and finally decided to put the gun away. We'd never taken the gun out. After a while, I think, we'd just decided to quit playing with toy pistols and let it be.

Nancy was looking across the high grass stretching eastward to the lagoon. She was wearing a Marimekko long-sleeved shirt, her hair falling to her shoulders.

"Don't you hear something?" she asked.

Faintly, I could hear hooves on the gravel driveway and voices laughing. Asha was saying, "Don't go too fast."

I turned the burner off, and we walked to the deck. Lis was leading a procession up the driveway, Asha perched on Queen Toots with Lis's English-style riding helmet on her head, Ruth and Neva following.

For most of the past two years, much of Lis's life had revolved around Queen Toots. The mare was nearly sixteen hands tall and had a wonderful disposition. Almost seventeen, she was long past her prime, but Lis schooled her carefully to take advantage of her natural gifts as a jumper. With her mane and tail braided and Lis in a borrowed saddle, she'd won several firsts at local horse shows. We didn't own but only "sponsored" her, buying hay and oats, pasturing her in the field across the road for a few dollars a month. On weekends, Lis rode her on trails in Point Reyes National Seashore, only half a mile distant. They had become close pals, but now Toots was being left behind as Lis changed. A year younger than Toots and a high-school sophomore, Lis was blossoming. Boys and music were replacing Toots. This afternoon she looked terrific in blue shorts and black Taqueria of Marin T-shirt, leading Toots up the driveway by her bridle.

The procession curled around the house to the field in back. Lis walked the mare in wide circles, and Asha grinned proudly, holding onto Toot's mane with her right hand. It was slippery up there without a saddle, and I was glad when Lis let Toots' head drop to graze. Finally Lis helped Asha off, and stood by the horse's head, petting her behind the ears. A few moments later Nancy called from the deck where we were sitting, "Better take Toots back now. Dick Werthimer will be here in half an hour, and we've got to get cleaned up."

Asha was both guest of honor and spark plug of the dinner. Before Dick arrived, she sat on the floor making *chapatis* for the Indian meal Neva and Ruth had prepared. Nancy and I tried to help but ended up getting in the way. Asha circled the table, chattering nonstop as she doled out *chapatis*, while the rest of us worked on the curry and sauces, washed down by the champagne Dick brought. Then she handed a jar of chutney to Dick.

"Can you open this?" she asked, grinning impishly.

He turned the top, and a jack-in-the-box placed there earlier by Asha and Lis popped out and bounced to the floor. It lay on a plank in a patch of sunlight, the jester on the spring grinning strangely under its fool's cap. I had difficulty taking my eyes off it until Lis scooped it up and gave it to Dick to examine.

After dinner we moved into the living room. Ruth started stroking an Indian drone instrument, and Lis joined in, picking up the same melody on her flute. Neva and Nancy began stacking the dishes in the dishwasher. Dick and I moved out on the deck.

"Baker-roshi asked me to thank you for bringing Neva into the city," he said.

"That's my job," I answered, thinking how frustrated I'd felt sitting in Mel's Coffee Shop two days before, waiting for Baker-roshi. I'd wanted to get outside so I could watch his arrival, checking to see whether he'd picked up a tail driving in from Green Gulch. It was a longshot Krishan could have organized anything this quickly, and a longer one that anyone he'd hired would have the resources to put a tail on Baker-roshi. So I'd temporized, telling myself I was being paranoid, and had sat there chatting with Neva so as not to alarm her even though my instincts told me I should be outside, watching.

"He also told me," Dick went on, "that Green Gulch had gotten a couple of calls inquiring about Neva."

"You mean from Krishan?"

"No. He said they were local calls and the caller didn't have an Indian accent. The woman who took the call did what you said and told the guy they didn't know where Neva was, that she'd packed up and left."

"Good. I'll get over there Monday and talk to them. Krishan has some friends in the Bay Area. Probably one of them."

"That's what I was thinking. You might take a look at this," he said pulling a telex out of his pocket. "Remember, before you left, we were joking about causing an international incident? Close call, apparently. But don't worry. The judge isn't concerned."

The telex was addressed to Neva at Green Gulch Farm. Across the top were the letters: *"TLX SECSTATE WSH,ZC2C 0224,GOVT PD SD WSH DC."*

"Am I crazy," I asked, "or is this from Senator, now Secretary, Muskie?"

"Would appear to be so. Apparently Krishan is well connected in Delhi."

I read on: *"FATHER OF ASHA SAHNI, KRISHAN CHALAM SAHNI, IS INQUIRING ABOUT WELFARE OF DAUGHTER WHO HE CLAIMS WAS RECENTLY KIDNAPPED IN BOMBAY. PLEASE INFORM EMBASSY IN NEW DELHI IF YOU KNOW HER CONDITION AND WHEREABOUTS."*

"I really like that verb *claims*," I said. "It shows they don't fully believe him. What worries me is that he's going to get tired real quick of getting jerked around by the bureaucracy and start free-lancing. That is, if he hasn't already. Does he know you're Neva's attorney?"

"If he doesn't, he could find out from his attorney."

"Why don't you telex the embassy, then? You might tell them Neva has custody and there's a warrant out for him in California."

"You read my mind. I just wanted to check with you first."

Ever since we'd gotten back, Werthimer had been deferring

to me about Neva's arrangements. Evidently he figured her security was my province.

"Damn," I said. "I wish we'd been able to get him charged with passport fraud. INS would hold him at the airport. As it is, there's nothing stopping him from waltzing right in. He might be here now. If I were him, damn straight I'd be here now."

"Isn't that a bit paranoid?"

"Maybe. Hell, I don't know," I said, looking out at the brown grass where Allegro was crouched over a gopher hole. "This case has been going on too long. We're getting sloppy."

"It won't be much longer. We'll find them a place to stay."

"Monday early, I'll take Neva over and wipe out all her bank accounts. Last Friday we canceled her credit cards. I don't want any tracks. And I want to see if anyone goes for a phone when we close out the bank accounts. By the way, when the cutoff and the hiding place are set, I want to take them there and make sure there aren't any screwups."

"I don't know," he said. "The bills are up around thirty grand now, and we can't charge Krishan for anything but the kidnapping itself. I know you're not milking this case, but—"

"You know right," I said, cutting in angrily. "If Neva had done what I told her, we wouldn't even be having this conversation. I'm a detective, not a fucking baby-sitter."

Dick didn't reply. Sulking, I looked out over the field. Allegro made a jump at the hole but came up with nothing. Damn cat never could catch anything.

WEDNESDAY, JULY 2

If it were you sitting back there, I told myself, that's exactly how you'd do it. You wouldn't crowd in two or three cars behind. You'd hold about a quarter of a mile distant. Just close enough to see if we pulled off at one of the exits. You'd hold back there just like he's doing with the speedometer dead on sixty, speeding up when we sped up, slowing down when we slowed down. But what would you do if we pulled off for gas? Would you follow us into the station and gas up at another island? You'd be real tempted wouldn't you? On the other hand, you could pass up the stop and pull over a mile or two farther along, top off from the spare tank in your trunk, and wait. That'd mean losing contact. Risky. But you still might try it. In any case, you'd stop before the exit on the chance we got off there. And you'd have to sit there by the side of the highway, waiting until we cruised by. Considering all that, it looks like now would be a fine time for us to tank up.

"Asha," I said, half turning in the seat, "How'd you like a Pepsi?"

She didn't say anything. She'd been owlish since leaving Brooklyn three hours earlier. Something to do with the visit to her grandmother. Maybe she hadn't slept well. I flipped on the turn signal and got in the exit lane for the filling station off I-95. I checked the mirror, but the dark-green Ford was too far back for me to see anything.

We got out, and I moved to the passenger side so I could scan the parkway without appearing obvious.

"We'll be back in five minutes," said Neva, taking Asha by the hand and stepping around an oil slick.

No green Ford came into the plaza. Where was he? That truck had been just in front of him. He wasn't there. He wasn't going by. I knew we shouldn't have stopped in Brooklyn. I knew the grandmother's place would be hot. But after all that had happened, how could I tell Neva and her mother they couldn't meet, that the grandmother couldn't see Asha with her own eyes? He must have stopped up the road, maybe watching through binocs, ready to pick us up after the stop. I hadn't thought of that. If this fucker was really there, he was good. I'd picked up nothing earlier, and we'd been in heavy traffic getting out of New York. I'd first noticed him just after New Haven. Construction work had narrowed traffic to one lane west of the Connecticut River Bridge, and he'd been forced closer as the traffic bunched. That was the closest he'd come to us, crawling along between a Volvo station wagon and a Toyota.

Whoever he was, he'd better have a big spare tank; the Pontiac held twenty gallons, and we weren't stopping again until we got there. I paid for the gas and went into the station to hit the men's room and get sandwiches.

We pulled out of the station, and I kept my eye pasted to the mirror. There was a dark, big American car back there, but I couldn't tell if it was the Ford. I thought about getting off at an exit and waiting. But that would alarm Neva and Asha. I also didn't want to let the tail know he'd been burned; better to lose him in Providence traffic in a way that wouldn't signal we'd seen him. But I couldn't be sure. He was too far back.

Asha was happier now. Earlier, her blood sugar must have been down, because the sandwich cheered her up. Neva seemed content. Over the last few weeks her strength had been coming back. Losing Asha must have deadened some nerve, making her not care for anything. With Asha back, things had changed. It wasn't just that she seemed more animated; she seemed stronger too, moving to take charge of her life. I'd seen it in San Francisco, in the letter she'd sent to Krishan along with a note from Asha, and again the day before, at her mother's apartment. When her sister had complained about not getting any advance notice of our visit, Neva had moved in, defending me.

Asha was settled down with her coloring book in the backseat, and Neva wasn't saying anything, just watching the Rhode Island landscape drift by the windshield. The silence between us was almost comfortable.

The last two weeks in Bolinas had seemed interminable. I'd found a place nearby and had rented it by the week for our little group. But I'd known in my bones they should be out of the Bay Area, and each day had ground on my nerves. Finally Bakerroshi had produced a hiding place. A couple close to the Zen Center conducted seminars on Cuttyhunk Island, a nineteenth-century resort community off the Massachusetts coast. They had agreed to find a place for Neva and Asha and to watch over them through the summer. Dick Werthimer knew a young lawyer in Philadelphia who consented to act as cutoff, taking mail and phone messages for Neva. Philadelphia also seemed like a good place to end the false trail I was laying for Krishan. With that in mind, I'd asked Neva not to tell her friends where she was going, but to have them see her off at the airport. On Monday morning a group of ten or fifteen people, many of them from the Zen Center, had said their goodbyes to Neva and Asha at the TWA gate. The destination sign above the counter showed the flight was nonstop to Philadelphia.

Philadelphia also permitted me to wrap up another loose end. On the tape Henry had made of our session with Krishan in the Blue Ballerina, he'd referred to me in Krishan's presence as "Yo-see-ah." That's where Don Gilchrist came in. Good old Don. A professor at Haverford, he'd been willing to go to Western Union in Philadelphia and send off a cable to Krishan telling him, "Neva and Asha are together, well, and happy at an undisclosed location." Following my instructions, he'd signed the cable "Yossarian" and paid for it in cash. I'd already checked and made sure there were no Yossarians in the Philadelphia phone book. But when Don sent me a copy of the cable, I saw it bore the name Dave Yossarian and what looked like a real address and phone number. We had a few chuckles over that when Gilchrist explained he'd picked the phone number and address of the Cheese Shop, a local gourmet food boutique.

Those were the only chuckles I'd had over the last two weeks. The previous week, Henry's reports arrived by air mail. Somehow or other he'd been able to throw another shill into the game, an operative named Deepak Jolly who'd signed an affidavit certifying what Krishan told him the day after being released. Most of it was familiar stuff, but the last sentences were disturbing. *"According to Mr. K. C. Sahni,"* Jolly had written, *"by tactfully getting rid of the wife would mean 100% victory. In this way, he can get the daughter, full property and disputed money and still settle down in America."* I wondered what Krishan had had in mind that prompted Jolly's choice of the word *tactfully*. A staged accident, perhaps, failed brakes or a fall down some steps instead of the nastiness of a gun or a knife? I knew now what it was Henry had said over that bad connection in Hawaii.

True, these were only words, disgruntled words from a man who had just lost the biggest gamble of his life. As Henry suggested, the whole thing might pass; it might be only "the devil barking in him." Just rolling that phrase over in my mind made me look again in the mirror.

There was no dark car back there. Its place had been taken by a light-colored sedan. I watched for a moment or so. It maintained its distance, cruising along at our steady sixty. Could it have replaced the dark-green Ford? Could they be using two cars? If Krishan was shelling out enough money to put a surveillance on the Brooklyn apartment, they could have laid on two cars. Overnight would have given them enough time to set up properly.

I went over in my mind the precautions we'd taken.

Monday night I'd met Dick's friend at a fern bar in Philadelphia. It was late when we got in, and he worked there evenings as a bartender. We'd laughed over Gilchrist's cable, and then I'd shown him Jolly's affidavit. He'd agreed to keep Neva's address and phone number in code in his wallet, never to call her from his office or home, and to use no return address on her mail packets.

Then there was the car. You can't rent a car without a credit card, and I had to assume my credit-card slips could fall into Krishan's hands. With that in mind, I'd rented the Olds from a small, local outfit where I hoped the bookkeeping would be sloppy. If he got to them, all he'd be able to learn was the round-trip mileage on the car. He could halve that distance and use it to draw a radius around Philadelphia. But that would still take in too much territory to give him any idea where to begin. Later that evening I'd register us on the coast under phony names and pay in cash.

So far, so good. But all these precautions would be worthless if we were still being shadowed. I looked in the mirror. If the light-colored sedan was still there, it was too far back to be seen.

In Providence I did a cute little number, pretending to take a wrong turn near the Civic Center. By the time we got back onto the interstate, I'd jogged around enough back streets to feel comfortable.

Soon we crossed into Massachusetts. When we turned off onto Route 88, I started to enjoy the scenery. Three years before, this landscape with its weathered wood and heavy vegetation had reminded me of an Andrew Wyeth painting. It still did.

The road was familiar. It was, in fact, that same road I'd traveled to Nonquitt Harbor three years earlier. Coincidentally, the ferry to Cuttyhunk Island left from South Dartmouth, only a few miles down the road from the house where Nancy and I had stayed. When the road widened and the shopping center came into view, I glanced in the mirror and pulled into the mall.

Making the turn, my eye caught on a blurry dark shape that was closing rapidly. By the time we were turned around facing the road again, I could get only a quick glance as the car went by. There was a man in the passenger seat, but I couldn't tell about the driver. The plate was hidden by the following car, but it could have been New York. There was no question it was a dark-green Ford.

My first instinct was to bolt, to gun the engine, catch the green light at the entrance to the shopping center, and keep going. Then my mind braked to a stop and I recognized that losing them was the last thing I wanted. In the same instant I knew exactly what I was going to do.

"I need some shaving cream," I said, pulling up in front of the Finast.

I got out and checked to make sure the back of the car with its Pennsylvania plate could be seen from the entrance to the mall. Then I walked into the store and bought a can of shaving cream. Nobody else wanted a doughnut, but I did, and that used up eight more minutes. When I finally opened the driver's door, fourteen minutes had gone by since the Ford had passed. He must have seen us make the turn; that was why he'd been closing so fast when I saw him. He'd had fourteen minutes to get himself turned around and in position to pick us up when we came out of the lot.

"There's a place near here I want to show you," I said, turning the key in the ignition.

Sedately, we eased out of the parking lot, stopped at the light, and then headed straight through on the road around the point. We dipped to pass over the bridge, then curved up the other side to the intersection with the lane. Flat granite stretched off to the left, the tide lapping at its edge. The house loomed in front, still painted blue. A Peugeot was parked in its circular driveway. We jogged a bit to the left, past the Carvells' house and barn, and pulled to stop in the gravel by the inn. A sign that said *"Woods Rest"* hung at an angle from a single eyebolt. Stuck in the ground by the front steps was another sign saying the place was for lease or sale.

We walked to the nearby dock. The surface of the water was gently stirring. Just under the surface, heavy clumps of seaweed rose and fell in the tidal surge. "Three years ago I found thirty thousand dollars in a paper bag hidden in that house up there," I said, and began telling them an expurgated version of the Reynolds case.

Wisps of fog were drifting in. The evening was going to be like that first Sunday night when I'd gone crawling around in the bushes. I kept watching the lane. This was my hole card, and the next minute or so would tell whether I'd played it correctly. The people in the Ford couldn't possibly know the lane was a cul de sac that ended over there beyond the trees. They would have to come in after us, and when they did I'd have my answer. The most dangerous thing was not to know. I couldn't deliver Neva and Asha to the island if there was the remotest chance we'd been tailed. All day I'd seen only ambiguous shapes in mirrors. I had to make the world disclose what those shapes meant. The trip down the lane was going to be my Michelson-Morley experiment. If a dark-green Ford with what I expected would be New York plates came cautiously nosing its way down the lane, then I'd know where we were and what I had to do.

"I don't know about your stories, Tink," Neva was saying. "Sometimes I think I ought to believe only half what you say."

The minutes stretched out. Nothing. Finally a pickup pulled up to the Carvells' back door, and a young man in his twenties got out and went inside. Probably their son. We waited another ten minutes, and then I took the long way around into South Dartmouth.

I paid in cash at a motel with a big lobster on the chimney, unloaded our suitcases, and parked the car in a restaurant lot up the street.

Dinner that night was subdued. Asha kept wanting to go back and watch the lobsters in the salt-water tank with the fake seaweed floating on top. I was distracted, chewing over the trip, wondering what to do. Neva was also quiet, undoubtedly wondering what sort of arrangements she'd find on the island the next day. We talked a bit about the cutoff in Philadelphia and the rules of the game. She'd be isolated for the next few months, and wasn't happy about it. Underneath it all was the fact we'd been together long; everything that could be said had already been said. The conversation dragged, and I was glad when dinner was over and we could get back to our rooms, side by side in the section of the motel away from the street.

I turned on the TV, but after half an hour shut it off and lay back on the bed. I was bewildered. I didn't know what was going on.

We shouldn't have gone to the Brooklyn apartment. That was my fault. I should have been smart enough to work out an alternative. I could have picked up Neva's mother and sister myself, shaken any tails, and taken them to a hotel in Manhattan for the visit. I'd been sloppy, and now it would be Neva and Asha, not me, who would pay. I shouldn't have taken the case. I should have encouraged Baker-roshi at the beginning. His snatch team would have failed, and that would have been the end of it. Our success had just raised the cycle of violence one level. The *Oresteia* all over again. First there had been only child-stealing; now the furies had been let loose. And I was responsible for that. Where would it end? I didn't know. That would depend on Krishan, and where, I wondered, was he tonight? India? San Francisco? Down the street? Henry's words kept circulating in my mind: "Otherwise, he will go mad." What did Henry know that I didn't?

Around ten-thirty, I switched off the light, but I couldn't sleep.

"The awful ambiguity of immediate experience . . ." In college, I used to quote that line from Robert Penn Warren to dates from Smith or Holyoke. Back then, I thought it might make me seem "poetic" and interesting. Now it burst into mind again. What I'd seen in the mirror was ambiguous and was getting more so the more I thought about it. I couldn't call this off on the basis of a couple of cars a quarter of a mile back. It had probably been nothing, just my febrile imagination. There was, however, the green Ford. Why had he sped up just when we turned off? He'd probably wanted to catch the light; if he'd been tailing us, he would have followed us up the lane. Or was there something I hadn't thought of?

By midnight I'd decided to call Fechheimer. He might be able to think of it.

The relays clicked, and David's phone began to ring. We had the same answering service, and on the third ring Iris picked up. Bad handwriting and all, she had outlasted Cathy. Iris recognized my voice and was willing to tell me Fechheimer was out of town and hadn't called in yet with a contact number. I thanked her and hung up.

A mosquito was buzzing in the corner. I walked into the bathroom, pulled the cellophane off the plastic cup, and ran water into it.

Then I had it. It was a beeper! They'd put a beeper on the car. That was how they'd been able to maintain the tail from so far back. That was why I hadn't lost them in Providence. That was why they hadn't come down the lane; they'd known the car wasn't moving. When had they put it on the car? I'd spent the previous night with friends who lived only a couple of blocks from Neva's mother's place. I'd left Neva and Asha at the grandmother's and gone to the car, parked two blocks away on a cross-street. I'd opened the trunk, pulled out my suitcase, and walked the block and a half to my friends' townhouse. I hadn't even moved the car. They must have tailed me to it and then had all night to put on the beeper. That was it!

I pulled on my pants and headed for the car. The fog had rolled in dense and heavy, but the streetlights helped me find my way. With the flashlight from the glove compartment, I started with the inside of the rear bumper. Then the same for the front bumper. I got down and looked up into the wheel wells. It was hard work. Beepers could be made as small as a quarter, and the Pontiac was a big car. Underneath was heavy

gravel, and the fog had moistened it. I rolled under and shined
the light up at the gas tank. Then I felt around on top of the
tank. I squeezed further in and shined the light up around the
rear axle, at the same time scraping my forehead on the chassis.
Nothing.

Ten minutes later I stood by the rear bumper, breathing hard
and sweating. A brake support had put a small rip in the elbow
of my tweed jacket, and I was dirty from the gravel. The fog
had made everything wet. I felt the way I'd felt that Sunday night
three years before, only now I'd come up blank.

A hot shower helped, but still I couldn't relax. The town had
shut down, and even the mosquito had quit buzzing. The silence
was getting to me. It was intractable. You couldn't argue with
it.

THURSDAY, JULY 3

I woke early the next morning. The sun was streaming in, and
for a moment I didn't know where I was. Then I remembered.
My torn jacket was hanging over the back of a chair, my dirty
cords in a pile by the door. I pulled them on and rummaged
around in my briefcase for an old sweater. It was just before
seven.

People get up early in New England, so it didn't take long to
find an open filling station. It was diagonally across the street
from the hardware store with the Gliden paint sign. The one
where I'd bought the crowbar and the extension cord.

I paid the attendant ten bucks to put the car on a hoist just
high enough so I could feel around in the areas I hadn't been
able to get to the night before. There was a lot of grime on the
undercarriage; it made the work dirty, but also made it easy to
see if any of the nooks and crannies had been touched. I couldn't
feel or see into all of them, but twenty minutes later I was pretty
sure there was no beeper on the car.

I drove around for a while, checking motel parking lots, hoping to find the green Ford. When that proved fruitless I parked
down by the waterfront, near an old home with a giant oak in
front. I sat in the car and looked at the house and the water
lapping against the rocks beyond. Along one side of the house
leaned an old grape arbor. Vegetation struggled up its side, and
between it and the street lush grass grew. It struck me again that

winter was always present in New England, that something in the plants' DNA knew it was coming and told them to grow with a kind of desperate energy. The house was painted dark red, and against it the morning light etched each leaf with a hard, sharp line. It was California light, giving objects an incandescent purity like they might have had in Eden. I sat in the car for twenty minutes, smoking a cigarette, thinking.

By the time I got back, Neva and Asha were up. I showered and changed, and we had breakfast in the coffee shop. The meal was different from the one the night before. Neva was refreshed and anxious to begin the adventure that would start for her that day. Asha was her usual impish self, drawing on the napkin and asking all sorts of questions. For the first time in weeks she told us a dream she'd had, a nice dream. "There were children all the way to there," she said, pointing to the street sixty feet beyond the window. "Lots of children. Children all the way to Ravi's house. And I was the leader. Miss Mackintosh gave me a stuffed dinosaur this big." She opened her arms wide. "Mommy was waiting outside. I took her the presents, and we went into a room. There were two men in there. But they were nice men, not *goondas*. They played with me. And then I was hiding behind the curtain." She stopped, but it didn't seem as though the dream had stopped.

There was nothing else to do. We stepped out of the restaurant, into the sunlight, and walked back to the motel. Neva and I stood by the trunk of the car while Asha went to the bathroom.

"There's always the outside chance we were followed," I said. "That's why I made the wrong turn in Providence yesterday. But I don't think anyone was there. Probably just my imagination."

She brushed a wisp of hair back from her forehead, squinting into the sun.

"It's OK, Tink," she said smiling. "I can take care of everything now. Thank you, thank you for everything."

It struck me that up to this point Neva had never thanked me. I looked away quickly, closing the trunk lid over my suitcase.

We sat on straight benches in the sunlight, waiting for the ferry to get under way. As it left the harbor, we faced aft and watched the boarding dock get smaller. I looked to the left at some restaurants lining the shore. The tourists were crowding in for breakfast now, and the parking lots were full. I counted three or four green sedans scattered here and there. My father's glasses were in my suitcase; with them I could have seen if any were Fords. Never mind, I told myself, let it be.

Off the point, the wind picked up, and a good chop was running. As we got further out, the sea became cobalt blue and seabirds followed the wake, diving on the scraps passengers threw to them. Asha was wearing a cotton-print sundress, so we put a sweater over her shoulders. After a while that wasn't enough, and we went below.

In midafternoon I left them there on the island. Love affairs and books and cases all have to end, and there's no good way to end them. Perhaps they all end a little too late, a bit after their time is up. We walked together down the rutted gravel to the dock where the ferry was loading. We hugged, and I got on board. As the ferry pulled away, I looked back at them standing on the dock, framed between oil drums and a rusting davit. Asha was holding on to Neva's skirt. They were both waving and smiling.

I looked for the green Ford as the ferry rounded the point into South Dartmouth. Nothing. Did that mean I'd guessed right? No. Whether I'd guessed right or wrong was something I couldn't know. At least not now.

I had to let go, I told myself, I had to let things be. Later that afternoon I tried to do that.

John and Elizabeth McClelland had a summer place on the next peninsula south. John taught British history at Haverford, and we'd been comrades-in-arms through several skirmishes with the college's administration, back in the days when such things mattered.

Their house had been an eighteenth-century inn, and we drank gimlets on its porch, overlooking the barnacle-encrusted granite that shelved down to the water. Their kids liked my stories, and I enjoyed playing the mysterious detective. We ate lobster on a refectory table under ax-hewn oak beams, and when I looked over Elizabeth's shoulder I could see the lights of the harbor across the bay.

At dinner, they insisted I stay over. But somewhere between the coffee and the brandy a shadow crossed my mind, and I knew this wasn't where I wanted to be that night. It was too safe and cheery and pleasant, too distant from where I'd been in my own mind the past few days and weeks. So I made my excuses and left shortly before ten.

Almost involuntarily I headed back to Nonquitt Harbor on

the off-chance of finding the Ford. Once again I came up blank, and now, shortly after midnight, I was watching the black ribbon of Route 88 unroll before my headlights. I didn't know where I'd sleep. It didn't matter.

I flipped on the radio. The announcer on a Boston classical station was talking about this being the Fourth of July. I'd forgotten that. Andover would be deserted the next day. It would be nice to swing by there, sit in the dark chapel, and pay my respects to Henry L. Stimson.

Fourth of July. Twenty-two years earlier, Nancy and I were to be married on the Fourth of July, and then I'd been sent off to Lebanon with a UDT detachment. On the June morning I'd left, Nancy had been standing on the dock in a blue summer dress. All the night before we'd made love in a motel in Virginia Beach. Exhausted, we'd watched the sun rise red over the Atlantic. The band had played, and I'd started missing her before the *Fort Snelling* cleared Little Creek harbor. I missed her now. I wondered what she and the kids were doing.

Back in Bolinas, I'd been a bear these past two weeks, fretting over Neva and Asha. When I'd been there, I hadn't been there. It was like being in a tunnel and not being able to find your way out. What kind of life was this, anyway? Coming back from India, I'd imagined mine would be like Odysseus' return to Ithaca. It hadn't been like that at all. I'd consoled myself with the thought Odysseus hadn't had a crazed Indian architect to worry about. Now I laughed, remembering Fechheimer's remark in San Francisco. "It's a great tale of derring-do," he said. "Just leave out the part about him weighing only a hundred thirty pounds and pare down the number of goons you had helping you."

The announcer said something about the traditional Boston Pops concert in the Hatch Shell and then put on the 1812 Overture. I hated the 1812 Overture. I hated Tchaikovsky and his Romantic posturing. The Marseillaise theme was drifting up from the speakers. *"Allons enfants de la Patrie . . ."*: the spirit of the Enlightenment and all that.

Maybe that was what made me think of Spade. For I thought of him then, and of the last scene in the *Falcon*. Hammett really had gotten it right, gotten the bleakness right. Especially that last scene in Spade's office.

Effie's sitting there. It's the day after Spade turned in Brigid to the cops. He loves Brigid, but he can't trust her, and you get the idea he doesn't much trust the love bit either. Effie has read the newspaper, so she knows what Spade has done. It's cold, she thinks, inhumanly cold, what he's done. He tries to put his arm around her, but she'll have none of it. *"Don't touch me now,"* she says, *not now."*

On the radio, the Overture began driving toward its conclusion. The theme was building again in the background, no longer tentative but exultant, victorious. Soon they would be ringing the damned church bells.

Spade and Effie hear the knob rattle on the corridor door. Effie goes out and then reappears in the doorway.

"Iva's here," she says.

Spade looks down at his desk.

Iva? Imagine him thinking, Is that what I've got to look forward to for the rest of my life? No more Brigids, just Ivas? A succession of shallow, manipulative bitches and two-A.M. phone calls telling me my partner's been murdered? Just more lies and intrigue and more times when I've got to cover my ass or get it chopped off? Just that? Nothing more?

Bleakly, still looking at his desk, he nods to Effie and delivers the last line:

"Yes," he said, and shivered. "Well, send her in."

I'd always liked that line. Especially the *shivering* part. It showed Hammett had gotten it all right.

The cannons fired, and then there was silence.

EPILOGUE

REPORT OF INVESTIGATION

T*he information below was developed through interviews with the individuals named. In those instances where interviews were not possible, facts were developed through inquiries with third parties or public-record searches.*

Neva and Asha Sahni remained on Cuttyhunk Island into the late summer of 1980. When the "summer people" left, the two of them moved to a small town in Connecticut, living under aliases and communicating with friends and family through the cutoff in Philadelphia. Krishan Sahni entered the U.S. early that same summer and immediately initiated legal proceedings to establish contact with Asha. In May and June of the following year he was permitted supervised visits with Asha, the first at a private home in Mill Valley, California, the second at an amusement park in San Jose, California. Neva was present with Asha during the second visit.

When further legal efforts by Krishan compromised her and Asha's security, Neva broke off communication with the California court and left Connecticut. With assistance she was able to construct a new identity for herself and settle with Asha in a different state under that identity. Krishan remarried and resumed his career as an architect in the San Francisco Bay area. He died of natural causes in September 1984. After his death Neva and Asha retained their aliases as a matter of convenience but resumed direct communication with friends and family.

On March 21, 1980, the district court of appeals upheld Judge
Karlton's reversal of Chol Soo Lee's conviction in the Chinatown
killing. Although technically no longer subject to the death penalty, Lee was housed at San Quentin in an annex to death row,
essentially in solitary confinement. In December 1980 the court
appointed Leonard Weinglass to represent Lee in the retrial of
the Chinatown case, set for March 23, 1981.

Continuances postponed the retrial until August 1982. Weinglass
withdrew in early 1982 and was replaced by San Francisco attorneys Tony Serra and Stuart Hanlon. In March 1982 the California Supreme Court ruled in People vs. Shirley that a
previously hypnotized witness could not testify about matters
discussed under hypnosis, thus removing Steven Morris from the
case. Even without Morris's testimony, Lee was acquitted in the
Chinatown killing on September 3, 1982. Five months later
the district court of appeals reversed his conviction in the prison
killing. In a plea bargain, Lee pled guilty to second-degree murder. With credit for time served, he was released from San Quentin in the summer of 1983. He now lives in Los Angeles.

During Lee's retrial on the Chinatown killing in August 1982,
this investigator contacted an associate of Danny Choi who was
with Choi shortly after Tak's murder. He said Choi described to
him how Choi and another youth pursued Tak near the Ping
Yuen Bakery, how the one youth disappeared into the crowd as
Choi fired three bullets into Tak, and how Choi made his escape,
throwing away the gun in Beckett Alley and joining up with the
other youth later that night. The informant also provided a photograph of Choi taken in the summer of 1973. It shows what
appears to be a mole at four o'clock under Choi's right eye.

Wylie's lawsuit against Green collapsed as the criminal prosecution of Wylie moved forward. The criminal case against Wylie
was dismissed when Dr. Walker declined to come to San Francisco a second time to testify.

A search of public records in Hennepin County, Minnesota (Minneapolis), disclosed little concerning the war between the Cutlers. A Petition for Dissolution charging adultery was filed on
September 19, 1977. It is unclear whether the absence of additional documents in the file means they are still married.

Hal Lipset continues to run the Lipset Service from the Victorian on Pacific Avenue. David Fechheimer, now remarried and the father of two boys, still lives and works in the home built for Robert Louis Stevenson at the corner of Hyde and Lombard. In 1984 Henry Bawa was elected president of the World Association of Detectives.

Investigation is concluded.

JOSIAH THOMPSON
San Francisco, California
December 1987

ABOUT THE AUTHOR

Josiah Thompson works out of San Francisco, where he was named "Best Detective of 1987" by the *Bay Guardian*. He taught philosophy at Yale and Haverford before resigning eleven years ago to become a detective. The author of several books, he has been the subject of numerous articles, including a profile in *The New Yorker*.